THE B SIDE

ALSO BY BEN YAGODA

How to Not Write Bad:
The Most Common Writing Problems and
the Best Ways to Avoid Them

Memoir: A History

When You Catch an Adjective, Kill It:
The Parts of Speech, for Better and/or Worse

The Sound on the Page: Style and Voice in Writing

About Town: The New Yorker and the World It Made

Will Rogers: A Biography

The Art of Fact: A Historical Anthology
of Literary Journalism (coeditor)

THE B SIDE

THE DEATH of TIN PAN ALLEY

and the REBIRTH of the

GREAT AMERICAN SONG

BEN YAGODA

RIVERHEAD BOOKS

a member of Penguin Group (USA)

New York

2015

RIVERHEAD BOOKS
Published by the Penguin Group
Penguin Group (USA) LLC
375 Hudson Street
New York, New York 10014

USA · Canada · UK · Ireland · Australia
New Zealand · India · South Africa · China

penguin.com
A Penguin Random House Company

The author gratefully acknowledges permission to quote lyrics from the following:

"Dancing in the Street," written by Ivy Hunter, Marvin Gaye, and William Stevenson.
© 1964 Jobete Music Co. Inc., MGIII Music, NMG Music, and FCG Music. All rights adminis-
tered by Sony/ATV Music Publishing LLC, on behalf of Jobete Music Co. Inc., MGIII Music,
NMG Music, FCG Music, and Stone Agate Music (a division
of Jobete Music Co. Inc.). All rights reserved. Used by permission.
"I Get a Kick out of You" (from *Anything Goes*), words and music by
Cole Porter. Copyright © 1934 (Renewed) WB Music Corp.
All rights reserved. Used by permission of Alfred Music.
"Mr. Cole Won't Rock and Roll," written by Joe Sherman and Noel Sherman. © 1959
Sony/ATV Tunes LLC. All rights administered by Sony/ATV Music
Publishing LLC. All rights reserved. Used by permission.
"To Each His Own" (from the Paramount Pictures film),
written by Jay Livingston and Ray Evans. Copyright 1946 Sony/ATV Music
Publishing LLC. All rights administered by Sony/ATV Music
Publishing LLC. All rights reserved. Used by permission.
"What Happened to the Music," written by Carolyn Leigh, Nacio Brown,
and Robert Sadoff. Used by permission of Alley Music Corporation.

Pages 309–310 constitute an extension of this copyright page.

ISBN 978-1-59448-849-8

Printed in the United States of America
1 3 5 7 9 10 8 6 4 2

BOOK DESIGN BY AMANDA DEWEY

To Bob Dorough, Ervin Drake, Dave Frishberg,
Norman Gimbel, Sheldon Harnick, Johnny Mandel,
Randy Newman, Curly Putman, Charles Strouse,
Allen Toussaint, and Jimmy Webb

CONTENTS

Prologue
Premises, Premises

I n the second decade of the twenty-first century, the pianist Keith Jarrett sat down for an interview with Robert Siegel of National Public Radio. Jarrett had just released an album called *Somewhere*, which included his trio's rendition of the songs "Between the Devil and the Deep Blue Sea" (written in 1932), "Stars Fell on Alabama" (1934), and "I Thought About You" (1939). Jarrett has a reputation as an avant-garde jazz artist, but this was only the latest of a series of albums—others include *Standards, Vol. 1*; *Standards, Vol. 2*; and *Setting Standards*—that featured his trio's renditions of classic American popular songs written roughly in the second quarter of the twentieth century. That is, standards.

Siegel started off by saying, "Standard tunes, first of all, what do they mean to you and why have you recorded so many of them on this disc?"

"First of all, they are anything but standard by today's standards," Jarrett replied. "They're exceptional. There was a period of time in

American history where so many things came rushing in, especially in popular music."

Siegel wondered, "Do we not have more songs like this for lack of people trying to write them? Is it unfashionable?"

"Yes, is the short answer to that," Jarrett said. He suggested parts of a longer answer as well. First, in that long-ago period of time, there were "people who were actually good at writing melodies." Second, he talked about the importance of singers. He recounted that Miles Davis was once asked who he learned his phrasing from. His answer: Frank Sinatra. Today, Jarrett said, "there are also no important singers, so maybe it's all part of the same pancake mix. If there's no singers and there's no good songs, which came first?"

The pianist said it once occurred to him to try to write a standard, a song that had the quality of having "existed before." He eventually came up with a tune he called "No Lonely Nights."

"But it wasn't that easy to do," Jarrett said.

The standards, as Jarrett said, "came rushing in"—from the 1920s through the 1950s, but most quickly and intensely in a two-decade span starting in about 1925. The best of them are said to make up the "Great American Songbook" (the term was first used as the title of a 1972 album by the jazz singer Carmen McRae), the size of which varies depending on who's counting. In his definitive book *American Popular Song*, Alec Wilder puts forth about three hundred entries.

What are the attributes of these few hundred songs? The composer Jule Styne once gave a concise definition to a young friend of his, the jazz pianist Bill Charlap: "What's the secret to a great popular song? It must be melodically simple and harmonically attractive." Expanding on that, standard songs are sophisticated (in several senses of the word) and melodic, constructed with, at the minimum, superior craftsmanship, and sometimes with remarkable innovation and artistry. Charlap is speaking of Styne's "Just in Time," but he could be referring to any of hundreds of songs: "It has an innate sense of structure. There are rests, points of emphasis, and overall balance and taste. It's so pliable, and very American." Although the standards are roughly divided into ballads (slow) and rhythm tunes (fast), the categories are fungible and a given tune can be interpreted in many different ways. Fast or slow, standards are jazz-inflected in rhythm and harmonic possibilities and, especially in later years, show the influence of modern European composers like Ravel and Debussy. The main criterion for songs' status as standard is the music, but most of them have lyrics that rise to the occasion and are wedded to the melody: sophisticated, once again, and sometimes dazzlingly inventive. The internal rhymes and wordplay from a Cole Porter or Lorenz Hart can suggest W. S. Gilbert with an American accent. But even when dealing with commonplace tropes of love and longing, as in Irving Berlin's "Always," "How Deep Is the Ocean," or "Count Your Blessings (Instead of Sheep)," a standard can have a palpable honesty and conviction and can be emotionally affecting without being schmaltzy. Or at least it can be delivered that way by the right singer.

The melodies were written—to start naming the great names—by Berlin, by George Gershwin, by Jerome Kern, Cole Porter, Richard Rodgers, Duke Ellington, Arthur Schwartz, Harry Warren, Hoagy Carmichael, Richard Whiting, Vincent Youmans, Walter Donaldson, and Jimmy McHugh. They went with lyrics by Ira Gershwin (George's brother), Lorenz Hart, Oscar Hammerstein II, Howard Dietz, and E. Y. "Yip" Harburg. Those men were all born within a seventeen-year span, from Kern in 1885 to Rodgers in 1902. A slightly younger group, consisting of Harold Arlen, Vernon Duke, Dorothy Fields, Frank Loesser, Johnny Mercer, Jule Styne, and Fats Waller, were born between 1903 and 1910. Burton Lane and Jimmy Van Heusen came on the scene in 1912 and 1913, respectively, and that was pretty much that. To be sure, not all their songs were gems, and even in the very heart of the golden age, a lot of hack tunesmiths turned out reams of lesser material. But not every painter in Renaissance Florence was a Leonardo or a Botticelli. The comparison might raise your eyebrow, or both of them. But the more you ponder the short list of places where intense creativity emerged from a core group of artists in a limited amount of time, the less far-fetched it begins to seem.

The place from which the Great American Songbook emerged was New York City. The highly concentrated music industry originated around the turn of the twentieth century on one Manhattan block, West Twenty-eighth Street between Broadway and Sixth Avenue, called "Tin Pan Alley" for the cacophony that blew out of music publishers' offices. The designation persisted even after the publishers moved uptown, to various outposts centered around the Brill Building on Broadway at Forty-ninth Street. From the 1920s on, a growing number of the best songs originated in the scores of New York musical shows or revues. Henceforth, an ambitious fledgling songwriter's goal was to have his number in the Broadway spotlight, figuratively and literally—clearly, a big step up from being a mere assembly-line worker in the pop music factory.

The first talking motion picture, in 1927, was a musical called *The Jazz Singer*, and for two decades after that, Hollywood was the western outpost of American songwriting, the home base for such outstanding practitioners as Warren, Mercer, Arlen, and Van Heusen, as well as lesser artisans. Bigfoot New Yorkers periodically went west for short sojourns. Some of the biggest furnished just three 1930s films starring Fred Astaire and Ginger Rogers with an astonishing number of standards of the highest caliber: Irving Berlin's score for *Top Hat* ("Isn't This a Lovely Day [to Be Caught in the Rain]?," "Cheek to Cheek," "Top Hat, White Tie and Tails"); Jerome Kern and Dorothy Fields's for *Swing Time* ("The Way You Look Tonight," "A Fine Romance," "Pick Yourself Up"); and the Gershwin brothers' for *Shall We Dance* ("They All Laughed," "Let's Call the Whole Thing Off," "They Can't Take That Away from Me"). But gems popped up even in films that were less than classics. I'll cite three examples from hundreds. Kern and Oscar Hammerstein's timeless "The Folks Who Live on the Hill" was introduced by Irene Dunne in a forgotten 1937 film, *High, Wide and Handsome.* "There Will Never Be Another You," with music by Harry Warren and lyrics by Mack Gordon, is recognized as one of the greatest songs ever; go to a jazz gig in any city in the world, and you are likely to find it on the setlist. It first appeared in a 1942 Twentieth Century–Fox B movie called *Iceland*, starring skater Sonja Henie and John Payne as a U.S. Marine posted in—that's right—Iceland. Another from the same year: the timeless "Moonlight Becomes You," by Johnny Burke and Jimmy Van Heusen, originated as filler in a Bob Hope–Bing Crosby comedy, *Road to Morocco.*

The parity among the three sources of standards—Broadway shows, Hollywood movies, and one-off Tin Pan Alley compositions—is illustrated by a recent book of sheet music, *The Great American Songbook: The Composers.* The Hal Leonard Corporation book includes one hundred songs, from "Ac-cent-tchu-ate the Positive" to "You'd Be So Nice to Come Home To." The roster is highly selective and (obviously) subjective, but it's credible, and useful for giving a

· · · 5 · · ·

sense of where standards originated. Eighty-two songs in the book were written in 1950 or earlier. Of them, 33 percent came from Broadway, 33 percent from Tin Pan Alley, and 34 percent from Hollywood.[*]

The songs were composed with sundry goals in mind, producing great art rarely being one of them. But the songs—the best of them, anyway—took on lives of their own: it turned out they lent themselves to being interpreted in different styles and with different approaches by a range of singers and musicians. They became a repertoire, a canon, repeatedly redefined by distinctive performances, some of which were, in fact, works of art: Coleman Hawkins's "Body and Soul," Teddy Wilson and Gerry Mulligan's "As Time Goes By," Bunny Berigan's "I Can't Get Started," Fred Astaire's "Cheek to Cheek," the Boswell Sisters' "The Object of My Affection," Artie Shaw's "Begin the Beguine," Billie Holiday's "They Can't Take That Away from Me," and so on. It was more than a matter of individual renditions. The songs provided the foundation of myriad laudable and important American enterprises: not only jazz and the Broadway and Hollywood musical, but popular dancing, the recording industry, radio (or the significant part of it devoted to music), and the crafts of singing, playing instruments, and arranging and conducting music for big bands. Collectively, they constituted one of the great cultural achievements of the United States in the twentieth century.

The most successful songwriters in the Great American Songbook period were recognized for their achievements, repeatedly interviewed

---

[*]It's interesting to compare the provenance of songs that would become standards with the general run of songs. Near the height of the Great American Songbook era, a researcher analyzed songs played on the radio and determined that 8 percent came from "musical revues" (that is, Broadway shows), 25 percent from films, and 67 percent from "pops" (Tin Pan Alley). The unsurprising conclusion is that, compared with the typical Alley number, a Hollywood song was more likely and a Broadway song much more likely to "last."

in the popular press, and periodically turned into the subjects of biographical movies. Their names went above the titles on billboards for shows and movies. They garnered fortune as well as fame, through a number of different streams of revenue. The best-known but least common was the long run of a Broadway musical in which their songs appeared. Hollywood work was compensated by a weekly salary or a per-picture contract, so the upside was less spectacular, but the terms were generous and the work steady. The biggest potential financial boon was via United States copyright law and the efforts of a collective organization called the American Society of Composers, Authors and Publishers (ASCAP). Composers and lyricists were paid a few pennies each time a recording of a song they'd written was played on the radio or bought at a record store. When a song was played and bought a lot— when it became a hit, as measured by the charts in the weekly *Billboard* magazine—the pennies added up to a huge payday.*

In the Music Division of the Library of Congress in Washington, D.C., you can request to see Irving Berlin's ledgers. Berlin published his first song, "Marie from Sunny Italy," in 1907, when he was nineteen, and his first big hit, "Alexander's Ragtime Band," four years later. Not long after that, he was acknowledged as the king of American songwriters, a designation he retained until his death at 101 in 1989. The ledgers are mammoth books, bound in red, the entries penciled in precisely by what must have been a small army of accountants. Slowly lifting the cover of the 1950 book, you will see royalties from record and sheet music sales broken down by song—from "White Christmas,"

Billboard started publishing reliable charts in the early 1940s. The categories of the charts, in terms of type of music (pop, rhythm and blues, country and western, etc.) and platform (record sales, radio or jukebox plays), were frequently shuffled and changed. In this book, unless otherwise indicated, I refer to the chart showing sales of single records—at first in the 78-rpm format, then, starting in the 1950s, the 45-rpm.

which netted Berlin $13,293.95 for the year, down to "Marie from Sunny Italy," which earned a total of two cents (from foreign sheet music sales). The total royalties for the year amounted to $78,079.31, which translates to $771,030.67 in 2014 dollars. That figure does not include Berlin's payments from ASCAP, which were about $72,000, or his earnings from the Broadway hits *Annie Get Your Gun* (which closed in 1949 after a three-year run) and *Call Me Madam* (which opened in September 1950).

Berlin's "White Christmas" mechanical royalties were almost all due to Bing Crosby's Decca recording of the song, originally released in 1942 and hauled out every yuletide. It hit the top spot on the *Billboard* charts for several years running, but in 1949 (the year reflected in the 1950 royalties) it was pushed aside by another holiday song and peaked at number five. The other song was the creation of a tunesmith named Johnny Marks, who was several rungs on the ladder down from Berlin. He had put to music a humorous poem, "Rudolph, the Red-Nosed Reindeer," written by his brother-in-law; cowboy singer Gene Autry's recording reached number one on December 31, 1949. Despite the fact that, like Berlin and most other songwriters, he was Jewish, Marks would repeatedly return to this particular well, writing "Rockin' Around the Christmas Tree," "A Holly Jolly Christmas," and other holiday songs. But none reached the heights of his first hit. A 1980 *People* magazine interview with Marks contained some illuminating statistics. To that point, Autry's version of "Rudolph" had sold more than 12 million copies, and records by some five hundred other performers 130 million more. The magazine didn't say how much money Marks had made from the song in total but did report that, at the time of the interview, it was netting him some $600,000 a year. That suggests his total "Rudolph" proceeds, by the time of his death five years later, had probably reached eight figures.

. . .

draw these examples from 1949 and 1950 for a reason. In his scholarly book *The American Popular Ballad of the Golden Era*, Allen Forte, a professor of the theory of music at Yale University, defined that golden era as lasting from 1924 through 1950. In *American Popular Song*, published in 1972, Alec Wilder covered work only by songwriters who were already established by 1950. When an interviewer asked why he instituted the cutoff date, Wilder said, "After that, the amateurs took over." The statement is hyperbolic and a bit unkind, but its core of truth can be seen in the repertoire of singers and jazz musicians who have the luxury of performing the very best songs. From the 1950s through the present day, the concerts and CDs of Tony Bennett—the most justly celebrated singer of standards—have been dominated by songs written in the second quarter of the twentieth century. In 2014, Bennett released a collaboration with the pop singer Lady Gaga. Thirteen of its fifteen songs were written between 1928 ("I Can't Give You Anything but Love") and 1947 ("But Beautiful" and "Nature Boy"). The many singers from other genres who have turned to the American Songbook usually follow similar parameters. In 1978, the country singer Willie Nelson released *Stardust*, which was on the *Billboard* list of top-ten albums for two consecutive years and was ultimately certified as quadruple platinum, meaning that it sold more than four million copies. Of the ten songs on the record, six (including the title song) were composed between 1926 and 1931. Three of the remaining four were written in 1944 or earlier. The outlier was "Unchained Melody" (1955). The pop singer Linda Ronstadt's nearly as successful 1983 album, *What's New*, consisted of standards all written before 1950. Subsequently, virtually every aging rocker, most egregiously Rod Stewart and most recently Annie Lennox, has

· · · 9 · · ·

released one or more albums dominated by pre-1950 selections from the Songbook.

It's not uncommon to hear statements to the effect that the American Songbook constitutes a towering achievement in the history of this country, equal to or greater than any of our other cultural or artistic endeavors. William Zinsser and Wilfrid Sheed, among others, have made that case and made it well. I am sympathetic to the argument but I don't intend to make it again, and this book does not depend on a reader's agreement with it. However, it does proceed from certain premises: that it is possible, legitimate, and useful to make judgments about works of art, including songs; that there was something special— very special—about the Great American Songbook; that musical and lyrical sophistication in popular music is a valuable and maybe even precious thing; and that its demise and reemergence in the United States over the course of a couple of decades in the middle of the twentieth century is worth tracking. If you accept the premises, I welcome you aboard and make a pledge: I will formulate my judgments judiciously and provide evidence for them to the extent I can.

The B Side has some of the elements of a nonfiction mystery. What causes an artistic phenomenon such as the body of standards of the twenties through the forties? How much is due to a fortuitous arrival of geniuses on the scene, how much to external factors, and what might those factors be? More generally, what are the elements of good popular music? What are the elements of bad? How much does, or can, the ratio of one to another change from one era to another? How and why does this happen—and how and why, precisely, did pop music get so bad in the 1950s?

And bad it got. Alec Wilder's remark about amateurs taking over elides the fact that some writers did emerge composing pop songs in the classic manner in the fifties. However, as the decade progressed, with very few exceptions (Rodgers and Hammerstein, Jule Styne, Lerner and Loewe), the established songwriters had a tough time of it—on Broadway, in Hollywood, and on the pop charts. There weren't very many young writers wanting to bring the tradition forward, and the majority didn't do very much exceptional work. Even when first-rate songs *were* recorded, as often as not they flopped. Instead, America seemed to want to listen to banal jingles or turgid laments like "Cry" and "Que Sera, Sera (Whatever Will Be, Will Be)" and the Patti Page jingle whose refrain was "How much is that doggie in the window?"

The malaise was vague and inchoate at first, but starting in 1955 a clear "other" crystallized: Bill Haley, Elvis Presley, and the music that was starting to be called rock and roll. And let me put another card on the table: I love rock and roll. I understand that the standards are not the last word in great songs, or even great popular songs, or even in great American popular songs. Even in the years when Tin Pan Alley held sway, writers and performers who were literally and figuratively miles away—think Jimmie Rodgers, Bill Monroe, Robert Johnson, or Muddy Waters—were scaling artistic heights with very different kinds of music. In the 1950s and into the mid-1960s, these men's heirs produced "Jambalaya" and "Johnny B. Goode" and "Blue Suede Shoes" and "That'll Be the Day" and "Twist and Shout" and "Surfin' U.S.A." and "I Want to Hold Your Hand" and "(I Can't Get No) Satisfaction" and "My Generation" and "Like a Rolling Stone," all of which are great songs. But they are a different kind of song, their amazing energy generated by an emotional release expressed in three chords, a pounding beat, and shout-out-loud vocals.

The seeds of those songs had been planted over the decades by various southern whites and blacks (not Tin Pan Alley, Broadway, or Hollywood denizens), and this new garden ever more luxuriantly blossomed till the Beatles' invasion in 1964. The work of John Lennon and

Paul McCartney was actually evidence that, with the dust having cleared from the rock explosion, a space had emerged where it was possible to create songs with some of the qualities that marked the earlier tradition. In the span of a few years in the early 1960s, Willie Nelson wrote "Crazy," Brian Wilson "Caroline, No," Burt Bacharach "A House Is Not a Home," Smokey Robinson "The Tracks of My Tears," and McCartney "Yesterday." A wide range of remarkably talented songwriters of popular songs has emerged since then. But it isn't possible for them to write a standard—or, as Keith Jarrett found out, it is possible, but really hard.

By the time the Beatles played on *The Ed Sullivan Show*, the people who had written the words and music to the standards—those who were still alive—had lost the game, decisively. In retrospect, it's touching to observe the stages of grief, as it were, experienced by those old-line songwriters as the world over which they had held sway receded in the distance: ignorance, dismissal, bemusement, mockery, rage, attempted alliance, resignation, capitulation.

If you had to choose a moment that represented the beginning of the end of the old order, you make a case for a business meeting. The place: Columbia Records' headquarters in Manhattan. The year: 1954.

I
....

Mr. Miller and Mr. Schwartz
1954

Like, "You know, all those songs on the Hit Parade are just a
bunch of shit, anyway." . . . You know, "If I give my heart to you,
would you handle it with care?" Or "I'm getting sentimental over
you." Who gives a shit! It could be said in a grand way, and the
performer could put the song across, but come on, that's because
he's a great performer, not because it's a great song. . . . So a lot of
us got caught up in that. There ain't anything good on the radio. It
doesn't happen.

· Bob Dylan

Come on-a-my place, my bambino.
All those crazy sound effects they use.
I'd give a million dollars for a good old-fashioned blues.

· "What Happened to the Music" by Carolyn Leigh,
Robert Sadoff, and Nacio Herb Brown, 1953

While not quite on the level of a Richard Rodgers, a Cole
Porter, or an Irving Berlin, Arthur Schwartz was certainly
in the top echelon of American songwriters. Born at the
turn of the century, by the mid-1950s he had been producing wonderful melodies for decades, and he was known for the sophistication,

range, and quality of his work. Alec Wilder observed in *American Popular Song* that Schwartz "wrote with total self-assurance and high professional skill. . . . His published record contains some of the finest American songs in existence." (Although Wilder used the past tense, when he was writing those words the composer was still alive. He died in 1984.) Schwartz's father was a lawyer in Moscow. In this country, the only job he could get at first was as a buttonhole maker. But eventually he became a lawyer, and Arthur grew up in a middle-class New York family, graduated from New York University and Columbia Law School, and practiced law himself before turning to songwriting full-time. His first published song, in 1923, was "Baltimore, Md., You're the Only Doctor for Me." Since then, he had moved up in several different worlds, and he had the well-groomed look of a professional man. His son Jonathan wrote that in his (and the) forties, his father "cut a suave path. He was cultivated, as suggested by his unaccountable, ever-so-slight British accent. He was always wonderfully dressed. He moved gracefully with cigarette in hand, a man in honorable thought. His dark hair was turning gray; his light blue eyes held no venom. He was alive and ready for conversation, by all accounts a marvelous listener."

Schwartz was an important member of a second wave of American songwriters, who came on the scene after Berlin, Kern, and the Gershwins had established the principle that popular songs could be simultaneously successful, sophisticated, and artful. These men—they were all men, except for the lyricist Dorothy Fields—were born around the turn of the century, often to middle-class Jewish families in New York; a striking number attended Columbia University. Schwartz's first collaborator, back when both of them were counselors at an Adirondacks camp called Brant Lake, was Lorenz Hart, a New Yorker and a Columbia man. Together they composed a number called "I Love to Lie

Awake in Bed" (second line: "Right after taps I pull the flaps above my head") that I sang as a Brant Lake camper in the 1960s and is still in the repertoire there. Hart went on to team with the prodigiously talented Rodgers (Upper West Side, Columbia), and Schwartz started contributing to the Broadway stage in 1926; his main collaborator was Howard Dietz, Columbia School of Journalism, class of 1917. Schwartz and Dietz's standards included "Dancing in the Dark," "You and the Night and the Music," and "I Guess I'll Have to Change My Plan," which had the melody of "I Love to Lie Awake in Bed" with new lyrics by Dietz. (The second line—"I should have realized there'd be another man"—didn't scan as well as the original, but played better in nightclubs.) Schwartz moved to Hollywood in 1938, following a path worn by many New York songwriters. By that time Dietz was fully occupied with his job as publicity director of the Metro-Goldwyn-Mayer movie studio, but most of the best lyricists eventually made their way west from New York, and Schwartz worked with most of them: Frank Loesser, Yip Harburg, Ira Gershwin, Oscar Hammerstein, Leo Robin, and Johnny Mercer. He also was an occasional film producer, his best credits being the Cole Porter biography *Night and Day* and the 1944 musical *Cover Girl*.* After World War II, like his colleagues Harold Arlen, Loesser, Harburg, Jule Styne, and Burton Lane, Schwartz shifted his base of operations from Hollywood back to New York. Over a seven- or eight-year period he had written the music for a series of Broadway shows, most recently *A Tree Grows in Brooklyn*. His lyricist on that production was Dorothy Fields, and their new musical *By the Beautiful Sea*, starring Shirley Booth, had just now, in

---

*Schwartz was offered the job of collaborating with Gershwin on that film's score, but according to Jonathan Schwartz, he responded, with characteristic modesty and grammatical meticulousness, "There's a better man than I available." The man was Jerome Kern, who produced at least two timeless songs for *Cover Girl*: "Long Ago (and Far Away)" and "Sure Thing." Kern died the year after the film's release.

the spring of 1954, opened on Broadway. Schwartz was at Columbia to meet with Mitch Miller, head of popular music at the label, who had the power to choose songs Columbia artists would record.

The foregoing gives a somewhat misleading impression of the state of Schwartz's professional life on the day of his meeting with Miller. To be sure, he enjoyed status and prestige. He had been a close associate of both Kern and George Gershwin (whose death in 1937 shocked the songwriting community), of Ira Gershwin, Rodgers, Arlen, and the other princes of Tin Pan Alley. He had just stepped down as president of the League of New York Theatres, was a council member of the Songwriters Protective Association, and had an AA classification— one step down from the highest, AAA—from ASCAP, the forty-year-old association that collected songwriters' royalties from the radio stations that played their songs. He was getting musicals produced on Broadway, which was what every songwriter aspired to. And he was still feeling a bit of the glow from a Fred Astaire film MGM had produced the year before, *The Band Wagon*. It featured a raft of old Schwartz and Dietz songs—plus one new one, "That's Entertainment"—and it was a big hit at the box office.

For some time, however, Schwartz had had an unmistakable sense that things were slipping away from him. For one thing, his Broadway musicals never managed to do very well. *Inside U.S.A.* had a respectable run, but *A Tree Grows in Brooklyn* had played for less than a year, failing to recoup its investment. That was disturbing. "He viewed himself as a theatrical writer," said his other son, Paul. "He looked down on 'pop' songs, said they were for people like Jimmy Van Heusen and Sammy Cahn. I told him that was bullshit. 'No no no,' he'd say. 'I worked in the theater.' The music *business*, to him, was déclassé."

That's not to say he didn't want his songs recorded or played on the radio. And in recent years, that simply wasn't happening. What seemed so vexingly different now for Schwartz—and, as a matter of fact, for many of his peers—was that, in marked contrast to previous times, his songs never seemed to live on *after* the show. The gatekeepers of the record industry, who decided which songs singers would record as singles—and thus which songs would even have a chance of being hits on the radio—were the artist and repertoire (A&R) men; Miller occupied that position at the most powerful label, Columbia. The A&R men were not buying what Schwartz had to offer. The previous year, he had met with a man from RCA Victor, who flatly turned down a batch of songs from *A Tree Grows in Brooklyn*. Not a single song from that show had so much as made an appearance on the charts that appeared each week in the trade magazine *Billboard* showing the most popular recordings. Indeed, only one song from his recent shows had charted—a sweet and simple ballad from *Inside U.S.A.* called "Haunted Heart," Perry Como's version of which had peaked at number twenty-three in 1948.

Possibly even more annoying was the fact that Schwartz's old songs—his *standards*—weren't doing much in terms of any of the three streams of a songwriter's income: recordings, radio play, and sheet music sales. (In earlier years, sheet music had accounted for the biggest stream. That had diminished with the advent of new technologies and changes in family life—no one had time to sit around the piano anymore—but still could be significant.) And again, he was far from alone in feeling marginalized. A year later, some staffers at ASCAP put together figures showing how many radio "plugs," or plays, a group of the most glorious American standards got in 1948 and then in 1955. The drop-off was shocking. And the higher 1948 numbers couldn't be explained by saying the songs were then fresh. As the following examples show, they got airplay in that earlier period *despite* being long in the tooth.

	1948	1955
"A Pretty Girl Is Like a Melody" (Irving Berlin, 1919)	31,518	5,478
"Always" (Berlin, 1925)	81,808	7,210
"I Got Rhythm" (George Gershwin, 1930)	18,474	7,115
"More than You Know" (Vincent Youmans, 1929)	9,987	899
"Night and Day" (Cole Porter, 1932)	41,769	11,722
"Over the Rainbow" (Harold Arlen, 1939)	28,704	12,228

What *was* getting played? When he turned on the radio, Schwartz could only shake his head. What came out of the box—and had been coming ever since the end of the war, it seemed to him—were novelty numbers, lachrymose ballads, simplistic jingles, hillbilly hokum. The smash hit of the previous year, 1953—number one on the charts for eight consecutive weeks and in the top ten for a total of seventeen—was Patti Page's "The Doggie in the Window." The writer was not a cowboy or a hick but a thirty-two-year-old Atlantic City native and Tin Pan Alley pro named Bob Merrill. Merrill (born Henry Levan) specialized in novelty numbers, most of them recorded by Columbia artists, and many of them vaguely regional or "ethnic": "If I Knew You Were Comin' I'd've Baked a Cake," a hit for Eileen Barton in 1950; "Feet Up

(Pat Him on the Po-Po)," recorded by Guy Mitchell in 1952; and "Ooh Bang Jiggilly Jang." In 1954, Rosemary Clooney's record of Merrill's geographically puzzling "Mambo Italiano" made the top ten. But "Doggie," with its insistent waltz beat, simplistic melody, and nursery school lyrics—which, once heard, positively could not be extracted from a listener's head—was somehow emblematic, not only of Merrill's output, but of this particular moment in American popular song.

Interviewed by *Cue* magazine in 1953, Merrill said, "Don't get me wrong. I'm no Tchaikovsky. I can't read or write a note. I compose all my songs on this toy xylophone I bought at the five-and-ten for $1.98." He said he put numbers on the xylophone keys so he could easily transcribe the melody. "You can't fool yourself with fancy arranging," he said. "All my hits have a very simple, hummable melody." At that point Merrill claimed he had earned more than $250,000 from his songs. That emboldened him to purchase a new, better xylophone, which cost $6.98.

By way of explaining his success, Merrill told *Cue* his songs were "all about America, they are all wholesome, and they are all happy."

Had the world turned mad, or just imbecilic? That was the basic question the old-line songwriters continually asked one another over corned beef sandwiches at Lindy's or Nate 'n Al's, or in brief conversations in the lobby of the Brill Building, the Times Square office building that for decades had been the epicenter of songwriting and music publishing. The whole thing was a mystery. As Schwartz later said, referring to his colleagues, "Their conclusions were the same as mine, that the simultaneous change in our position as writers of songs that could receive exploitation could not be coincidence or the result of the atom bomb or the Russian preparation for the next world war. . . . It must be somebody's doing."

Another veteran songwriter, Jack Lawrence, the lyricist of "All or

Nothing at All," "Tenderly," and "Beyond the Sea," described his own experiences in a similar way:

> I took a Broadway show score and a Hollywood picture score to both Columbia Records and NBC-RCA-Victor records. This represented over a total of twenty-odd songs and perhaps two years' work or more. In both instances I got not one single recording. Now, perhaps it is true that I've lost my touch for writing and creating hit songs in my twenty-odd years of writing professionally. And it could be true that two or three or four of my fellow writer-members have also lost their talent for writing hits. But when you see hundreds of premium quality writers who have written great songs, memorable songs that have lasted for years and years, suddenly confronted with an accusation of having lost their touch and talent, or their feeling for what the public wants today, I think this is too great a coincidence.

You will note that neither the phrase "rock and roll" nor the name Elvis Presley is mentioned by Lawrence or Schwartz as a possible reason for the change in their and their colleagues' fortunes. In 1954, Elvis was just commencing his recording and performing career in Memphis. And "rock and roll" would, at that moment, have produced a blank look on the face of most Americans.

At this point, the "somebody" who had sabotaged the songwriters, in their increasingly certain estimation, was actually an interwoven collection of entities: the biggest radio networks, CBS and NBC; the record companies they owned, Columbia and RCA Victor, respectively; and a song-licensing organization they had collectively formed more than a dozen years earlier, Broadcast Music, Inc., commonly known as BMI. BMI was a competitor to the venerable association Arthur Schwartz, Jack Lawrence, and everybody like them belonged to. A long-standing financial dispute between ASCAP and the radio networks—which depended on ASCAP songs for the bulk of their programming—had come to a head in 1941, and then, for about a year, the networks banished ASCAP material from the airwaves. In its place, listeners heard classical pieces, works in the public domain, and songs that had been hurriedly signed to the brand-new BMI. BMI writers were not the likes of Arthur Schwartz. Rather, they were people who had been unable to crack ASCAP (the membership policies of which were reminiscent of the most restrictive country club) or who hadn't even thought to try. A lot of them were from places other than New York City—*very* other. They were African-Americans like Lead Belly, whose song "Good Night, Irene" was number one for the Weavers in 1950, westerners like cowboy crooner Gene Autry, and outliers like Pee Wee King, a Polish-American accordionist from Milwaukee (birth name: Julius Frank Anthony Kuczynski) who reinvented himself as a country-western singer-songwriter. (His song "The Tennessee Waltz" would be a number-one record for Patti Page in 1950.)

The ASCAP ban lasted only ten months. And since 1942 the two organizations, ASCAP and BMI, had coexisted on the airwaves and among the music publishers of Tin Pan Alley. But the radio stations still owned BMI. Radio stations determined what would be played on their air. Didn't it stand to reason that they would favor songs licensed to the organization they owned: BMI?

It certainly did to Schwartz and his peers. In April of 1952, *Billboard* reported that ASCAP had filed a complaint against BMI for "antitrust violations." The magazine commented ominously: "ASCAP has tried to live with the BMI competition, but it is no secret that a segment of Tin Pan Alley's upper crust has come to the conclusion that the battle must be to the death." In the middle of 1953, a group of top songwriters met in Oscar Hammerstein II's house to discuss strategy;

among those present, *Variety* reported, were Hammerstein's partner, Richard Rodgers, and another titan of popular song, Cole Porter. In November a group of thirty-three composers and lyricists brought a $150 million antitrust suit against BMI; the four major broadcasting networks (NBC, CBS, Mutual, and ABC, which had grown out of NBC's Blue Network); RCA Victor and Columbia Records; and sundry other parties. The $150 million figure derived from the plaintiffs' claim that they collectively had been denied $50 million in revenues from a conspiracy against them and their works; the Clayton Antitrust Act empowers injured parties to sue for treble damages.

The lead plaintiff was Arthur Schwartz, whose law degree had finally come in handy! He was joined by Alan Jay Lerner, Ira Gershwin, Dorothy Fields, Virgil Thomson, Gian Carlo Menotti, and others from both the popular and classical worlds. (*Variety* noted, "While top names like Rodgers & Hammerstein, Cole Porter and Irving Berlin do not appear among co-plaintiffs, they have contributed to the legal war chest, which is now variously estimated at around $300,000.") The lawsuit claimed that the radio networks and record companies had conspired to give "preference to the performance of BMI controlled music." A widely publicized statement signed by the plaintiffs alleged that the defendants had been guilty of "placing American music in a strait jacket manipulated through BMI."

After generating a flurry of publicity, the lawsuit adopted the petty pace that would characterize it till its resolution, which took a *Jarndyce v. Jarndyce*–like eighteen years. Slowing things at the outset was the discovery process, which in just five years would generate "20,000 pages of testimony, some 11,000 exhibits consisting of approximately 55,000 pages, and almost 3,000 pages of answers to written interrogatories." Schwartz's reading of this material gave him to understand that it wasn't just the conspiracy to favor BMI songs that was holding him back. There was *another* kind of conspiracy. In a deposition for the suit, Mitch Miller testified that in his capacity as head of artist and repertoire for Columbia, none other than Bob Merrill would customarily bring him songs intended for Guy Mitchell, a Columbia recording artist. "I made many suggestions, and he was very grateful for them," Miller testified. "He asked me to be part writer. I said no; I was only doing an editor's work." But then, lo and behold, after "Mambo Italiano" and "Make Yourself Comfortable" became hits (the latter for Sarah Vaughan), Miller starting receiving checks from Merrill's publisher, totaling about $4,000. Schwartz took that to mean Miller was protesting too much: the payment was a kickback, pure and simple— or, to call it by the term that *Variety* had been using since the late 1930s and that had been a characteristic of the music industry for years before that, payola. A similar thing happened in 1952, Miller testified. During World War II, GIs had turned the old English folk song "A Knave Is a Knave" into a bawdy ditty called "A Gob Is a Slob"; a young American singer and writer named Oscar Brand had recorded it on an obscure folk label in 1949. He brought a cleaned-up version called "A Guy Is a Guy" to Miller, who showed it to the Columbia singer Doris Day. Miller testified that she "didn't like the lyrics as they were"— presumably feeling they needed even more cleaning up—"so we had it changed." Day's record did well, and Miller "received compensation" of $1,200.

Miller's willingness to take and maybe even solicit such payments wasn't the only thing that made him a controversial figure. A graduate of the Eastman School of Music, he started out as a classical oboist and became a highly respected one, playing on recordings under Leopold Stokowski's baton and for over a decade in the CBS Symphony Orchestra. But his career changed in 1948, when his friend John Hammond recruited him to head the pop A&R department at a new label, Mercury. Miller created two number-one hits—a sort of folk spiritual called "That Lucky Old Sun" and a cowboy number, "Mule Train"— for the singer Frankie Laine (born Francesco LoVecchio), who had previously had middling success at Mercury with a series of jazzy numbers. Miller's Eastman School classmate Goddard Lieberson lured him to Columbia in 1950 to spearhead a new approach to popular music for the label. "Hereafter," Lieberson said in an announcement, "more emphasis will be placed on selecting the right artist for the right tune and an imaginative, creative effort to produce the best records possible will be made at the main source of every successful record—the recording studio."

Lieberson made an intriguing analogy: "A record is in a sense like a play. It requires a beginning, a denouement and an end."

The strategy worked. Within a year and a half, the label's pop music sales had increased 60 percent, catapulting the company from last to the first among the four major labels. (The others were RCA Victor, Decca, and Capitol.) Miller—commonly referred to as "the Beard" because of his trademark goatee—was responsible for a series of smashes, including Johnnie Ray's "Cry," Rosemary Clooney's "Come On-a My House," Tony Bennett's "Because of You" and "Rags to Riches," and "I Saw Mommy Kissing Santa Claus," which sold more than three million copies and was sung by a thirteen-year-old freckled Mississippian named Jimmy Boyd. (When the record was first released, the Catholic Archdiocese of Boston banned it because it mixed sex with Christmas.)

Miller, forty-two years old on the day he was to meet with Schwartz, was considered the "golden boy" among the A&R men, in the words of a 1954 *Vogue* magazine article about the music industry. But he was not so well liked by people, such as Arthur Schwartz, who felt, whether they put it this way or not, that a popular song could reach the artistic heights of classical music.

Miller's attitudes and actions had brought him into conflict with some of the singers Columbia had under contract, notably Frank Sinatra. Sinatra was the greatest singing star of the forties; his intimate, exquisitely controlled tones made girls scream and swoon and earned him the nickname "the Voice." But by the early fifties he had fallen on hard times. The Voice's voice was in poor shape, and Sinatra chafed at the fluff and novelty tunes Miller gave him to record, such as "The Hucklebuck," "Bim Bam Baby," and "Mama Will Bark," a duet with a buxom television personality named Dagmar, the gimmick of which was that dogs actually barked in the background. In every possible way, the Beard annoyed the Voice. Drummer Johnny Blowers remembered years later that at one recording session Miller fiddled so incessantly with the dials that Sinatra "looked in the control room, pointed his finger, and said, 'Mitch—out.' When Mitch didn't move, Sinatra turned to Hank Sanicola [a longtime Sinatra associate]. 'Henry, move him.' To Mitch, he said, 'Don't you ever come in the studio when I'm recording again.'"

Columbia dropped Sinatra in 1952; soon afterward he signed with Capitol Records and his career began to turn around. But the singer's grudge against Miller remained. During a Copacabana engagement in 1953, according to author Arnold Shaw, the singer "donned a coonskin hat, snapped a bull whip, and honked derisively like a wild goose." (The whip was a reference to "Mule Train," which very prominently featured the sound of a whip—created by wood blocks—and the honk to another folksy hit Miller had with Frankie Laine, "The Cry of the Wild Goose," in which the wild goose's cry was simulated with French horns. The Davy Crockett craze would not occur for another two years, but coonskin hats had become a trademark of Tennessee senator Estes Kefauver, so Sinatra may have worn one as an act of general rural derision.)

Songwriters, for their part, couldn't afford to affect disdain for Mitch Miller; they needed him. He needed them, too. Every Monday afternoon he opened his doors and let the writers' representatives, publishers, show their wares. Robert Rice of *The New Yorker* sat in on one five-and-a-half-hour session—during which Miller smoked five cigars—and his account is worth quoting for the general sense it gives of the tenor of Tin Pan Alley in 1953, when the Korean War was in full swing and rock and roll was a whisper in the air that was just out of hearing:

There were publishers of almost every possible age, size, shape, and costume, most of them carrying demonstration records but some with piano or guitar players in tow. There was a tall young crew-cut publisher in a regimental tie who crooned; a short, fat, middle-aged publisher in orange slacks and a hound's-tooth sports jacket who bounced; and a tieless, cauliflower-eared, mash-nosed, ex-prizefighter of a publisher who bellowed. There was a businesslike publisher who said, "Mitch, I have two things here, one extremely important"; a highbrow publisher who said, "Mitch, this thing is melodically unoriginal but lyrically powerful"; a timorous publisher who said, "I've got a beautiful little thing here, Mitch, that you're going to turn down"; an aggressive publisher who said, "Let's get lucky together, Mitch"; and an articulate publisher who said, "They all flip for this thing, Mitch." There was a publisher with a number called "Korean Love Song"; when Miller said that it was difficult to associate Korea with love these days, the publisher asked why. There was a publisher with a song called "Off the Coast of Capri on the Way to Sorrento"; when Miller said to him, "Capri yet! Why not Brighton Beach? Why does it all the time have to be so arty?," he replied, "Why, Mitch, nobody's ever used Sorrento before." There was a publisher with a song called "Cigarette, Cigarette," which was about a wild gypsy girl and whose tune was a theme from Mozart's symphony No. 40 in G-Minor; when Miller said, "Mozart's ode to nicotine, eh?," the publisher answered, "Why not? I made money with Tchaikovsky and Rachmaninoff." There was a publisher with a song called "Till I Waltz Again with You," written in fox-trot time; when Miller protested against this anomaly, he said, "But, Mitch, that's the whole kick." . . . There was a young and excited publisher who sprinted in waving a record of a song called "Heartbroken Me and Brokenhearted You." "Mitch," he said breathlessly, "I got a sensational switch on heartbreaks." From this welter, which he bore with astonishing meekness, Miller extracted just two faintly possible songs.*

The fact that Arthur Schwartz was granted a private audience to play the songs from *By the Beautiful Sea*, rather than having to troop in with the rest of the Monday supplicants, was in accordance with his stature and his body of work. But the composer couldn't help approaching the meeting with mixed feelings. Private audience or no, it seemed less than respectful that he, Arthur Schwartz, was still forced to appear before this crass A&R man and depend on his good graces. And it was slightly awkward that he had just very publicly sued Miller's employer, Columbia Records.

His trepidations were confirmed when, after hearing all the songs from *By the Beautiful Sea*, Miller said only one of them was a possi-

---

*It turns out Miller made a mistake with "Till I Waltz Again with You." As recorded by Teresa Brewer on Coral Records, it was the country's best-selling record for five weeks.

bility, a ballad called "More Love Than Your Love." But even that needed "work."

"I like the song but I think you ought to make a change in the melody," Schwartz remembered Miller saying. "I don't think that the second eight measures should do what they do; I think maybe you should repeat the first eight measures where you now have a new eight-measure section."

The composer immediately thought of Miller's testimony about the payments he got from Merrill's and Brand's publishers. It was a shakedown, pure and simple.

"I will think it over," Schwartz replied. "Thank you for the suggestion."

Thank you, indeed. One can imagine the boiling of Schwartz's blood, the iciness of his words. This goateed vulgarian whose claim to fame was insinuating a whip in "Mule Train," who had been responsible for "Come On-a My House" and "Mama Will Bark," having the nerve to tell Arthur Schwartz, friend and colleague of George Gershwin and Richard Rodgers, to write a song in AABA—the elemental form of American popular song since Irving Berlin and Jerome Kern were starting out—as if this were some kind of brilliant and original insight! And if the "improvement" was accepted, no doubt expecting his palm to be greased!

"I thought it over and decided I did not want to make the change," Schwartz said.

No Columbia artist would record "More Love Than Your Love." As a matter of fact, only three recordings of it have ever been made, to the best of my knowledge. It appeared on the cast album of *By the Beautiful Sea*, released by Capitol on a 1950 78-rpm record by Les Baxter and His Chorus and Orchestra; as a filler instrumental track on a 1954 Capitol album by Stan Kenton and His Orchestra; and, improbably, on a 2005 CD by the singer Andy Bey. Lyrically and musically, it is an undistinguished song, sentimental and plodding. It is hard to imagine how it might be improved. Possibly if the first eight bars had been repeated, but probably not.

By the Beautiful Sea got mixed reviews, but Shirley Booth's star power kept it going till November, when it closed after a seven-month run.

II
....

I Get a Kick out of You
1885–1933

The word for Dick Rodgers' melodies, I think, is holy. For Jerome
Kern, sentimental. For Irving Berlin, simplicity. For my own,
I don't know.

• Cole Porter

n order to understand how popular songs got so bad, it makes sense
to give some attention to how they got so good. A useful place to start
is with the first songwriter to make a significant living at the trade,
a Milwaukeean named Charles K. Harris. (The greatest songwriter of
the nineteenth century was Stephen Foster. The median total payment
Foster received from his songs was $36, and he died penniless in 1864
at the age of thirty-seven.) Sometime around 1885, Harris hung out
a shingle that read: "Charles K. Harris—Banjoist and Songwriter—
Songs Written to Order." "After the Ball," his 1891 waltz-time tear-
jerker about lost love, was this country's first million-selling song. He
followed it up with another hit, "Break the News to Mother," in which
the words of the title come from the lips of a dying soldier. In his 1926
autobiography—naturally titled *After the Ball*—Harris observed: "I

find that sentiment plays a large part in our lives. The most hardened character or the most cynical individual will succumb to sentiment sometime or other."

Harris's phenomenal success introduced the idea that one could make money, even a good deal of money, by writing popular music. It also spawned a whole new style of song, with such self-explanatory titles as "The Picture That Is Turned Toward the Wall," "The Letter That Never Came," and "The Pardon Came Too Late." The last two were the creations of Paul Dresser, who surpassed even Harris as an apostle of sentiment. He was known to burst into tears at the sound of a touching song, especially one of his own compositions. His brother the novelist Theodore Dreiser, on the other hand, described Dresser lyrics as "mere bits and scraps of sentiment and melodrama in story form, most asinine sightings over home and mother and lost sweethearts and dead heroes such as never were in real life."[*]

The American songs of the period that are still sung, or hummed, today display a kind of forced nostalgia, hammered home by their customary 3/4 waltz time. They put forth a rural or (less often) urban ideal; when they express longing or love, the object is idealized, sentimentalized, and/or distant. The following were all Tin Pan Alley productions written between 1892 and 1910 but somehow seem much older, as if they had emanated from a prehistoric period of pure Americana: "In the Good Old Summer Time," "Down by the Old Mill Stream," "Daisy Bell (Bicycle Built for Two)," "The Sidewalks of New York," and "Let Me Call You Sweetheart."

Charles K. Harris couldn't read or write music and did not consider that an impediment. He wrote in *After the Ball*: "The reader will naturally wonder how it was possible for me to write music to a song when

---

[*]It was Paul who changed the spelling of the family name.

even to this day I cannot distinguish one note from another. The answer is simple. As soon as a melody occurred to me, I hummed it. Then I would procure the services of a trained musician . . . hum or whistle the melody to him and have him take it down on paper, with notes. He would then arrange it for the piano. This method is known as arranging." His compositions' lack of musical complexity not only wasn't a problem, it was a virtue. In an era before radio or recordings, songs were disseminated by means of sheet music, bought in music shops and department stores. Middle-class families customarily had pianos in their parlors and one or more members with the ability to play them. "Ability" was a relative term, and therefore most songs were fairly basic melodically and harmonically. The lyrics, too, had to be simple enough for memorization.

The trade grew year after year. "Nowadays," *The New York Times* remarked in 1910, "the consumption of songs in America is as constant as their consumption of shoes, and the demand is similarly met by factory output." The high-water mark was 1917, when more than two billion copies of sheet music were sold in the United States; it had become common for a popular individual title to sell five million. In fairly short order, a new group of entrepreneurs took over the major publishers, many of them having come from backgrounds in selling: Isidore Witmark had sold water filters; Joseph W. Stern and Edward B. Marks, neckties and buttons; Leo Feist, corsets; Max and Louis Dreyfus, ribbons and picture frames. These men were resourceful and opportunistic, and in its mature phase the song industry was more vertically integrated than the shoe industry, with the sheet music publisher controlling the structure and taking a cut of every transaction.

Once a song met a publisher's approval, a complicated chain of events was set in motion. The publisher might suggest or demand changes to the song itself or the title. Upon taking it on, he would commission an illustration (very important, since music was often an impulse buy), then print copies, frequently offering a variety of orchestrations. Then it was time for the song plugger to do his stuff. In his 1930 study *Tin Pan Alley: A Chronicle of the American Popular Music Racket*, Isaac Goldberg gave a good description of this vital job: "He it is who, by all the arts of persuasion, intrigue, bribery, mayhem, malfeasance, cajolery, entreaty, threat, insinuation, persistence and whatever else he has, sees to it that his employer's music shall be heard." "Bribery" is a harsh word, but without a doubt, in order to get vaudeville and dance-hall entertainers to add the song to their repertoires, pluggers customarily provided them with substantial amounts of what would come to be called payola.

Given the scale of the enterprise, it's not surprising that songwriters were near or at the bottom of the ladder in terms of power and money (they generally sold a publisher all rights to a song for a modest sum, plus a royalty of a penny or two per copy sold). In the words of a 1908 book, "With a few notable exceptions, America's popular songwriters are unknown. Such songs are almost impersonal. They do not bear the stamp of the composer's individuality so much as they reflect the taste of the day." Some of the "notable exceptions" have been mentioned. Another one is George M. Cohan, who established his own lucrative corner of the industry in the last decade of the nineteenth century and the first two decades of the twentieth with rousing numbers like "Give My Regards to Broadway," "The Yankee Doodle Boy," and "You're a Grand Old Flag."

The lack of respect accorded to songwriters didn't stop waves of hopefuls from showing up on Tin Pan Alley to sell their wares like so many Fuller Brush men. Songwriting presented an attractive prospect to ambitious young folk with no other prospects, especially New York City's hundreds of thousands of immigrants and immigrants' sons from eastern and southern Europe. The upside potential was so high— you could get a good payday with just one thirty-two-bar hit song—and the barrier to entry so low. *Anyone* could offer his wares—that is, any- one who could handle the indignity of knocking on door after door and being summarily rejected time and again.

In the first two decades of the new century, the hallmark of Tin Pan Alley was novelty. Writers and publishers searched relentlessly for the angle, the pitch, that would sell, and when one of them hit on it, he was slavishly and copiously imitated. One year it was dream songs: "Meet Me Tonight in Dreamland" was a hit, and so it was succeeded by "Girl of My Dreams," "My Little Dream Girl," "Sweetheart of My Dreams," "When I Met You Last Night in Dreamland," "You Tell Me Your Dream and I'll Tell You Mine," and more. According to the publisher Ed Marks: "The jobbers became so confused that they num- bered the dream songs and sold them by number instead of by title."

The Alley was also keyed to goings-on in the world at large. No significant event, fashion, or trend escaped a musical commentary, including the conflict in Europe, which spawned Al Piantadosi's mildly pacifistic "I Didn't Raise My Boy to Be a Soldier." But when the United States entered the war in 1917, songwriters immediately adopted an extreme patriotism. Certainly, the pitch was right in George M. Cohan's wheelhouse. "I read those war headlines and I got to thinking and humming to myself—and for a moment I thought I was going to dance," he recalled. That same morning he wrote "Over There." Within a week of the U.S. entry, "Good-bye Broadway, Hello France" was on the department stores' sheet music counters, followed in short order by "I'm Glad I Raised My Boy to Be a Soldier," "I Didn't Raise My Boy to Be a Slacker," "We Don't Want the Bacon (What We Want Is a Piece of the Rhine!)," and scores of others. The war also made its way into love songs, including such kitsch classics as "Your

Lips Are No Man's Land but Mine" and "If He Can Fight Like He Can Love, Good Night Germany!"

A half-dozen years later, Gershwin, Porter, and Rodgers had joined Berlin and Kern in producing songs that do not seem quaint and are still being sung, played, and enjoyed. How did we get from "If He Can Fight Like He Can Love, Good Night Germany!" to this remarkable work? In hindsight, it's possible to identify an array of interwoven factors.

Individual

The quintet of writers just named represented a rare flowering of genius; as noted, a comparison to Renaissance Florence may seem excessive, but then again it holds up to scrutiny. Unlike Italian painters, they did not all undergo extensive training. But the trailblazer, Jerome Kern, certainly did. Born to a middle-class German Jewish family in New York in 1885, he studied music in the United States and Heidelberg, worked as a Tin Pan Alley song plugger, and contributed numbers to Broadway and London shows as early as 1905. His 1914 song "They Didn't Believe Me"—with its stately, lingering melody; its 4/4 rhythm that could go fast or slow, syncopated or straight; and its simple, conversational ("and I'm certainly going to tell them . . ."), resonant lyrics by Herbert Reynolds—has been credibly nominated as the first modern American popular song. By his early thirties, Kern was the dean of Broadway composers, unmatched in the way he combined the influences of operetta, English music hall, and ragtime to create a new American sound.

Comparable in genius, close in age, Kern and the second great figure were different in almost every other way. Israel Baline, the son of a cantor, was born in Temun, Russia, in 1888. He came to New York at the age of four and by fourteen was on his own, with a new name—Irving Berlin—working as a saloon pianist and a singing waiter in a Chinatown joint called Nigger Mike's. He had no musical training, and his piano skills were the most rudimentary of all the great composers, but he had an ear for melody and soon he began writing music as well. (Famously, Berlin only ever learned to play in the key of F-sharp, and had a specially designed piano that allowed him to transpose keys by turning a small wheel.) In 1911 came "Alexander's Ragtime Band," which, while not technically a rag, had a syncopated vitality the American popular song had never seen before and which singlehandedly changed everything. Over the next forty years, Berlin produced hundreds and hundreds of first-rate songs. Alec Wilder said, "I can speak of only one composer as the master of the entire range of popular song—Irving Berlin." Berlin appears in retrospect as a freak of nature. The combination of his lack of training, on the one hand, and seemingly inexhaustible, high-level production, on the other, spawned urban legends, which would persist his whole life, that he had between one and three "colored boys" in the back room who wrote his songs.

The Gershwins' parents were Russian immigrants as well. But both George and Ira were born on this side of the Atlantic (Ira in 1896 and his brother two years later), and their father worked steadily and earned enough money for the family to buy a piano, which George learned to play magnificently. Rodgers (born 1902) came from a well-to-do German Jewish family in New York, and Porter (born 1891, a comparatively late bloomer), whose grandfather was known as the richest man in Indiana, went to Yale. Rodgers, Porter, Gershwin, and Kern all had significant musical training, were familiar with classical composition, and were amenable to incorporating the innovations of classical modernists into popular songs.

Genius is seldom a discrete phenomenon. It certainly wasn't in the case of these groundbreakers. They were inspired and goaded to greater achievement by each other; Gershwin once remarked that it was Kern's music that made him realize most popular songs were of an inferior quality. And their presence, in and of itself, inspired other talented young people to go into the field, where the bar of acceptability, and the bar of excellence, were now considerably higher than they had been. Among all songwriters, there was an implicit and sometimes explicit competition to advance the craft. With one exception, the inspiration these men provided was a result less of their personalities than of their artistic example. Kern and Rodgers were introverts, as was Berlin, whom many colleagues found cold and distant, especially as he got older. Porter tended to consort more with upper-class socialites than songwriters. The exception was Gershwin, who was charismatic, glamorous, and generous in encouraging younger songwriters such as Arthur Schwartz, Harold Arlen, and Vernon Duke. If he hadn't died young, in 1937, he would have encouraged even more.

Technological

Early-twentieth-century changes in the way music was delivered generally disadvantaged publishers, favored the songwriters (or at least the best songwriters), and led to creative innovations. The first such change was the 78-rpm wax record, introduced in 1902. The technology had not matured very much by 1909, so when the Copyright Act of that year specified that copyright applied to "mechanical" reproductions of a musical work, what it had in mind were piano rolls. Nonetheless, the act applied to records as well, and Congress established a system whereby publishers received two cents for each recording or player piano roll. The Victor Talking Machine Company dominated the manufacture of both phonographs and records. The number of records it sold increased by an average of 20 percent each year from 1902 to 1923, from 1.7 million to 40.5 million. A milestone could be glimpsed in two 1920 hit songs ("Whispering" and "The Japanese Sandman"), which sold two million records each. By 1929, more than 105 million records and 750,000 phonographs were manufactured in the United States, together valued at $100 million.

The Alley had to make one compositional accommodation to the 78. Disks ran four minutes or less, so the old-fashioned song with endless verses and choruses was now out of the question. The slimming down was salutary. The jazz bandleader Paul Whiteman observed in 1926, "Previous to 1897 every song had to have six or seven verses and each verse had six or seven lines. Now there are two verses of a scant four lines each, and even at that, the second verse counts scarcely at all. The whole story must be told in the very first verse and chorus and usually there is very little to it anyway, the music being what matters."

Presently the verse itself disappeared, or at most retained a vestigial presence, often skipped in recordings or performance. The meat of a typical standard song, it became understood, was four sections of eight bars each, most commonly in AABA form, with the B section, known as the bridge or release, sometimes modulating to another key. As Charles Hamm observed, "The skill and genius of Tin Pan Alley composers (and lyricists) was revealed by what could be done within a tightly constricted formal structure, rather than by flights of fancy soaring to new and complex designs. One is reminded of similar restrictions embraced by writers of sonnets, by the Japanese poets of haiku verse, and by the great American bluesmen."

A characteristic example is Cole Porter's "I Get a Kick out of You," from the 1934 show *Anything Goes*, which is simple in structure yet, in its way, perfect.

Verse:

My story is much too sad to be told,

But practically everything leaves me totally cold.

The only exception I know is the case

When I'm out on a quiet spree,

Fighting vainly the old ennui,

And I suddenly turn and see your fabulous face.

Chorus (A):

I get no kick from champagne.

Mere alcohol doesn't thrill me at all.

So tell me why should it be true

That I get a kick out of you?

A:

Some, they may go for cocaine.

I'm sure that if I took even one sniff

It would bore me terrifically, too.

Yet I get a kick out of you.

Bridge (B):

I get a kick every time I see

You standing there before me.

I get a kick though it's clear to see

You obviously do not adore me.

A:

I get no kick in a plane.

Flying too high with some guy in the sky

Is my idea of nothing to do.

Yet I get a kick out of you.

At the upper end of royalties, songwriters got two cents per piece of sheet music sold (three for Broadway show writers) and up to one-third of the publisher's cut of a recording. By the end of the decade, a hit could earn writers $5,000 to $10,000. But only the most consistently successful of them, such as Berlin (who was savvy enough to start his own publishing house), Walter Donaldson, and Gus Kahn, could expect to earn as much as $150,000 in a very good year. Even so, the music industry continued to foster the idea that "popular songwriting is the most highly overpaid form of writing in the world," in the words of Abel Green, then music editor of *Variety*.

The Copyright Act of 1909 set the term for copyright of a musical composition to twenty-eight years, renewable for an additional twenty-eight, and for the first time included under copyright "public performance for profit." That is, anyone playing or singing a copyrighted song had to pay for the right to do so. "Had to" but often didn't: many bandleaders—and the restaurants and nightclubs that employed them—resisted paying anything to copyright holders, sometimes offering the justification that public performances stimulated sheet music sales. In 1913, a group of songwriters and publishers met in Lüchow's restaurant in New York to talk about how to collect; out of that dinner came the founding, the following year, of the American Society of Composers, Authors and Publishers. ASCAP actively attempted to collect money from restaurants and hotels that offered live music. Some of the proprietors refused, and the matter went to the courts. In 1917 the Supreme Court ruled in ASCAP's favor and thus established the foundation for the organization's future existence, its subsequent power and influence, and, in some measure, a new respect for songs as individual artistic creations. Justice Oliver Wendell Holmes Jr. ruled that establishments, notably restaurants, had to pay for music even if they did not charge an entry fee: "It is true that music is not the sole object, but neither is the food, which probably could be got cheaper elsewhere. . . . If music did not pay, it would be given up. If it pays, it pays out of the public's pocket. Whether it pays or not, the purpose of employing it is profit, and that is enough."

Radio began commercial operation in 1920, three years after the court's ruling, and soon established itself as an important cultural and commercial institution. About 190,000 radio units were produced in 1923; by 1929 the number was almost 5 million. Radio was free of charge to listeners, of course, but when radio stations sent copyrighted music over the airwaves, the same pay-to-play principle would seem to apply. The stations, predictably, balked, sometimes claiming that all they were doing was broadcasting "ether." ASCAP responded with a series of (ultimately victorious) lawsuits against the radio interests. With the rulings in hand, ASCAP undertook to monitor the musical offerings of all the stations in the country. By the mid-1930s, ASCAP was annually collecting some $10 million.

It distributed that money to songwriters by means of a complicated classification system. An internal committee placed every member into one of thirteen separate classes, from AAA to 4, based on achievement over the course of a career: number of songs written, sales, and hits. An individual writer's classification determined both voting power within the organization and the share of ASCAP-collected money he received. For example, in 1929, when there were still only four classifications, the quarterly payments were as follows: Class A, $2,000; Class B, $1,000; Class C, $500; Class D, $250. The system was not only undemocratic but also unfair and would eventually be scrapped in 1952.* Yet at the outset it helped solidify the idea that popular song-writing wasn't a monolith but a skilled endeavor with practitioners operating at many different levels.

ASCAP was also important for lyricists, giving them, for the first time, a chance to receive recognition, respect, and a decent paycheck. In the original Tin Pan Alley model, a lyricist got a flat fee (for many years the going rate was five dollars) for a song, covering all rights for the rest of time. ASCAP's decision early on to award "authors" equal royalties to "composers" not only represented recognition of the importance of lyrics but also served as an enticement for talented young scribblers to enter the field.

The steady growth in record sales was accompanied by a sharp decline in sheet music sales. As life become busier and less rural, and mechanical devices like the radio and the record player started to beckon, fewer families had the time or inclination to sit around the piano of an evening. As Isaac Goldberg put it in 1930, "People buy music because they desire to have it at hand when they feel like hearing and playing it. When a song is dinned into their ears around the

---

*Some of ASCAP's flaws can be seen in its treatment of African-Americans, perhaps most egregiously in the case of the pianist, prolific composer, and jazz pioneer Ferdinand "Jelly Roll" Morton. Of the nearly two hundred charter members of the organization, only two were black: classical baritone Harry T. Burleigh and classical composer James Weldon Johnson. Born in 1890, Morton started writing songs in the first decade of the twentieth century but did not earn any royalties from them until 1939, when ASCAP finally allowed him to become a member. He had applied five years earlier but had been rejected, in a letter reading: "Please be advised that all applications must be proposed and seconded by members of this Society." In 1939, he was placed in category 3, then the lowest designation. In a letter to a friend, he reported that he expected to get $120 a year from ASCAP. The organization is notoriously secretive about its classifications and its members' earnings, but Oscar Hammerstein II subsequently testified in a court case that, at the time, ASCAP members in the top category—such as Cole Porter and Irving Berlin—received an average of more than $15,000 a year. Morton died in 1941.

face of the clock, they have no need of buying the printed form." The change hurt publishers more than songwriters, who received significantly more favorable royalties on mechanical reproduction and public performance than they did on sheet music.

There was a big difference between having family members pound out a song on the parlor piano and listening to professional renditions on the phonograph or radio, and the professionalization of music delivery had a big impact on the quality of songs. In the earlier model, publishers subsidized professionals to perform songs with the goal of selling sheet music to amateurs, who were seduced into thinking they could bring the piece off as well. Now writers and publishers were making their money through fees linked to professional performance and recording. Popular songs no longer had to be elementary enough for mother or sister to play them at the family spinet. Professionals could carry off complexity, and, in the case of jazz virtuosos, do it brilliantly. The widespread use of microphones was significant as well. In the early days, even the best singers had to be belters, which didn't leave much room for subtlety or nuance. The personification of the change is the transition from Rudy Vallee to Bing Crosby and such subsequent masterful interpreters as Frank Sinatra, Billie Holiday, and Ella Fitzgerald.

Institutional

The Italian Renaissance was facilitated by enlightened patrons, gatekeepers, popes, and Medicis. American songwriters had no such benefactors in their own renaissance, with one notable exception, who deserves a bit of attention. That was Max Dreyfus, who was born in

Kuppenheim, Germany, in 1874, the son of a cattle dealer, and came to America at the age of fourteen. After peddling picture frames through the South, he unsuccessfully tried to make it as a songwriter. Unlike most Alley denizens, he could read music, and after Witmark's rejected some of his tunes in 1895, the house did accept him as a pianist and arranger. He moved on to T. B. Harms, where he started as staff arranger, advanced to professional manager and 25 percent partner, and in 1904 became full owner.

Dreyfus turned the floundering firm around. Where it had previously been an Alley song mill like any other, it now became closely associated with the stage, underwriting Broadway shows both as investments in themselves and as a means of securing the publishing rights to the highest-quality songs. Dreyfus was unusual if not unique among publishers in recognizing that popular music could be art (though he probably wouldn't have used that word), and his ear for talent was unequaled. In 1904, nineteen-year-old Jerome Kern walked into the office. "He said he wanted to imbibe the atmosphere of music," Dreyfus recalled years later. "I decided to take him on and to start him off by giving him the toughest job I had—selling music." That is, he hired Kern as a song plugger. For a salary of twelve dollars a week, the young man peddled song sheets up and down New York's Hudson Valley and demonstrated Harms tunes at local department stores.

In 1912, Dreyfus—along with the publisher Gus Schirmer—commissioned Rudolf Friml, an immigrant from Prague, then a concert pianist and teacher who had composed no popular music, to write the score for an operetta, *The Firefly*, a gamble that paid off handsomely. Twenty-two-year-old Vincent Youmans had published but one tune when Dreyfus took him on as staff pianist and song plugger. When Cole Porter was struggling and unknown, Dreyfus sustained him with continual advances. A younger man, E. Y. "Yip" Harburg, the lyricist for "Brother, Can You Spare a Dime?" and "Over the Rainbow," recalled: "Max signed me up when nobody else would. He didn't give me much, but it was enough to keep me alive when I had nothing."

In the winter of 1918, George Gershwin appeared at T. B. Harms. He had already been a plugger, rehearsal pianist, arranger, and piano roll artist; as a composer he had published but a handful of songs. Gershwin played a couple of numbers, Dreyfus was impressed, and the upshot was described by Ira Gershwin in his diary: "George has been placed on the staff of T. B. Harms Co. He gets $35 a week for this connection, then $50 advance and a 3 cent royalty on each song they accept. This entails no other effort on his part than the composing, they not requiring any of his leisure for plugging nor for piano-playing. Some snap."

As Dreyfus put it at the time, "I feel that you have some good stuff in you. It'll come out. It may take months, it may take a year, it may take five years, but I'm convinced that the stuff is there. You have no set duties. Just stop in every morning, so to speak, and say hello." What's more, he accepted two Gershwin–Irving Caesar collaborations on the spot—"I Was So Young (You Were So Beautiful)" and "There's More to the Kiss Than the X-X-X." Gershwin remained dedicated to the publisher for the rest of his life, and in 1931 dedicated his *Second Rhapsody* to Dreyfus.

According to Irving Caesar, who was still regularly coming in to his Brill Building office when I interviewed him in 1982, "To get into the orbit of Harms was every composer's dream." Dreyfus managed to make the Harms offices on West Forty-fifth Street the Tin Pan Alley equivalent of the Algonquin Round Table that convened one block to the south. The music historian David Ewen described the "professional parlor" there this way:

Important composers and lyricists of that day made it a habit to drop in at Harms during the noonday hours for some music, shoptalk, social palaver. George Gershwin could be found there several times a week. Harry Ruby, Bert Kalmar, Joe Meyer, Buddy DeSylva, Vincent Youmans, Irving Caesar, Paul Charig—later on, Arthur Schwartz, Vernon Duke and Harold Arlen—hovered around Gershwin like satellites. . . . Caesar was something of the court jester, delighting the group with impromptu parodies and improvised opera arias.

Not coincidentally, Dreyfus was the most financially generous publisher. His habit was to pay more than the standard royalty, and "was considered radical for this abuse of custom."

The theatrical emphasis of Harms under Max Dreyfus was no coincidence, for the most significant broad-based institutional spur to first-rate songwriting in the 1920s was the stage itself. In the 1920s in particular, musical comedies were the rage in New York, with 432 of them mounted on Broadway over the course of the decade. Berlin and Gershwin in their early days were part of the Tin Pan Alley song factory, but both switched early to Broadway, where Kern, together with the librettists and lyric writers Guy Bolton and P. G. Wodehouse, had changed the rules of the game, replacing the antique Mittel-European operettas of Friml and Herbert, on the one hand, and the one-number-after-another revues and follies, on the other, with integrated, unmistakably American theater pieces in which character, dialogue, and songs were integrated. Rodgers and Porter presently joined in.

It was understood that these musicals needed songs of a certain quality not only to fit into the libretto but because the audience *expected* them. Moreover, in contrast to Tin Pan Alley, where a song got little more than a surface polish before being handed off to a plugger, a show tune was shaped—"workshopped" in a later parlance—by directors, producers, librettists, and performers until it reached what they deemed to be its best form.

As usual, there was also an economic impetus. On Broadway, song-writers worked for a share of box-office receipts and thus, in author Gary Rosen's words, "were no longer subsistence piece workers prized for their conformity to accepted norms, or for their ability to crank out knockoffs of the latest hit, or to cater to the latest dance craze." They could make quite a bit of change: Sigmund Romberg grossed more than $1.5 million for three musicals: *Blossom Time* (1921), *The Student Prince* (1924), and *The Desert Song* (1926).

From the 1910s through the 1930s, Broadway musicals mainly served as settings for the song and dance numbers and had inane stories and dialogue. The eventual standards in the Gershwins' *Lady, Be Good!*, produced in 1924 and starring Fred and Adele Astaire, included the title song, "Fascinating Rhythm," and "The Girl I Love." (The last was dropped from the score before its opening and became a classic under a new title: "The Man I Love.") The plot, typically, was less timeless: "Angry because Dick Trevor has not returned her affections, property owner Josephine Vanderwater evicts Dick and his sister Susie from her apartment building and they take residence on the sidewalk until the crafty lawyer 'Watty' Watkins comes up with a plan. He has Susie disguise herself as a Mexican wife so that Watty can collect his fee from a divorce case. The ruse causes complications when . . ." Slowly, the stories of American musicals became more mature, complex, and worthy of the songs in them, key points along the way being *Show Boat* (1927), *Porgy and Bess* (1935), *Pal Joey* (1940), and *Oklahoma!* (1943).

The lyrics matured more quickly than the scripts; indeed, writing for Broadway elevated the work of lyricists as much as if not more than that of composers as the operetta style was replaced by more down-to-earth fare. The plots may not have been Shakespeare, but they were complemented by songs in chest-voice vernacular, in contrast to the high-pitched heavy vibrato of yore. That vernacular touch meshed well with the wordplay, unexpected metaphors, and intricate rhyme schemes ("I'm sure that *if* I took even one *sniff* / It would bore me te*rrif*-ically, too") with which the best lyricists began to do great things. That inventive language itself was characteristic of the era, now long gone, when young wordsmiths vied to publish their light verse in *The New Yorker* and Franklin P. Adams's column in the New York *World*.

Hollywood, in its way, also advanced the craft of songwriting. At the very beginning of talking films in the late twenties, music publishers reaped a windfall as producers bid against each other for the rights to existing songs. Eventually, the movie studios realized that it was better to own songs than to rent them. Starting in 1928 the studios began buying almost all the important publishing firms, including Harms, which Warner Bros. snapped up in 1929 for an estimated $8 to $10 million. (The studio retained Max Dreyfus as a consultant, but as he said later: "This was all hooey. Picture people don't take advice. They give orders.") They quickly exhausted the existing catalogs and began bringing composers and lyricists out to Hollywood as staff songwriters. By 1929, some 320 composers and lyricists were working for the studios, some at impressive salaries. Whereas a staff writer for a Tin Pan Alley firm could expect to make a maximum of $200 a week (in the rare case of a hit, their royalties could exceed that), Warner Bros. paid the team of Harry Warren and Al Dubin $3,000 a week each and a younger duo, Harold Arlen and Yip Harburg, $2,500 a week each. Irving Berlin got $75,000 for a film score, plus a percentage of receipts. The sun-drenched security brought on creative paralysis in some writers, but for others, such as Warren and later Jule Styne, Johnny Mercer, and Jimmy Van Heusen, the orange groves and the ocean seemed to be a powerful muse.

Cultural

One of the many new ideas of the American 1920s, as seen in the work of such critics as Edmund Wilson, Constance Rourke, Vachel Lindsay, H. L. Mencken, and especially Gilbert Seldes (author of the 1924 book *The 7 Lively Arts*), was that popular culture was in fact culture, that a "low" art could still be an art. The vitality and occasional vulgarity of movies or popular music, far from disqualifying them, were admirable attributes. This idea was felt and expressed most intensely in New York City—also, of course, the location of Tin Pan Alley, to which it gave an energetic burst of legitimacy.

In a 1925 diary entry, Wilson traced the "progress" of a prototypical popular song "from fall in New York to summer throughout the country." It reads like a movie montage, with soundtrack, and gives a vivid, Gatsbyesque feel of the various channels of dissemination and the way a song could take hold of the popular consciousness and imagination:

Harlem cabarets, other cabarets, Reisenfeld's classical jazz, the Rascoe's private orchestra, the hand organs, the phonographs, the radio, the Webster Hall balls, other balls (college proms), men going home late at night whistling it on the street, picked out on Greenwich Village ukuleles, sung in late motor rides by boys and girls, in restaurants, Paul Whiteman and Lopez, vaudeville, played Sundays by girls at pianos from sheet music with photographs on the cover, of both the composer and the person who first sang it—first sung in a popular musical comedy (introduced several times—at the end of the second act pathetically—and played as the audience are leaving the theater)—pervading the country through the movie pianists, danced to in private houses to the music of a phonograph—the Elks fair—thrown on a screen between the acts at the National Winter Garden Burlesque and sung by the male audience.

Wilson's description gives a sense of the polyglot nature of the culture at the time. Linda Ronstadt started her career forty years after his journal entry and, until her retirement in 2012, sang virtually every style of music. She regards the standard song as "maybe the greatest gift of American culture to the world at large in the early twentieth century." She sees it as a "sandwich" with ingredients from different cultures: "The first piece of the bread is New Orleans Creole culture—their knowledge of European instrumentation met West African rhythms—with the five-beat, the talking drums—and that's when jazz was born at the end of the Civil War," she said. "Layered over that were the Polish immigrants, Irish immigrants, Italian immigrants. A very sentimental working-class kind of song—longing for home, for love. Over the top, the last layer of bread is the Jewish migration, who were fleeing from the pogroms and had terrible sadness as well. They had great rhythms going on in central Europe, too—they had syncopation, they had gypsy rhythms—so the West African five-beat was easy to glom on to. Somebody like Benny Goodman sounds like klezmer music grafted onto an African rhythm."

By the 1890s, the African-American influence started to make its way into mainstream popular music as black musicians thrilled their audiences to ragtime and other kinds of syncopated rhythm: "displacement of beat, anticipations of rhythmic resolutions at the ends of phrases, and the use of triple figures in duple time," in Charles Hamm's words. White songwriters with good ears absorbed all of it, usually without acknowledging the source. Irving Berlin proclaimed, "Syncopation is the soul of every American; pure unadulterated ragtime is the best heart-raiser and worry-banisher that I know." In many of Gershwin's early songs—"I Got Rhythm," "'S Wonderful," "Fascinating Rhythm," and "Somebody Loves Me," for example—the melody seems to proceed from the rhythm rather than the other way around.

The particular harmonies of blues and jazz, and the uncanny improvisations of jazz instrumentalists, were important, too. The first blues song to reach a wide audience was Mamie Smith's 1920 recording of "Crazy Blues," which sold an estimated million copies. Other African-American singers, including Ethel Waters, Alberta Hunter, Ma Rainey, and Bessie Smith, had crossover success during the twenties. In 1921, two black songwriters, Eubie Blake and Noble Sissle, had a smash Broadway revue, *Shuffle Along*. The effect on white songwriters and arrangers was evident to Gilbert Seldes, who concluded, "Our whole present music is derived from the negro." Gershwin, especially, appreciated black musicians and throughout his career made a point of seeking them out. His disciple Harold Arlen carried on the tradition, writing for Harlem Cotton Club revues in the early 1930s, where his and Ted Koehler's classic "Stormy Weather" was first performed by Ethel Waters. Gershwin's "American folk opera" *Porgy and Bess* opened in 1935 with an entirely African-American cast and a score that probably represented the artistic zenith of this cross-cultural project.

As first- or second-generation Jewish immigrants, Berlin, Gershwin, and Arlen were on the edges of mainstream American culture themselves, and thus inclined to be comfortable with such excursions. But the prominence of Jews among songwriters of the post-Berlin generation was a broader phenomenon than that, and lends itself to no single or simple explanation. The fact that the entertainment industry generally and Tin Pan Alley specifically didn't discriminate on the basis of religion (the same could not be said of race) was surely relevant, as was the respect accorded to both words and music in Jewish and Yiddish culture. And so was the nature of the music in that tradition: soulful, rhythmic, often minor-key, and, as it turned out, well suited to the bluesy, jazzy harmonies that were beginning to take hold of Americans' imaginations. Sometimes forgotten is the fact that Jews were well represented in every corner of Tin Pan Alley, not only as writers and publishers, but as pluggers and performers as well. Hazel Meyer observed, "In the search for song-pluggers so vital to the exploitation of their songs, Tin Pan Alley publishers shrewdly led frequent raids on the Lower East Side synagogues. . . . The boys who chanted the Hebrew refrains had what today's musicians call a schmaltzy delivery, a style eminently suitable for the soddenly tearful songs of the early 1900s." Many of the top singers of the first few decades of the century were Jewish, including Al Jolson (a cantor's son), Fanny Brice, Libby Holman, and Sophie Tucker.

Cole Porter, of course, was one of the few major songwriters who *wasn't* Jewish. Richard Rodgers recalled in his autobiography that, on their first meeting, Porter announced he had discovered the secret of writing hits:

As I breathlessly awaited the magic formula, he leaned over and confided, "I'll write Jewish tunes." I laughed at what I took to be a joke, but not only was Cole dead serious, he eventually did exactly that. Just hum the melody that goes with "Only you beneath the moon and under the sun" from "Night and Day," or any of "Begin the Beguine," or "Love for Sale," or "My Heart Belongs to Daddy," or "I Love Paris." These minor-key melodies are unmistakably eastern Mediterranean.

Harold Arlen, born Hyman Arluck and a cantor's son, once played a Louis Armstrong record for his father. After hearing one "hot lick," Mr. Arluck said, "Where did *he* get it?"

The greatest lyricists of the great age of songwriting, by most accounts, were Lorenz Hart, Ira Gershwin, Yip Harburg, Dorothy Fields, Oscar Hammerstein II, Johnny Mercer, and Cole Porter. The first five were all Jewish New Yorkers—the first three born to immigrants, and Fields and Hammerstein to prominent theatrical families—and a good case has been made linking their masterful wordplay and delight in the English language to the outstanding public education that New York City offered its children in the early twentieth century. Howard Dietz sat in the same classrooms, as did such subsequent stellar lyricists as Alan Jay Lerner, Frank Loesser, Sammy Cahn, and Carolyn Leigh.

Music, especially folk and popular music, has historically had a strong connection with dance, probably never more so than in the Great American Songbook era. Before 1913, in the United States, popular songs and dancing had only a tenuous association, with about as much space between them as separated the partners in one of those waltzes those songs lent themselves to. The change can be traced to a particular year because 1913 marked the beginning of the remarkable popularity of Vernon and Irene Castle. First in public "tea dances" and then in a series of Broadway musicals, the couple introduced a series of fast-time dance steps in 2/4 or 4/4: the fox-trot, the bunny hug, the grizzly bear, the turkey trot. The dances required lively, sometimes syncopated songs that made you want to get up and move your feet; Tin Pan Alley supplied them.

The composer and historian Mark N. Grant has made a strong argument that the fox-trot, introduced by the Castles in 1914 and inspired by dances popular among African-Americans, was especially important. The step, Grant writes, "combines slow and fast, rhythmic flexibility and downbeat regularity, in a unique way. It can be made to swing or syncopate yet it gives off a subtle lilt even when the rhythm is foursquare and unswinging. It can be elegant and romantic or peppy and jazzy with a simple alteration of the basic tempo. It can equally be swank or earthy because it mixes courtly and folk dance elements in a way that no other dance ever has."

In many cases, a song's versatility wouldn't become evident until years or even decades later. Will Friedwald observes of the twenties, "Love songs, like every other kind of music then, were also meant for dancing, and the idea of a band or jazz-influenced pop singer doing a number in slow rubato . . . was all but unknown." Hoagy Carmichael's 1927 song "Stardust" is known today as a ballad—maybe the quintessential ballad—but Friedwald notes that Carmichael's original recording "moves along at a comparatively fast clip." In his memoir, *Lyrics on Several Occasions*, Ira Gershwin recalled his brother George composing a "fast and jazzy" tune. As the composition of "Someone to Watch Over Me" proceeded (Ira supplying the lyrics), the tempo slowed down. But just a bit: the sheet music for the song, which premiered in the 1926 Broadway show *Oh, Kay!*, carried the notation "Scherzando"— meaning that it was to be played in a light and playful manner. In 1939, the singer Lee Wiley took it down to an even slower, ballad tempo. Margaret Whiting and Frank Sinatra followed suit, in 1944 and 1946, respectively, and the standard was set. The online reference source allmusic.com lists 1,868 recordings of the song, which is at the very core of the Great American Songbook. All but a handful—if that many—are ballads.

Tempos moved in the other direction as well, thanks to jazz, bands, musicians, and arrangers. Dick Hyman, a pianist born in 1927, says, "Cole Porter had no particular interest in jazz, and if you go back and hear the original recordings of songs by him and other composers, it's not the way we play them today. All those old songs were revised by Fletcher Henderson," whose influential arrangements were a foundation of his New York–based band of the 1920s and, later, of Benny Goodman's band.

Henderson's group, the Casa Loma Orchestra, and Paul Whiteman and His Orchestra were just three of the most celebrated of the dozens of bands that sprang up over the course of the decade, appearing in dance halls and nightclubs, always with an implicit invitation for couples to come out on the floor. Customarily, they played Tin Pan Alley songs; after a series of choruses were played purely instrumentally, a male or female singer would step up to the microphone and supply the vocals. Over time, bands became the main way songs were disseminated, not only in these live dance performances, but also on records and over the radio.

A significant number of the great songs of the period took dancing itself as their subject, including a remarkable number of Berlin classics: "Change Partners," "Cheek to Cheek," "Steppin' Out with My Baby," "Let's Face the Music and Dance," and "It Only Happens When I Dance with You." It isn't jumping out on a limb to say that "dancing," in the lexicon of popular music, had become a euphemism for "making love." It may seem strange now, but the fixation on love in lyrics of post–World War I songs was a new thing, and to some people an uncomfortable one. In 1934, a cultural commentator named Kenneth S. Clark wrote an essay called "Why Our Popular Songs Don't Last," in which he complained that song subjects were "all too often ultra-sentimental, the almost unvarying theme being love—particularly the unrequited or unsatisfied love of the 'torch' song. Who is going to take any pleasure in singing such songs ten years from now!"

The songs did "last," of course, and helping them to do so was the agreed-upon convention that, a few novelty numbers and other odd exceptions aside, love was the only true subject for a pop song. It ended up being a salutary restriction, just as religious scenes had been for Florentine painters and love (again!) for Elizabethan sonneteers. For some commentators in the early thirties, these songs went too far in terms of sexual explicitness. Prominent among these was the great humorist Ring Lardner, who used the radio column he wrote for *The New Yorker* in 1932 and 1933 to very seriously bemoan the fact that Tin Pan Alley was "polluting the once-pure air of Golly's great out-of-doors with a gas barrage of the most suggestive songs ever conceived, published, and plugged in one year." Lardner felt that merely listing some titles was sufficient evidence for his contention: "I'll Never Have to Dream Again," "Good Night, My Lady Love," "Let's Put Out the Lights and Go to Sleep," "Love Me Tonight," "I'm Yours Tonight," "And So to Bed," "Take Me in Your Arms," "What Did I Get in Return?," and "Thrill Me!" In retrospect, of course, the songs of the period are positively demure. So much was felt in the loins, so little of it could be explicitly described, and—as in Hollywood films of the Hays Office era—the conflict between those two propositions yielded creative sparks for decades.

III

....

Jukebox Saturday Night
1925–1942

Goodman and Kyser and Miller
Help to make things bright,
Mixin' hot licks with vanilla,
Jukebox Saturday night.

• "Jukebox Saturday Night,"
by Al Stillman and Paul McGrane

ven golden ages are not uniformly golden. A glance at a list of the
most popular songs of the 1920s and 1930s—as collated and
compiled by Joel Whitburn, a prolific popular-music historian
and archivist—confirms that this is true of the golden age of popular
song. Catchy but silly novelty numbers, cute and bouncy jingles, and
sentimental laments are heavily represented among the biggest hits of
the twenties, including such numbers as "The Love Nest," "Wang-
Wang Blues," "Ain't We Got Fun," "Toot, Toot, Tootsie (Goo' Bye!),"
"Yes! We Have No Bananas," "That Old Gang of Mine," "Yes Sir, That's
My Baby," "'Gimme' a Little Kiss, Will 'Ya' Huh?," "Ida! Sweet as
Apple Cider," and "Tip-Toe Thru the Tulips with Me," a 1929 hit for

Nick Lucas, known as "the Crooning Troubadour," that was un-accountably revived four decades later by a ukulele-strumming figure called Tiny Tim. The following year, 1930, was in the very shank of the golden age. Here are the songs that reached number one that year, in Whitburn's calculation: "Chant of the Jungle," "The Man from the South (with a Big Cigar in His Mouth)," "Happy Days Are Here Again," "Stein Song" (the official song of the University of Maine, as recorded by Rudy Vallee, and the biggest hit of all, with ten weeks at number one), "When It's Springtime in the Rockies," "Dancing with Tears in My Eyes," "Little White Lies," "Three Little Words," "If I Could Be with You (One Hour Tonight)," and "Body and Soul." Of all the songs named in this paragraph, Alec Wilder thought only the last two worthy of mention in *American Popular Song.*

The truth that this was a remarkable period in popular music is universally acknowledged now, but was not at the time. One of the rare critics who glimpsed the grandeur was a lawyer named Abbe Niles, who in his column for the *Bookman* magazine, "Ballads, Songs and Snatches," reviewed contemporary recordings and sheet music with an unusually sharp eye. In one column, he apologized for only dipping into the heap of songs that had come his way: "There is better popular music today than in the Golden 'Nineties, the Elegant 'Eighties, and so on down," he flatly stated, "but its quantity is embarrassing." A wider strain of commentary was dismissive or, at best, condescending. Kenneth Clark, a Princeton man from the class of 1905, cited another reason "Why Our Popular Songs Don't Last": that "too many" current offerings were "entirely too intricate. . . . In the old days of Tin Pan Alley, many of the successful song-writers were merely 'two-finger boys' at the piano. . . . The trouble is that too many of the lads who now write songs really know something about music—orchestra leaders, jazz pianists, and so on. They know what modulation means and are expert in broken rhythms. The result is a 'Body and Soul,' with which little Nellie Green would have a terrible time, and a 'Night and Day,' which is nothing to strum by ear on your ukulele."

Those two examples of difficulty (written by Johnny Green and Cole Porter, respectively) refute Clark's title proposition, but plenty of songs supported it, including one he named as a top-seller at Macy's in the autumn of 1932: "Play, Fiddle, Play." Its story proves not only that there was chaff as well as wheat in the period but that, in many ways, Tin Pan Alley continued to operate much as it always had.

Jacob Schwartz was born in Brooklyn in 1912. As he came of age he set his sights on becoming a songwriter, and when he was twenty he wrote the words and Arthur Altman (another Brooklyn boy) the music to a minor-key concoction they called "Play, Fiddle, Play." Schwartz would ultimately change his name to Jack Lawrence, write the lyrics to such standards as "Tenderly," "All or Nothing at All," and "Beyond the Sea," and live nearly ninety-seven years. In his autobiography, *They All Sang My Songs*, he gives a good sense of how the non-Gershwin, non-Porter, non–Max Dreyfus division of the Alley operated when he was trying to break in. A musician named Emery Deutsch, known as "the Gypsy Violinist," had endorsed "Play, Fiddle, Play" but had somewhat overstated to the fledgling songwriters the influence he wielded in the industry. Lawrence writes:

> All those publishers he claimed owed him favors didn't seem to know it. He had neglected to tell us that many of them paid him a small stipend for playing their material, and in their minds, that canceled any debt. We three—Emery, Arthur, and I—made the rounds of music offices for months with discouraging results.

I recall some of the comments thrown at us. "Nobody dances to waltzes." "That kinda song is a ballbreaker." "A minor melody—and a waltz yet. Feh!" That should convey some idea of the classy publishers who ran the music business. Valiantly, the three of us continued, Emery even lugging his violin along to bolster our demonstrations.

The following is typical of the reactions we encountered. We were in a publisher's office. The firm was new and small. The man who ran it, George Marlo, was small of body and mind. The only big thing around was his oversized cigar, which he was able to afford due to his current, medium hit called "Home." We had just concluded our song—at least he had allowed us the courtesy of finishing, unlike other publishers.

George slowly removed the big cigar from his lips, flicked the ashes carefully on the floor, replaced the cigar, and spoke out of one side of his mouth. "What kind cockamamie song is that? Who the hell is gonna sing about a fiddle? Bring me a song like"—and in a raucous voice he spread his arms wide and bellowed:

"When shadows fall and boids whisper night is ending

My thoughts are ever wending . . . HOME!"*

He glared at us. "That's a song! That's what people wanna sing about—wending HOME!"

Similar routines were repeated at other offices, the only variation being each firm's respective hit song. I was still in great awe of these powerful tycoon publishers, little realizing what shallow, crass, un-

---

*Lawrence's depiction has Marlo accurately representing the sentimental verbosity but mangling the actual lyric of "Home (When Shadows Fall)," by Harry Clarkson, Geoffrey Clarkson, and Peter Van Steeden, which he had published in 1931 to great success. The actual line goes: "When shadows fall and trees whisper: 'Day is ending.'" *Variety*'s 1970 obituary of Marlo calls him "one of the most colorful song pluggers in the music business during the 1920s and '30s" and recounts that "Home" had been "introduced simultaneously on eight different network radio shows on Thanksgiving Eve, 1931, by Kate Smith, Bing Crosby, Rudy Vallee, Russ Columbo, and others. It was to become a legendary Tin Pan Alley exploit."

musical, but shrewd deal makers most of them were. Traits they seemed
to have in common: they were supersalesmen, connivers, manipula-
tors, and would have been equally successful selling toilet fixtures—
an area in which many of them would have felt more at home.

Lawrence, Altman, and the Gypsy Violinist were finally able to
convince a publisher to take "Play, Fiddle, Play." The man was Edward B. Marks, who had been in the business since the 1890s and who
ran his operation much as he had done back then. Like the other publishers Lawrence encountered, but maybe more efficiently, he worked
on the piecework rather than the quality model, looking for material
he could acquire on the cheap and driving a hard bargain. Lawrence
recounts that in return for taking on "Play, Fiddle, Play," Marks de-
manded some harsh concessions: "(a) Emery Deutsch was more important than Arthur Altman and Jack Lawrence combined, therefore
(b) Emery's name would appear in larger type as the composer, and
(c) our names would be lumped in tandem as the lyricists, and
(d) Emery would receive two-thirds of the royalties, and we would split
one third."

As Marks may have recognized, the song was actually well suited to
the cultural moment. Several performers went on to record it, in addition to Deutsch, including Ruth Etting, the popular tenor Morton
Downey, and a pseudonymous radio star billed as "the Street Singer"—
later revealed to be Arthur Tracy—whose other records included "I'll
Have the Last Waltz with Mother," "It's My Mother's Birthday Today,"
"When I Grow Too Old to Dream," and "Danny Boy." The Street
Singer (in Gary Rosen's description) "accompanied himself on the accordion, his voice and instrument blending to produce an ineffably
mournful timbre, in a repertoire that spanned the small space between
the maudlin and the lachrymose. . . . His unabashed sentimentalism

resonated with a large and appreciative audience as the Great Depression was bottoming out."[*]

Lawrence didn't have another success until teaming up with a composer named Peter Tinturin in 1937. Fats Waller had a hit with their "Do Me a Favor," and Andy Kirk and His Twelve Clouds of Joy, a swinging black jazz band featuring the pianist Mary Lou Williams, an even bigger one with "What Will I Tell My Heart." Those songs and a few others got the team a contract with Republic Pictures, and then in 1939 Lawrence cemented his success with a number-one song for the Ink Spots, "If I Didn't Care," for which he wrote both music and lyrics. That year he and Arthur Altman composed their last number together, "All or Nothing at All." The song, recorded by the Harry James Orchestra, featuring its skinny boy singer, Frank Sinatra, went nowhere at all at the time, but would have a second life in the years ahead.

"Play, Fiddle, Play" and "Home" were showcases for fiddler and vocalist, respectively, which put them in contrast to the dominant means by which songs reached the public. This was big, or at least biggish, bands. In the 1920s, these groups had a complicated relationship

---

[*]"Play, Fiddle, Play" is more famous in legal than in musical circles. A man named Ira Arnstein, who would become famous for his persistent and annoying litigiousness, sued Edward Marks, claiming that the song was plagiarized from an earlier work of his own, "I Love You Madly." A district court judge ruled against Arnstein; when he appealed to the Second District Court, his luck was no better. The ruling was written by the famous Judge Learned Hand, who, in discussing the possibility that Altman and Lawrence would somehow have gotten hold of Arnstein's composition, had some unkind things to say about the two young songwriters and about their trade in general: "Almost anything is possible; so is such a theory, but it is very unlikely. Altman was an entirely unknown person, a one-finger composer who had no reputation; the most he could do was to contribute the simple themes which by this hypothesis Deutsch intended to lift from the copyrighted song; that is to say, his only part could be just what Deutsch did not need, the melody. Lawrence could apparently write the kind of treacle which passes in a popular love song, but such mawkish verses are reeled off by hundreds of poetasters all over the country. Deutsch needed no help from either of these men." Arnstein's story is skillfully told by Rosen in *Unfair to Genius: The Strange and Litigious Career of Ira B. Arnstein.*

with the style of music—jazz—that later gave the age its name. A large subset had little or no improvisation or syncopated or propulsive rhythms, merely playing chorus after chorus of popular songs while couples made their way to the dance floor for the "businessman's bounce." But by the middle of the decade an awareness of jazz had developed to the extent that many white bandleaders, notably the aptly named Paul Whiteman (who was also heavily influenced by Art Hickman, from San Francisco, and who was eventually dubbed, with unintentional irony, "the King of Jazz"), felt they had to make some effort to accommodate it. These bands' output was given the designation "sweet." The 1930 edition of the *Encyclopædia Britannica* explained: "The present-day 'sweet' jazz, sprung from the Hickman–Whiteman reaction against cacophony, is opposed to 'hot' jazz." *The Bookman*'s Abbe Niles further elucidated:

> The "sweet" technique, hardly connected with true jazz save by its employment of saxophones and banjoes, consists primarily of hiring expert arrangers. These gentlemen proceed to take a given song, and do what they can to relieve the monotony of its fox-trot rhythm, and its usual lack of inspiration, by assigning successive choruses to different voices, writing in connecting passages between repetitions, changing keys, and so on. The result is refined, but still dull.

"Hot jazz" had emerged from New Orleans, Memphis, and other points in the South, and was mainly (but not exclusively) played by African-Americans. It was in origin a small-group form, but eventually black big bands emerged, including those led by Fletcher Henderson, Bennie Moten, and Duke Ellington, playing innovative up-tempo jazz. Of course, their music wasn't heard on network radio and their records didn't get wide distribution. In time, some white big bands adopted some of their styles, notably the Casa Loma Orchestra, which created a sensation in the early thirties by alternating up-tempo numbers with cleverly arranged ballads. In 1933, *Fortune* magazine observed, "The best white ensembles usually compromise by playing both sweet and hot music. This is true of Ben Pollack's excellent swing band of Chicago (with Trombonist [Jack] Teagarden and other crack soloists)."

A clarinet player named Benny Goodman, also from Chicago, broke through on a national level in 1935, playing hot jazz with a large ensemble. He very explicitly scorned the sweet bands, later calling their music "a weak sister incapable of holding its own in any artistic encounter with the real music of America." The style needed a name, and the one that emerged was a term that had for decades been part of the lexicon of African-American musicians, as noun, adjective, and verb, to describe rhythmic qualities of jazz, or sometimes jazz itself. The bandleader and pianist Duke Ellington used it in the title of a 1932 song: "It Don't Mean a Thing (If It Ain't Got That Swing)." No matter that Goodman stood on the shoulders of Ellington's and other black bands—and employed numerous Henderson arrangements. The press now determined he was "the King of Swing."

Many other swing bands, both white and black, followed Goodman, almost always taking the name of their leader: Harry James, Count Basie, the Dorsey brothers (together and separately), Artie Shaw, Charlie Barnet, Andy Kirk, and so on. They featured virtuoso soloists who sometimes became stars themselves, and in general focused on musicianship, arrangements, and rhythm rather than the song. They were able to take that approach in part because of the economic woes of record and music publishing companies, which previously had wielded a strong influence on singers' and musicians' choices of material. "The stranglehold music publishers had on the performance of popular songs was broken," recalled John Hammond, a young Yale graduate who actually arranged the introduction of Goodman and Henderson, and who would become an influential record producer. With the publishers thus weakened, Hammond observed, musicians could "take liberties with the melody."

Sweet bands did not go away, and in fact flourished. The long-forgotten Shep Fields had a number-one hit in 1936 (just as Goodman was breaking through) with "Did I Remember" and charted a total of thirty-eight times through 1943. The better sweet bands were given at least a modicum of respect by the jazz magazine *Metronome*, which conducted annual polls of best swing band, sweet band, and "favorite of all," but generally the more popular they got, the more jazz snobs loved to disparage them. "Hot musicians look down on sweet bands, which faithfully follow the composer's arrangements," *Vanity Fair* explained in 1935. (A favorite quip of swing fans: "What does Guy Lombardo's drummer tell people he does for a living?") The song was paramount for sweet bands—bandleaders commonly served as vocalist—and songwriters and publishers could claim success to the extent they could place tunes with one or more of these outfits. The most important chronicler of the big-band era, George Simon, provides a taxonomy of the sweet category: Isham Jones and Ray Noble "projected rich, full musical sounds. . . . Others played more in the society manner—Eddy Duchin with his flowery piano and Freddy Martin with his soft, moaning sax sounds. And then there were the extrasweet bandleaders. [Guy] Lombardo, of course, was one. So was his chief imitator, Jan Garber. So was the Waltz King, Wayne King." Other sweet bands were led by Sammy Kaye, Lawrence Welk, Horace Heidt, Fred Waring, Ozzie Nelson, Kay Kyser, Vaughn Monroe, and others whose names are even less familiar today.

Johnny Mandel, born in 1925, was a trombonist in Buddy Rich's,

Jimmy Dorsey's, and other swing bands in the 1940s; later he was an arranger, songwriter, and film composer. "In Chicago and the Upper Midwest," he recalled, "you had all these bands that really sucked when it came to jazz, but they had good music. There was a huge crowd that loved to dance to Blue Barron, Sammy Kaye, and Lawrence Welk in particular. We used to laugh at Guy Lombardo, but in retrospect, Gerry Mulligan and I came to the conclusion that Lombardo was a perfect museum piece of a band in 1920. This was what they also sounded like before swing came in. They always had a tuba bass, three-part harmony, and it got to [where] it sounded awful. But they were very good at it."

It's not as though the swinging bands threw songs overboard. Their most famous pieces tended to be instrumentals, but, in a given concert, vocal numbers predominated. For these, the band would play one or several choruses of the song, then a boy or girl vocalist—up till that point sitting demurely to the side, hands folded—would approach the microphone and sing one straight. In an eight-month period in 1941 and 1942, Benny Goodman made thirty-two recordings with vocalists and only twelve straight instrumentals. Goodman's singers weren't too shabby: at various times, Billie Holiday, Helen Ward, Martha Tilton, Mildred Bailey, Helen Forrest, Peggy Lee, and Dick Haymes were part of the orchestra. (As necessary as they were, singers were decidedly second-class citizens in the country of big bands. They were often paid lower salaries than instrumentalists, and in some cases did double duty as music librarians, instrument wranglers, or travel agents.)

Historian Lewis Erenberg has a good description of how the best bands deployed the best songs: "Swing fused love songs to a jazz style that gave ballads a lift and heightened their emotional power. Each band's use of individualized arrangements and versatile instrumentation helped make love songs seem more personal. Band singers performed a chorus of a song much as an instrumental soloist would, while the full band teased out the emotional nuances. At the end, no matter the sentiment, the band picked up the tempo as if to affirm that life goes on despite obstacles and that dreams come true."

Pop songs formed the basis of the repertoire of even the hottest bands of the period, and bands vied to see who could chart highest with a particular number. "Skylark"—music by Hoagy Carmichael, words by Johnny Mercer—is a quintessential standard. It was published in 1941, and almost immediately afterward the recordings started appearing. Glenn Miller, Harry James, Bing Crosby, and Dinah Shore all charted with the song in 1942; the bands of Gene Krupa, Woody Herman, Bunny Berigan, and Earl Hines didn't do quite as well with their disks. A subsequent Mercer song, "Blues in the Night"—music by Harold Arlen—was recorded thirteen times from September 1941 through March 1942 by such diverse artists as Cab Calloway, Guy Lombardo, Benny Goodman, and Big Joe Turner.

Swing or sweet, big bands became the country's principal popular music delivery system. Live bookings were helped by the repeal of Prohibition in 1933. By 1937, *Variety* estimated, some eighteen thousand musicians traveled the country in bands; the business as a whole grossed some $40 million in annual bookings. All the top bands were heard regularly on the radio, either via remote broadcasts of live shows in nightclubs or ballrooms or, in the case of the top dozen or so outfits, through their own weekly network shows. (By 1937, networks accounted for 88 percent of the total broadcast wattage.) These appearances served to promote their records, more and more successfully as the decade progressed. After falling to a low of about four million in 1933, national record sales rose steadily, reaching 130 million in 1941; an average hit sold about 250,000 copies. An important factor starting in the thirties was the introduction of jukeboxes; by the end of the

decade there were an estimated 500,000 of them, in taverns, bus stations, ice cream parlors, and even beauty parlors. They consumed
about 13 million records a year—over half of the industry's total production. The 1942 hit "Jukebox Saturday Night" offered a charmingly
self-conscious commentary on the cultural phenomenon they represented, especially how they turned music into a shared public experience. The song mentioned the top performers—and was ecumenical in
the sweet-swing controversy, endorsing a mix of the hot Benny Goodman, the "vanilla" Kay Kyser, and the down-the-middle bandleader
who had the biggest success with the song, Glenn Miller. It opens up:

> Moppin' up soda pop rickeys
> To our hearts' delight,
> Dancin' to swingeroo quickies,
> Jukebox Saturday night.
>
> Goodman and Kyser and Miller
> Help to make things bright,
> Mixin' hot licks with vanilla,
> Jukebox Saturday night.

The often unheralded keys to the big bands were the arrangers.
Johnny Mandel talked about realizing this when he was a kid listening
to broadcasts of the big bands night after night:

> Laying in bed after lights-out, I was glued to the radio, as most kids
> were then. Looking back on it, I realized this was the greatest labora-
> tory, because the focus was completely on radio—there was no tele-
> vision, nothing visual. Every band—from Goodman and Dorsey on
> down—was broadcasting, and the publishers were constantly forcing

songs on them. The whole idea was to get your song played on the radio. And the band's idea—especially if it was a struggling band— was to be heard more and more, so that when they went out on the road, they'd be able to get higher prices at better ballrooms.

I'd hear these different bands playing the same songs. That's what I mean by "laboratory." I would think to myself, "What's so great about this song that's supposed to be so popular? I think it's mediocre." Then another band would play the same damned thing, because everybody is restricted to those songs on the *Hit Parade*, and it would sound wonderful. And then another band would come on a half hour later, and that song would sound dreadful. At one point, a lightbulb went on over my head. I said, "Wait a minute. It's not about the song at all, it's about the way the band plays it."

The *Hit Parade* Mandel referred to was *Your Hit Parade*, a radio program that began in 1935 and would continue until 1953; a television version aired from 1950 till 1959. The show featured performances, by a regular cast of singers and musicians, of the top songs of the week; the formula by which they were picked was never revealed. *Billboard* magazine followed its example and in 1940 began publishing charts of the top-selling recordings. In contrast to the big-band dominance of the late 1930s and early 1940s, vocalists and vocal groups accounted for nine of the fifteen number-one records in 1945. The most successful group, Glenn Miller's, had thirty-six top-ten records from 1940 through 1943, including seven at number one. Miller had started as a trombone player with Ben Pollack's orchestra; when he formed his own group in the late thirties, he managed to achieve a sort of sweet-swing amalgam with tight arrangements, sophisticated harmonies, and a "silvery," reed-dominated sound. "When we started out . . ." Miller was quoted in a 1940 newspaper interview, "none of the big bands played pretty tunes . . . and the majority of people like to hear pretty tunes. We've tried to hit a happy balance between the two."

This was the environment in which the next cohort to contribute to the American Songbook reached their musical majority. In contrast to Kern, Gershwin, Rodgers, and Porter, who'd focused on the shows and revues that kept popping up in the twenties, this younger group often had early success writing for jazz bands, which consumed material at a rapid pace; consequently, they deeply understood jazz harmony and rhythm. And for these men the sign of arrival wasn't a Broadway show but a Hollywood contract. (All would find their way to Broadway in the late forties or fifties, with varying success.) A transitional figure was Hoagy Carmichael (born in 1899), an Indiana native who practiced law before moving to New York in 1929 to pursue songwriting full-time. He had success that year when Mitchell Parish wrote lyrics for a melody of his called "Stardust" (the bandleader Isham Jones had a hit with it in 1930, the first of hundreds of versions over the decades). Carmichael was hired as a staff writer by Ralph Peer's Southern Music, and composed such songs as "Rockin' Chair," "Georgia on My Mind," and "Lazybones"; lyrics to the last were written by a young Georgian named Johnny Mercer. In 1936, Paramount Pictures offered Carmichael a $1,000-a-week contract, and he was off to Hollywood.

Harold Arlen, born in Buffalo in 1905, was a real-life jazz singer not too far removed from Al Jolson's character in the first talking picture. From an early age he sang in the synagogue choir led by his father, the cantor, but jazz beckoned to him, and by fifteen he was playing the piano and singing in local cafés. He ultimately formed a band called the Buffalodians, which played several dates in New York City in 1925. Arlen stayed on in the city, singing and playing the piano in other bands. In 1929 he was working as a rehearsal pianist for a Broadway show, and one day he was fooling around with a rhythm and some chords that seemed like they could be a song. The result was "Get Happy," a propulsive jazz tune and a big hit; the lyrics, sort of anti-blues in spirit, were by Ted Koehler, Arlen's most frequent collaborator in his early career. Arlen was hired by a Tin Pan Alley publisher for a salary of $55 a week and with Koehler wrote scores for Cotton Club revues in the early thirties. Their songs of the period included "Between the Devil and the Deep Blue Sea," "I've Got the World on a String," "Let's Fall in Love," and "Stormy Weather," the classic torch song performed at the Cotton Club by Ethel Waters. Arlen was in Hollywood by 1934 and soon was working with the great lyricists Ira Gershwin, Johnny Mercer, and Yip Harburg, all of whom would be regular collaborators over the next two decades. In 1938, Metro-Goldwyn-Mayer hired Arlen and Harburg to write the music for *The Wizard of Oz*; their songs included, of course, "Over the Rainbow," which was ranked number one on the "Songs of the Century" list compiled by the Recording Industry Association of America and the National Endowment for the Arts and named the greatest movie song of all time by the American Film Institute.

Mercer moved from his Georgia home to New York in 1928, at the age of nineteen, to be an actor and singer; he had modest success, including landing a job as a vocalist with Paul Whiteman. But he had been writing lyrics on the side and struck gold with the 1933 "Lazybones," a hit for Whiteman. Launched as a songwriter, Mercer went to Hollywood the same year and over the next half decade produced a string of standards. For "I'm an Old Cowhand (from the Rio Grande)"— sung by Bing Crosby in the 1936 film *Rhythm on the Range*—he supplied both words and music, but his genius was in writing lyrics that combined wit, panache, and a wonderful ear for the American vernacular. Between 1934 and 1941, the following Mercer lyrics were sung on screen: "Goody Goody," "Too Marvelous for Words," "Jeepers Creepers," "Hooray for Hollywood," "I Thought About You," "Blues in the Night," and "Skylark."

Jimmy Van Heusen (born Edward Chester Babcock in 1913 in Syracuse, New York) was a rehearsal pianist in New York and scruffed about for a few years before scoring in 1939 with "Darn That Dream," written for Benny Goodman. By the end of the year he was in Hollywood. In 1939 and 1940, according to the Jimmy Van Heusen website, he published sixty songs, including "All This and Heaven Too," "Polka Dots and Moonbeams," and "Imagination." The lyricist for the last two was Johnny Burke (born in 1908), who in the thirties wrote (with other composers) big-band hits for Guy Lombardo, Ben Pollack, Paul Whiteman, and Ozzie Nelson. Burke went to Hollywood in 1936 and four years later formed an unbeatable combination with Van Heusen, often providing material for Crosby. Each member of the team brought, on the one hand, a purity and simplicity of emotion and, on the other, a mastery of his craft that together achieved near perfection in such songs as "Like Someone in Love," "Moonlight Becomes You," "But Beautiful," "Here's That Rainy Day," and "Swinging on a Star." Mercer collaborated with Van Heusen in 1939 on the enduring standard "I Thought About You" and later observed, "He seems to have a series of chords waiting at his command to which he can fashion a melody the moment his lyricist springs any idea on him. All of the highest quality, in my opinion."

Success took longer for Jule Styne, who was born in New York in 1905. He started out as an arranger and bandleader, moved to Hollywood to be a vocal coach and conductor, and began to get steady songwriting assignments as the thirties drew to a close, writing forgettable songs in forgettable pictures. In the early forties the pictures were still forgettable but the songs started to shine, especially on three collaborations with Sammy Cahn (born Samuel Cohen on New York's Lower East Side in 1913): "I've Heard That Song Before," "Saturday Night (Is the Loneliest Night of the Week)," and "It's Been a Long Time." Styne wrote "I Don't Want to Walk Without You" with Frank Loesser, yet another New York boy, born in 1910, who was also a relatively late bloomer. Loesser had little success as a New York songwriter in the early thirties but managed to get a Hollywood contract in 1936. He and Hoagy Carmichael wrote "Heart and Soul," "Two Sleepy People," and "Small Fry" in 1938, and he went on to work with Burton Lane ("Says My Heart"), Arthur Schwartz ("They're Either Too Young or Too Old"), and Jimmy McHugh ("Let's Get Lost").

A final composer in this group was an extraordinary musician and entertainer with a built-in outlet for his songs: his own band. Edward Kennedy "Duke" Ellington was born in Washington, D.C., in 1899; his parents were both accomplished pianists and he had extensive musical training. By the mid-1920s he was leading and playing piano for a top jazz orchestra. Like George Gershwin, Ellington straddled the line between popular and classical music, and throughout his career he composed ambitious orchestral pieces he sometimes called "suites." But he also wrote a collection of great standards, including, in the thirties alone, not only "It Don't Mean a Thing (If It Ain't Got That Swing)," but "Mood Indigo," "Sophisticated Lady," "Solitude," and "In a Sentimental Mood." Ellington's most recent biographer, Terry Teachout, writes that Ellington frequently relied for his melodies on the extemporaneous solos and improvisations of his band members, "who did not always receive credit—or royalties—when the songs were recorded and published." In 1939, Ellington began working with Billy Strayhorn—an inordinately talented young composer, lyricist, and arranger—and the two were creative partners until Strayhorn's death in 1967.

With the exception of Ellington, all these men (and one woman, the lyricist Dorothy Fields) were drawn to the West Coast, where they enjoyed a golden, sunbaked existence for a few years at least. Arlen later looked back:

> It was a great period! Maybe it was the accident of all of us working there because of the Depression. Practically every talent you can name. So many. Jerry Kern, Harry Warren, the Gershwins, Dorothy Fields and Jimmy McHugh, Oscar Hammerstein—even Berlin, although he didn't stick around. All of us, writing pictures so well. We were all on the weekly radio *Hit Parade*. If we weren't first, we were second; if we weren't second, we were fourth. A sensational period. Lovely for me. I went to the studio when I damned pleased, or when they called me. Got my check every week. And we were pouring it out! Oh sure, we all wrote picture scores that were bad. But people were having flops on Broadway, too, weren't they?

To be sure, there were flops and duds, but whether coming out of Hollywood or Broadway, the American Songbook was reaching its highest point of achievement and sophistication in the late 1930s. The Depression was rarely addressed in popular music, but perhaps its shocks and privations had some effect on the new ironies and twists songwriters were extracting from the familiar themes of longing and love. In any case, in 1937 the Gershwin brothers wrote one of their finest songs, "They Can't Take That Away from Me" for the Astaire–Rogers film *Shall We Dance*. In retrospect, it seemed to represent a new level of achievement, especially in the integration of words and music. Both of them show lightness of touch, technical mastery, and emotional depth. Throughout the song, Ira's words start with the quotidian, then stealthily deepen. It all leads up to the last verse, which goes from the mundane holding of a piece of silverware, to a romantic memory of dancing till the wee hours, to the devastating kicker: "The way you've changed my life . . ." Just as good, though a bit jauntier, was "Love Is Here to Stay," written that same year for the 1938 film *The Goldwyn Follies*.

Before the film opened, George, who had been suffering from severe headaches, was diagnosed with a brain tumor and died two days after being hospitalized. The country was in shock and was still dealing with denial three years later, when John O'Hara commented, "George died on July 11, 1937, but I don't have to believe that if I don't want to."

But Gershwin's generation, and the one coming up, continued to write deeper and better songs. Nineteen thirty-nine alone saw "Something to Live For," by Ellington and Strayhorn; "I Didn't Know What Time It Was," by Rodgers and Hart; "Darn That Dream" by the youthful Van Heusen and Eddie DeLange; "I Thought About You" by Van Heusen and Mercer; "Over the Rainbow" and the rest of the *Wizard of Oz* score by Arlen and Yip Harburg; and the work sometimes named as the greatest in the Songbook, "All the Things You Are," by Jerome Kern and Oscar Hammerstein II. None of these songs have in them a clichéd or even expected note. All of them can be and have been endlessly reinterpreted. As Charles Hamm put it, "The harmonic language of Tin Pan Alley had been so expanded that almost every chord could have added tones, nonharmonic tones, and dramatically altered notes, alone or in combination."

Lyrically, a clue to how refined the form had become was its intertextuality: the way a song would refer to other songs, or their writers, or itself. Ira Gershwin, in the verse to "They Can't Take That Away from Me," alludes to a Berlin classic: "The song is ended, but as the songwriter wrote, / 'The Melody Lingers On.'" Rodgers and Hart's funny 1939 "I Like to Recognize the Tune" protests against jazz combos that "kill the Arthur Schwartzes and the Glinkas." ("Don't be shtinkers," pleads the next line.) In "You're the Top," Cole Porter pairs "Waldorf salad" with "Berlin ballad" and refers to "gifted humans like Vincent Youmans." Porter's immortal couplet "But how strange / The change from major to minor," in "Ev'ry Time We Say Goodbye," is sung just as the key to the song *changes from major to minor*.

Only two decades had passed, but compared with the jaunty anthems of 1919, like "I Wish I Could Shimmy Like My Sister Kate" and "How 'Ya Gonna Keep 'Em Down on the Farm (After They've Seen Paree)?," these works seemed to represent a different category of human endeavor.

Of all American songwriters, Ray Evans was without question the biggest packrat. He held on to everything, from his mother's correspondence, to the Dear John letter he received in 1939 from the former Helen Ecker ("I know that you will understand why I pen this rather difficult note"), to the smallest *Billboard* clipping indicating that Tony Martin happened to perform an Evans song in a nightclub act in Toledo. After he died in 2007, his widow donated his papers to the University of Pennsylvania, from which he had graduated, and in whose library they can be perused. These documents allow one to get an unparalleled look at what it was like to try to break into songwriting in the late thirties and early forties.

Evans—a native of Salamanca, New York, near Buffalo—was a

lyricist; his composing partner was another Penn grad, Jay Livingston (born Jacob Levison in western Pennsylvania). In addition to having rhyming first names, they bore a physical resemblance—tall, bespectacled, conservatively dressed—and after they started achieving success, interviewers invariably commented about how hard it was to tell them apart. (The most reliable indicator was Jay's lack of hair.) They had started their collaboration at Penn, as fellow members of Beta Sigma Rho fraternity, then as musicians in a shipboard dance band that hit the high seas during vacations: one summer to South America, another to Russia and Scandinavia. They moved to New York after graduation, Ray's in 1936 and Jay's in 1937, and got—barely—enough intermittent positive reinforcement to keep trying to break into Tin Pan Alley. Their first really good news came in 1938, when one of their songs, the cleverly titled "Monday Mourning on Saturday Night," was recorded by a singer named Virginia Merrill. But the record went nowhere. Evans, always the more assertive of the pair, tried to follow up by contacting a top publisher, Jack Yellen, a fellow Buffalonian. (Yellen had migrated there from Poland in 1897, at the age of five. He'd entered Tin Pan Alley in 1915, writing the lyrics to three unlikely geographical numbers: "Alabama Jubilee," "Are You from Dixie?," and "All Aboard for Dixieland." He'd subsequently been credited with lyrics to "Ain't She Sweet," "Happy Days Are Here Again," "My Yiddishe Momme," and dozens more.)

Yellen's reply was encouraging, but, of course, encouragement and a nickel could get you a subway ride:

I read your lyric on "MONDAY MOURNING ON SATURDAY NIGHT" with a great deal of interest and satisfaction. It's certainly a novel idea and shows that your thoughts do not run in hackneyed grooves. You will find a demand for lyric writers who have a flair for new ideas.

You're tackling a tough racket—one which isn't as fruitful financially as it used to be—but if that's your chosen field, go to it. Don't get discouraged if success doesn't come easy. You never know when your lucky break will come. Get acquainted with the boys who write the tunes and the people who make them hits—and keep writing lots of songs. Good, bad or otherwise, keep writing and peddling.

You've overcome the toughest obstacle—getting your first song published. The rest is up to you—and Lady Luck.

Ray continued to commute every day from his Manhattan apartment to a dull clerical job in the accounting department of Edo Aircraft on Long Island. Back home at night, he worked on songs. Or at least, he did if he could rouse his partner/roommate, who put a few coins together by writing arrangements for others and working as a rehearsal pianist. One day Evans confided in his diary, "Came home late and Jay griped me by his indifference and apathy. I make suggestions, he rejects them, and that is as far as they get."

Ray's mother, Frances, back in Salamanca, was not the most stable person in the world, and her nagging letters only added to his anxiety. At one point she complained, "I visualized myself in expensive clothes, cars, money and everything else through you but I guess not." Her idea of advice was misguided, to say the least: "From now on, do not let any one know if you can help it that you are Jewish as I feel from the bottom of my heart that has been the greatest handicap you have had and if any one asks what church you go to tell them Christian Science."

In 1939 as today, however, contacts were priceless, and here Mrs.

Evans was helpful. She got in touch with a former mayor of Salamanca, George Abbott, whose son, also named George, was the biggest director and producer in New York. At that moment he had three productions running on Broadway, including Rodgers and Hart's *The Boys from Syracuse*, for which he'd also written the book. The elder Abbott replied to her that normally he didn't get involved in these matters, but "my son George Abbott of New York was a Salamanca boy; and, I make an exception by enclosing herewith the introduction you request." It seemed Ray and Jay's big break had finally come.

Evans's diary tells what happened next:

23 April: . . . Saw George Abbott Saturday afternoon. He was very friendly and courteous, and he had a pleasant laugh that made me feel entirely at ease. He said that no place of the theater has such a shortage as the music end. So he promised to call me for an audition.

1 May: Had our audition. He made no comment whatsoever, laughed at the risqué song and asked Love Resistance to be repeated. . . . After the audition was over George Abbott merely said "goodbye."

Four days later came a letter from Abbott. Ray ripped it open hopefully, then sighed when he read its brief contents. There would be no big break; even the praise the director could muster was profoundly faint. "I thought both the lyrics and the music were good, though not brilliant," he wrote. "I think you will both do better work as you mature, and I shan't forget you. There is nothing I have to suggest for the present."

A few months later, Ray saw a short news item saying that Olsen and Johnson, the vaudeville comedy team, were looking for new songs for their wacky revue *Hellzapoppin*, which had been playing on Broadway for nearly a year. Reflexively, Ray put a sheet of paper in his typewriter and pecked out a letter saying that Livingston and Evans were their boys. Of all unlikely things, Ole Olsen wrote back:

> Appreciate your frank and breezy letter and wanted to answer it personally to assure you that even though we have nothing immediate to offer, will be delighted to hear some of your material after some matinee (Wednesday or Saturday).
>
> Because even tho we have songs and material shot to us from forty different directions, I'm always glad to hear the other fellow's contributions. Sometimes you may find that "needle in a haystack"!

Jay and Ray worked on their material and their presentation for a month. Then, on Saturday, September 16, they went to the Winter Garden Theatre and were brought backstage. Ray described in his diary what happened next:

> *. . . Mr. Olsen saw us right away. He listened to everything, and it went over swell. There were a lot of people listening also, show people and others, and the songs brought laughs, the rhymes approval and the melodies, whistling. Olsen said we had the toughest thing to offer as everyone writes songs, but he had us to see the show and then come back to talk with him.*

Ray kept on coming to the Winter Garden; in one diary entry, he refers to his "nightly trip." On one night he met the cowboy actor Tom Mix; Wendell Willkie and Elliott Roosevelt were backstage another time. ("The latter looked like a wise guy," Ray observed.) Exasperatingly, Olsen and Johnson didn't buy any songs, but didn't kick the boys out, either. Once, Ray noted, "Oncle Oley put me immediately at ease by saying 'Hello Genius.'"

Eventually, Livingston and Evans were hired to score an ice show Olsen and Johnson were planning to produce. They wrote a full complement of numbers, but, in yet another case of good news/bad news, the show fell through.

This time, for once, it was good news/bad news/*good* news, as the boys benefited from the radio industry's boycott of ASCAP songs. The conflict stemmed from long-simmering trends in the music industry. At the beginning of the Depression, sheet music sales (and therefore royalties) had plummeted, falling from $16 million in 1929 to $2 million in 1933, and barely budging from then on. Through the thirties, there was just a trickle of income from record sales, or "mechanicals." That left—as far as songwriters' income was concerned—radio, which was booming and was absolutely dependent on music for its programming. Broadcasters paid ASCAP an annual percentage of revenues in return for the right to play its members' songs over the air. The percentage had steadily risen over the 1930s, reaching 2.75 percent in 1939—the year the networks, as a defensive and potentially offensive measure, formed a competing organization, BMI. In negotiations with broadcasters in 1940, ASCAP made a staggering demand: 7.5 percent of the networks' *gross* income. In response, beginning on January 1, 1941, American radio banished to silence the approximately 1.25 million songs in ASCAP's catalog. In their place, listeners heard classical pieces, songs that had been hurriedly signed to BMI, and works in the public domain. *Time* magazine noted late in January, "So often had BMI's Jeannie with the Light Brown Hair been played that she was widely reported to have turned grey." In addition, two important publishers signed with BMI: Tin Pan Alley veteran Edward B. Marks and Ralph Peer, owner of Southern Music, who had acquired the U.S. rights to thousands of Latin American songs.

Johnny Mandel, who was an ASCAP board member in later years, summarized the situation this way: "ASCAP finally got too arrogant. They thought the world centered around show writers. They wouldn't let the hillbillies in, and they didn't let the jazz guys in, with very few exceptions. The broadcasters finally said, 'You guys can shit in your hat—we're starting our own organization.'"

In the early months of 1941, with the ban newly in effect, BMI was desperately seeking songwriters and songs, and it snapped up Livingston and Evans's ice show score. One of the songs was "G'Bye Now," a clever number about the perennial awkwardness of saying good night, which showed Ray's knack for the vernacular and Jay's for melodic bounce. Horace Heidt, Jan Garber, Russ Morgan, and several other popular sweet bandleaders recorded it. Heidt's version eventually reached number one on the charts, and the title became a nationwide catch phrase. One night in March, Ray wrote in his diary, "Every announcer I heard ended his program 'G'Bye Now.'"

In May, the song was performed by none other than the King of Swing. Ray confided in his diary: "Got a big kick out of hearing Goodman did 'G'Bye Now' last night and hearing Heidt say that it 'stands a good chance of being song of the year.' Everything going along very well. Must there be a bad interruption or is this only delayed dividends on 3 years of struggle."

The song even roused the great George Abbott to write his fellow Salamancan, "Congratulations on having such a good hit as 'G'bye Now.'" Unfortunately, Abbott immediately followed that with "There is no possibility of my needing any music for sometime to come, since the score for YOUNG MAN'S FANCY has already been completed. I am glad, however, to be reminded of you again, and I shall certainly keep your telephone number close at hand." (The young team of Hugh Martin and Ralph Blane had written the songs for the show Abbott mentioned, which was ultimately retitled *Best Foot Forward*, opened on Broadway in October, and ran for about a year. Abbott never did call Ray.)

George Lilley, radio editor of the *Philadelphia Record*, wrote an article for the paper about the state of the ASCAP-BMI conflict; because he named "G'Bye Now" (albeit misspelled) as a sign that BMI might just be able to provide enough high-quality tunes for the networks to survive, Ray clipped the piece and kept it in his scrapbook:

"Basically the whole battle is simmering down to one affecting followers of the popular dance programs and the late evening, sustaining hours," Lilley wrote.

Most of the other music of importance on radio—the classic, the Latin rhythms, hillbilly tunes and many of the so-called old favorites—are in public [domain] and unrestricted. The Gershwin, Romberg, Cole Porter and other semi-sophisticated probably will not be missed enough by the general public to wreck the B.M.I.ers.

What B.M.I. needs badly to tide them over is a crop of 30 to 40 popular songs arranged and played—over the air and on records—by the top-flight dance bands. The life of the average popular song being about two months, lots of B.M.I. ditties can be made, with the proper bands playing them, lots of A.S.C.A.P.'s forgotten, in such a time.

The past few days B.M.I. has brought several numbers to the relief of their battle-worn "Practice Makes Perfect," "Jeanie with the Light Brown Hair," "Frenesí," and "Same Old Story." They are "A Stone's Throw from Heaven," "I Can't Remember to Forget," "Garden of the Stars," "Goodbye Now," "Let's Dream This One Out," and "The Last

Time I Saw Paris," all worthwhile songs, which is more than can be said of B.M.I.'s earlier offerings.*

But it turned out that Livingston, Evans, and the other BMI songwriters didn't get much time to make their mark. In late October 1941, ten months after the boycott began, ASCAP and the broadcasters agreed to terms much more modest than ASCAP's original demands. Under the new contract, the networks would pay the society 2.75 percent of *net* receipts.

BMI stayed around, and in future years would have a profound effect on popular music. But in late 1941, BMI writers went to the back of the line. Ray noted ruefully in his diary, "I suppose that kills whatever chance we had to get established."

---

*"Frenesí" was a tune by a Mexican songwriter, originally composed for the marimba; Artie Shaw had a number-one record with it. "The Last Time I Saw Paris" wasn't BMI but had come from the pens of quintessential ASCAPers Jerome Kern and Oscar Hammerstein II. The other songs mentioned were all conventional numbers that had modest success in record sales and airplay.

IV
....

As Time Goes By
1941–1948

The day after the Japanese attack on Pearl Harbor, ASCAP president Gene Buck called on songwriters to "do their bit in the present crisis by writing 'fighting songs.'" Tin Pan Alley gave it a try, with such numbers as "Yankee Doodle Ain't Doodlin' Now" and Irving Berlin's "We'll Wipe You off the Map, Mr. Jap," but it soon became clear that in this war, fighting songs didn't resonate. Only in the first year or so after Pearl Harbor did *any* explicit war songs have notable commercial success, and of them only Sammy Kaye's "Remember Pearl Harbor" had a jingoistic feel. Jimmy McHugh and Harold Adamson's "Comin' in on a Wing and a Prayer" and Frank Loesser's "Praise the Lord and Pass the Ammunition" expressed more of a can-do, gung-ho spirit; "When the Lights Go On Again (All over the World)," Kern and Hammerstein's "The Last Time I Saw Paris," and "(There'll Be Blue Birds over) The White Cliffs of Dover," were sentimental and elegiac.* For the rest of the war, the songs that achieved the greatest success followed that model. They brought the fighting home, addressing feelings of separation and loss, felt both by soldiers and the people they left behind. Indeed, just as the prewar songs by Jimmy Van Heusen and company represented new heights of melodic and harmonic sophistication, the war was a crucible in which popular songs were able to go beyond the easy sentimentality of "Play, Fiddle, Play" and the like and achieve a new level of emotional depth.

True, sometimes the treatment of the theme was jaunty—"Don't Sit Under the Apple Tree (with Anyone Else but Me)," Ellington's "Don't Get Around Much Anymore," "Saturday Night (Is the Loneliest Night of the Week)"—but more often the songs drew on and evoked strong feelings. Loved ones, separated by the (usually unnamed) war, reunited in memories, dreams, or an imagined future. Hits of this type included Loesser and Jule Styne's "I Don't Want to Walk Without You"; "I Had the Craziest Dream" and "You'll Never Know" (both by Harry Warren and Mack Gordon); "I'll Walk Alone" (Styne and Sammy Cahn); and, most powerful of all, Berlin's "White Christmas." Berlin actually wrote the song before Pearl Harbor. He was living in California at the time, and the singer of the opening verse laments being in Beverly Hills, with its sunshine, green grass, and palm trees. But Bing Crosby's performance of the song in the film *Holiday Inn* and his recording for Decca both came out in the summer of 1942, minus that verse. The geographical and meteorological nostalgia of the rest of the lyric effortlessly transformed into a wistfulness for Christmases past. Crosby's record was number one on the charts for eleven

---

*According to his daughter Susan, Loesser had written a "dummy tune" for "Praise the Lord"—a sort of placeholder until a proper composer came in. "My mother and some other people convinced him to keep the tune and not seek another composer," she recalled. "It was the first song he wrote both music and lyrics for."

consecutive weeks in the fall of '42, and by most accounts it is the most successful recording of all time. *Guinness World Records* estimates that various versions of the song have sold 100 million copies, with Crosby's record accounting for half of the total.

Other wistful yuletide songs followed. Crosby released "I'll Be Home for Christmas" in 1943; the lyrics appear to be transcribed from an overseas soldier's letter home. He starts off by making plans for his holiday return, but there's an abrupt kicker at the end of the second chorus: "I'll be home for Christmas / If only in my dreams." Ralph Blane and Hugh Martin's score for George Abbott's *Best Foot Forward* had gotten them a contract at MGM, and they wrote "Have Yourself a Merry Little Christmas" for the 1944 film *Meet Me in St. Louis*. The story is set in 1904, and the character played by Judy Garland sings the song to her little sister in an attempt to console her about an upcoming move to New York. But no one could mistake the emotional connection to contemporary wartime, as Garland hopes that "the fates allow" a reunion. "Until then," she concludes, "we'll have to muddle through somehow . . ."[*]

Older songs that tapped into such sentimental longing were revived during the war, finding a new resonance and new audiences. In 1942, Benny Goodman recorded a 1938 song, "Somebody Else Is Taking My Place," with vocals by Peggy Lee, and it hit number five on the charts. Another tune from 1938, "I'll Be Seeing You," a ballad of finely wrought nostalgia, reached number one, in the voice of Bing Crosby. Arthur Schwartz and Howard Dietz wrote "Something to Remember You By" in 1930; Dinah Shore's recording was a hit in 1943. The most

---

[*]In 1957, Frank Sinatra was putting together an album called *A Jolly Christmas* and asked Martin to provide some more upbeat lyrics. The writer provided some changes, including replacing the "muddle through" line with "Hang a shining star upon the highest bough." That became the most commonly performed version.

enduring example was a romantic lament from 1931. It was used prominently in a 1942 film about the war, and old recordings by Rudy Vallee and Jacques Renard charted the following year. The film was *Casablanca* and the song was "As Time Goes By."

A *Down Beat* writer summed up the situation: "Old songs and sentimental ballads as such have seen more interest than was ever thought possible in as desperately bitter a war as this. . . . War songs and patriotic marches by and large have fallen flat." The government was not especially pleased by the developments. Jack Joy, head of the Office of War Information's music committee, railed against music he called "slush." "The trouble, from the viewpoint of America's Ministry of Propaganda," *Variety* noted, "is that everything is too saccharine." But his objections were futile; the demand for this kind of stuff was just too strong. A woman wrote to her fiancé serving overseas about listening to "A Little on the Lonely Side," whose singer reads every letter from her loved one "a dozen times or more." The ballad, the woman said, "hits me right where it hurts. Me and a couple of million other lonely gals in this country." She added a bit of cultural analysis: "It's no wonder swing is on the decline and ballads are in again. It's the mood of the whole country with most of its lovers separated." The slush hit home with young men as well. *Down Beat* commented on the odd phenomenon of draft-age boys requesting sentimental ballads, noting that these young men weren't "so inclined to escape by means of 'Sing, Sing, Sing' with added anvils."

Ironically, Benny Goodman's "Sing, Sing, Sing" had no vocal; "A Little on the Lonely Side," like every other romantic ballad, did.* And that suggests an important reason why vocalists achieved an unprece-

*Louis Prima's version of "Sing," released in 1936 (a year before Goodman's), did have a kind of nonsense-rhyme lyric. Goodman wisely dropped it.

dented success during the war years: the human voice is the most efficient vehicle for evoking emotion in music.

In terms of performance, the pop music trend of the World War II years is simple to state: vocalists had great success at the expense of bands. The singer who led all the rest was Frank Sinatra. After singing for Harry James for less than a year, Sinatra went to work for Tommy Dorsey in 1939. Very quickly he became the band's prime attraction; in 1941, *Billboard* magazine named him Male Vocalist of the Year. Sinatra brought forth a special reaction in one particular segment of the listening public: teenage girls. At his performances, they would scream and swoon—a common reaction now, but unheard-of at the time. Rosemary Clooney, who was born in 1928 and thus squarely in the target demographic, compared Sinatra to the previous dominant vocalist, Bing Crosby. "I also think Frank showed a vulnerability that perhaps was not in Bing's makeup," she told Will Friedwald. "Bing wasn't able to come out and sing 'I love you' in a song. . . . Whereas Sinatra would be more vulnerable and feel very comfortable showing that vulnerability."* Another sometimes underappreciated factor was the liberal use of violins in Sinatra's numbers by Dorsey and his principal arranger, Axel Stordahl; they were so much more efficient at drawing out emotion than the customary brass and woodwinds.

In the summer of 1942, Sinatra left Dorsey to go out on his own (making sure to take Stordahl with him). This was a daring move. Jack Leonard, Edythe Wright, Ginny Simms, and Ray Eberle had tried it; the unfamiliarity of their names gives a sense of how successful they were. But it worked for Sinatra. Within a month he had his own show on the CBS radio network and, starting on New Year's Eve, an engage-

---

*Clooney's comment was perceptive. Crosby had once told his in-house lyricist, Johnny Burke, that the phrase "I love you" was never to appear in a Crosby song.

ment at the Paramount Theatre in New York. He didn't get top bill-ing, not with the Benny Goodman band playing the dates. Sinatra was even listed behind two comedy teams, the Radio Rogues and Moke and Poke. But from the very first performance he stole the show from Goodman and everyone else. His setlist was heavy with ballads: "I'll Never Smile Again," Jack Lawrence's "All or Nothing at All," "Be Careful, It's My Heart," "I Had the Craziest Dream," "Where or When," "The Song Is You." With each prolonged note—Sinatra knew how to take a ballad *slow*—the girls screamed and screamed. Between shows, they lined up around the block, waiting to get in. By July 1943, the Sinatra phenomenon had reached a point where *Time* magazine was compelled to comment: "In CBS's Manhattan playhouse, at the Paramount, at the Lucky Strike Hit Parade, hundreds of little long-haired, round-faced girls in bobby socks sat transfixed. They were worshipers of one Francis Albert Sinatra, crooner extraordinary. Their idol, a gaunt young man (25), looked as if he could stand a square meal and considerable mothering." (Sinatra was actually twenty-seven, but for some time had been shaving two years off his age so as to seem closer to his fans.) Very soon after that, "bobby-soxer" entered the American lexicon.

Sinatra's great success had ripple effects. His longtime saxophonist Ted Nash told Friedwald that Sinatra "put the kibosh on the big bands. Before, people went to see the band, and then they'd listen to a solo now and then or a singer here and there. The singers were strictly second-ary. But when Frank hit that screaming bunch of kids, the big bands just went right into the background." And sure enough, in short order, other vocalists followed Sinatra's lead, leaving bands and starting solo careers, including Ella Fitzgerald, Billy Eckstine, Dick Haymes, Peggy Lee, Helen Forrest, Dinah Shore, Perry Como, Jo Stafford, and Doris Day. They all did a good deal better than Ray Eberle and Jack Leonard.

The ASCAP radio boycott of 1941 also delivered a blow to bands. Most of them lost most of their best material, including in some cases their theme songs. Jumping into the breach was "hillbilly" music (what would later be called "country"). Roy Acuff, Gene Autry, Red Foley, Tex Ritter, and Bob Wills made the *Billboard* charts for the first time in the early forties, uniformly with BMI songs. Ernest Tubb's "Walking the Floor over You," which has been called the first honky-tonk song, was a hit in 1941, followed the next year by "Deep in the Heart of Texas," which charted in four separate versions. "Pistol Packin' Mama" reached number one in 1943 in a rendition by its author, Al Dexter. Kay Kyser's earwormy rendition of another cowboy tune, "Jingle Jangle Jingle (I Got Spurs)," was number one for eight weeks in 1942. "Jingle Jangle Jingle" was an ASCAP song that first appeared in a film called *The Forest Rangers*; the lyrics were by Manhattanite Frank Loesser, who never spent more than a couple of weeks inland in his entire life. But it demonstrated that hillbilly had gone mainstream, never to leave. Music performed by black musicians and singers, and intended primarily for black listeners, similarly reached a broader audience via BMI-licensed compositions, though, for the moment, it didn't penetrate to the extent of country. *Billboard* in January 1942 started covering records in both styles in a column called "Western and Race." Over the next decade and a half, BMI dramatically broadened the kinds of music Americans were exposed to. It encouraged writers of those sorts of music by giving them an economic and legal stake in their compositions, and implicitly encouraged performers of those sorts of music by strengthening their platform on radio and records.

An institutional manifestation of this openness to unfamiliar sounds was a new record company, Capitol, started in 1942 by two songwriters, Johnny Mercer and Buddy DeSylva, and Glenn Wallichs, a record store owner. Mercer's own compositions—and singing style—blended jazz and Tin Pan Alley, with a subtle down-home feel, and the label would reflect that eclecticism. Its first release was a disk by venerable jazzman Paul Whiteman; the next two were "Cow-Cow Boogie," by Freddie Slack and His Orchestra, with Ella Mae Morse on vocals, and Mercer's own "Strip Polka." Over the course of the decade, Capitol would sign and record Jo Stafford, Margaret Whiting, Stan Kenton, Peggy Lee, Merle Travis, and Nat "King" Cole. "We're going into the open market for the best songs and the best performers we can give the public," Wallichs told *Down Beat*. "We plan a complete catalogue that will offer sweet music, swing music, Hawaiian, hill billy and race music."

Just months after Capitol opened its doors, it had to close them because of the "Petrillo Ban." Angry that backing musicians and sidemen got no royalties on record sales—which had become especially important with the popularity of jukeboxes—James Caesar Petrillo, the head of the American Federation of Musicians, instituted a boycott of the major record companies, Columbia, Victor, and Decca. Decca and the newcomer Capitol settled about a year in, but the two biggest labels, Columbia and Victor, didn't come to terms until November 1944. Conventional wisdom holds that the ban was another important reason for singers' ascendance at the expense of the bands. It's true that a handful of a cappella records were successful during the strike, including Harry Warren and Mack Gordon's "You'll Never Know," another lament for an absent lover and a hit for both Sinatra and Dick Haymes, and Loesser's "First Class Private Mary Brown," recorded by Perry Como with chorus. Such vocal groups as the Song Spinners, the Mills Brothers (whose 1943 "Paper Doll" was one of the biggest hits of the decade), the Andrews Sisters, and the Ink Spots had substantial sales success during the ban. Mel Tormé, then a high school student in Chicago, later recalled, "Four- and five- and even seven-voice units were all over the place. The Merry Macs, the Pied Pipers, the Modernaires, Six Hits and a Miss, the Skylarks, the Town Criers, the Mills Brothers, the Andrews Sisters, the Dinning Sisters, Four Jacks and Jill . . ." They inspired him to form the influential jazz-inflected group the Mel-Tones in 1944, right after graduation.

But in the overall scheme of popular music, all-singing records didn't actually do very well; when the ban ended, they largely stopped. (The most important influence of this genre wasn't seen till a decade and more later, with the arrival of the harmonizing, finger-snapping doo-wop groups of the 1950s.) Moreover, the labels had plenty of advance warning about the strike and planned accordingly. As it approached, Milt Gabler was a new A&R man at Decca. He recalled the period in a single present-tense sentence: "We record like mad almost around the clock." Under Gabler's supervision, Decca pressed, before the ban, twenty-six albums of twenty-six songs each for a series called "Songs of Our Times." The other labels also were busy, and most of their releases during at least the first half of the strike were recordings they had stockpiled during the months before, or reissues of older songs.

The most significant factors in the bands' demise were dollars, cents, and bodies. As World War II progressed, more and more players were lost to the draft. Clubs and dance halls cut back their hours and sometimes went out of business altogether. Gasoline rationing meant that it was tougher to go on the road, and a 20 percent amusement tax hurt, too.

The result of all these trends was plain to hear on the radio, plain to see in the charts. In 1940, ten of twelve songs that reached number one on the *Billboard* charts were recorded by big bands. (Crosby was responsible for the other two.) Five years later, vocalists and vocal groups accounted for nine of the fifteen number-one hits. The most successful, that year at least, was Perry Como, a former barber from western Pennsylvania, who had started out as a singer with the Ted Weems band before going out on his own in 1943. He specialized in sentimental ballads whose tempos were so slow they almost seemed to stop in the middle. His "Till the End of Time," adapted from a Chopin polonaise, was number one for ten consecutive weeks in 1945. All told, that year Como sold 10 million records.

Songwriter Ervin Drake—born Ervin Maurice Druckman in New York in 1919—had a firsthand experience of all those developments. He had been drawn to the trade in part by his older brother Milton, who'd had some success on Tin Pan Alley, notably with "Java Jive," a hit for the Ink Spots in 1940. Like Livingston and Evans, Ervin didn't get his break until the ASCAP ban. Ralph Peer presented Drake with a traditional Brazilian song called "Tico Tico no Fubá." Drake supplied English lyrics, and the Andrews Sisters charted with the tune in 1944. He developed a specialty in providing English words to South American melodies, including "Yo Te Amo Mucho (and That's That)," which Xavier Cugat played in a movie called *Holiday in Mexico*, and "You Can in Yucatan," performed by Desi Arnaz. Also in 1944, Drake wrote the lyrics for Duke Ellington's instrumental "Perdido." Between the successes, there was a lot of hustling. "I put in nights sitting in places that were part restaurant, part dance halls," Drake recalled. "I'd try to get next to the bandleader and give him a song of my own."

In contrast to many Tin Pan Alley songwriters, Drake had a social conscience. In 1943, in reaction to the racial and religious segregation practiced by hotels and restaurants, he wrote a tune he called "No Re-stricted Signs (Up in Heaven)" and took it to Capitol Records. "I didn't want it to seem like a message song so I did it with a boogie-woogie tempo," Drake said in a 1996 interview. "Johnny [Mercer] wanted to record it. He showed it to his partner, and [Glenn Wallichs] said, 'John, the way things are in this country if you record that song we will lose our distributorship.'" So Capitol passed, but the musician and producer Enoch Light ended up taking the song to a gospel group called the Golden Gate Quartet, who released their version in 1946.

The biggest hit of Drake's early career, by contrast, would be un-playable today because it is almost entirely made up of crude racial stereotypes. While he was lying in the bathtub one day, as he recalled, the song came to him in its entirety: a novelty number titled "The Rickety Rickshaw Man," whose lyrics began, "There's a coolie name o' Chulee / Runs a rickety rickshaw south of Peking." Ralph Peer per-suaded sweet bandleader Eddy Howard to record the song; in return, Howard got half the songwriting royalties, a common practice known as a "cut-in." (Through the same custom, the lyrics to most of Elling-ton's early songs are credited to his manager, Irving Mills, who never wrote a lyric in his life.) The song reached number six on the *Billboard* charts in 1946.

As usual, Drake careered from the ridiculous to the sublime, this time drawing from his own life. He had been dating a showgirl named Edith Bein and fell deeply in love with her. But she began to be courted by "all these Wall Street types," Drake told Will Friedwald in 2009. "I felt like I couldn't compete, so I just withdrew from her life." In the midst of his subsequent depression, he heard a haunting melody by Irene Higginbotham. "It hit me—smack!" he said in the Friedwald interview. "This is exactly what I felt when Edith left me. So in about

20 minutes I wrote the whole lyric to 'Good Morning Heartache.'" A couple of months later, Billie Holiday made an immortal recording of the song, and it has since become a blues standard.

When I talked to Drake in his Great Neck, New York, home in 2010, sitting in on the conversation was his wife. She was none other than the former Edith Bein. The two had reunited in 1975, after their respective spouses had died.

Soon after Pearl Harbor, Jay Livingston was inducted into the Army, but Ray Evans was kept out of the service because of an old football injury. In '43, from his post at Fort Ontario, New York, Jay was so surprised at hearing a Syracuse radio station play their song "Hello There"—a follow-up to "G'Bye Now" that hadn't come close to matching its success—that he was inspired to put pen to paper. "These small stations play a lot of BMI music all day, and that explains where our performance royalties are coming from," Livingston wrote his partner. "The last check wasn't bad." (He added, "You better drown your troubles in sex as long as you have that place to yourself.")

Jay was out of the service by 1944. Songwriting prospects were sufficiently thin for the team that they took Ole Olsen up on an offer: If they would drive his car from Chicago to Los Angeles, they could stay at his house on the West Coast for a while. At first, amazingly and depressingly enough, L.A. felt like a reprise of their worst New York days, albeit with sunnier skies and some positive interactions with top Hollywood songwriters. Ray wrote in his diary about meeting the composer Burton Lane ("He was very nice") and the veteran lyricist Al Dubin, who "told us many anecdotes of old timers and lore of Hollywood. When he first heard [Lorenz] Hart's lyrics and it was the only time he felt discouraged—then Hart asks Mr. Dubin if they were okay."

Not so encouraging was their interview with Nat Finston, the head of music at the most prestigious studio of all, MGM. First, Finston kept them waiting for an hour. "Almost went crazy sitting there," Ray wrote that night in his diary. "But, finally he came and turned out to be good-natured but eccentric. He seemed to be surprised that we weren't members of Ascap, if we were 'amateurs,' what were we looking for etc." Whatever they were looking for, they didn't get it at MGM.

Ultimately, however, a chain of events led inexorably (or so it seems in retrospect) to the success they'd been pursuing for so long. The medley went something like this:

After months of scrounging and living in a five-dollar-a-week room in the Hollywood Hills, Ray and Jay were hired by a low-rent movie studio, Producers Releasing Corporation, or PRC, to write songs for some low-rent pictures: *Secrets of a Co-Ed*; *I Accuse My Parents*; *Crime, Inc.*; *Swing Hostess*; and *Why Girls Leave Home* ("The violent, unvarnished truth about the scores of thousands of young girls who recklessly toss away home ties for a life of dangerous thrills!"). The star of a couple of the movies was the former Benny Goodman singer Martha Tilton, who . . .

Recorded for Johnny Mercer's Capitol Records. Through Tilton (as Ray wrote in his diary), "we went to see Mercer. Surprise of surprises, we saw him and he was very enthusiastic about [the song] 'Cat and Canary.' It won't mean anything except his getting to know us a little better. But, it sure buoyed us up to have something favorable on the horizon." Mercer did in fact like "The Cat and the Canary" . . .

And ended up singing it, as well as some other Livingston and Evans tunes, on his radio show, *The Johnny Mercer Chesterfield Music Shop*—mentioning their names each time. A few months later . . .

Capitol called Jay and Ray asking if they had any songs for a new Betty Hutton record. The label took one, a swinging tune called "Stuff

Like That There." *Billboard* said of the disk, in characteristic lingo, "Here's a cinch for jukes. It's lady Hutton at her best. . . . It's definitely big-time. Once it catches on, it should go like a house-a-fire." The song reached number four on the charts. . . .

On the basis of the song and their past work, Livingston and Evans were finally elected to membership in ASCAP, the sign of having arrived as an establishment songwriter. Better than that, as ASCAP president Deems Taylor wrote to Jay, "the Writers' Classification Committee at its meeting held on December 7th, 1945, placed you in Class 3. . . . Ordinarily, new members are started in Class 4, but the Committee felt that the value of your contribution to the Society warranted their placing you in a more advanced class."

When Hutton was making a Paramount picture called *The Stork Club*, Mercer recommended Jay and Ray as songwriters. They auditioned for Louis Lipstone and Buddy DeSylva (a film producer as well as a Capitol Records co-owner), who took one of their songs, "A Square in the Social Circle."

About two weeks later . . . And here Ray Evans picks up the story (he's quoted in Gene Lees's biography of Mercer, *Portrait of Johnny*):

> We got a call from Louis Lipstone. He said, "I'd like to see you in my office. We need someone to write songs for the shorts and things like that. We can't pay you very much, two hundred a week. But if you like it, it's a nine-to-five job." We said, "Of course!" He said, "Okay, we'll give you a contract." On our way out of his office, Jay said, "Is it two hundred each or two hundred for both of us?" It was two hundred each.

The boys placed songs in a couple of Paramount films, notably Bob Hope's *Monsieur Beaucaire*. But their careers were not going "like a house-a-fire," and they were painfully aware that their contract had an option, which Paramount could renew—or not—at its pleasure. Not long before the telltale date, the studio's publicity department had the bright idea to create a song called "To Each His Own," the title of one of its forthcoming movies. The song wouldn't be in the film, which was already in the can. The hope was that it would get recorded, receive airplay, and thus provide free advertising for the picture. The flacks started at the top of the songwriting pecking order and went down the line. Everybody turned them down. Evans later recalled that "Victor Young, who had written the movie's score, said, 'I won't write a song with that dumb title.'" But Ray and Jay, at the very bottom, couldn't afford to say no.

Nearly seven decades after its creation, "To Each His Own" does not impress. Its melody is singsongy (though not entirely uncatchy), its lyrics sentimental and just this side of banal: "Two lips must insist on two more to be kissed / Or they'll never know what love can do." The year after its release, George Frazier wrote in *Variety*, "It was not, as one realizes in retrospect, an especially good record, but it presented a personality and, what is as important, it was part of the postwar trend toward sweeter music." For whatever reason, it struck a nerve, especially in sweet singer and bandleader Eddy Howard's version. (Howard recorded the tune on the same day as Ervin Drake's "The Rickety Rickshaw Man.") The song hit at a moment when, due to increasing competition among labels, cover versions of top tunes were rampant. In 1946, "To Each His Own" battled it out for preeminence with another bit of treacle, "The Gypsy," which had two number-one versions, one by Dinah Shore and one by the Ink Spots, the latter topping the charts for a remarkable thirteen straight weeks. But Howard's "Each" was number one for eight weeks, and versions by Freddy Martin and (again) the Ink Spots also reached the top spot; close to a dozen singers and sweet bands ended up recording the song. By the following March—according to a *Los Angeles Daily News* article Ray saved—"To Each His Own" had sold four million records and a million pieces of sheet music, and had earned its writers $30,000. The article did not specify if that was $30,000 each or $30,000 for both of them.

Better yet was a brief item in the trades: "Jay Livingstone [*sic*] and Ray Evans, songwriters, options lifted, Paramount."

"To Each His Own" would have a profound effect on Hollywood music. In the words of a 1946 Billboard headline, "TO EACH" CLICK MAY CUE MORE TITLE TUNES. Translation: All the studios started taking a page from Paramount's book and commissioning songs to play under the credits of their films; if it had the same title as the picture, so much the better, but there was definitely no need for it to have anything to *do* with the picture. Ray and Jay became the go-to guys for this sub-genre. Over the next five years they wrote title songs for the films *Golden Earrings*; *Easy Come, Easy Go*; *The Big Clock*; *Beyond Glory*; *Copper Canyon*; *Song of Surrender*; and *When Worlds Collide* ("When worlds collide and mountains tumble, I'll stop loving you"). Ray later said that the only title song assignment they ever turned down was *Desert Fury*. One wonders why.

One day in 1948 at Paramount, a producer on a forthcoming Bob Hope film came to their office, ordered up a song, and, wonder of wonders, left the title up to them. In an interview years later, Ray remembered that the producer said, "Why don't you write a song about Bob being a tenderfoot in the Wild West, way out of his element? And he wishes he were back East where life is civilized." Out of that came "Buttons and Bows," a small gem of a character song and another example—in the tradition of Cole Porter's "Don't Fence Me In," Johnny Mercer's "I'm an Old Cowhand," and Frank Loesser's "Jingle Jangle Jingle (I Got Spurs)"—of East Coast tenderfeet writing cowboy numbers. Dinah Shore got hold of the sheet music and made a record that shot to the top of the charts in September 1948 and stayed there for ten weeks. Sensing a potential waste of good publicity, Paramount speeded up the release of the Hope picture, *The Paleface*, and featured "Buttons and Bows" in every bit of advertising. Reviewing the movie in *The New York Times*, Bosley Crowther wrote:

> The historic thing about "The Paleface" is that in it is tucked away, as though it were a thing of no consequence, the sensational "Buttons and Bows." This song, which, our seasoned sources tell us, is now the all-time all-time hit, is brushed off in one casual chorus by—of all people!—Mr. Hope. Twiddling a concertina and comically mouthing the words, Mr. Hope tosses off the number and indifferently leaves it lie. Nobody picks it up later. That's all they originally thought of it when "The Paleface" was put together more than a year ago.
>
> The great things in human progress—and in art—usually happen this way. "The Paleface" deserves primarily a marker as the birthplace of "Buttons and Bows."

Three months later, "Buttons and Bows" earned Livingston and Evans the Academy Award for Best Original Song. Their jobs at Paramount were secure and their career was set.

However, Hollywood was not doing so well by other songwriters. As a 1947 *Billboard* article reported, "Only four studios today have a cleffer team apiece on a yearly contract basis as opposed to the golden era of movie musicals when some flicker factories boasted as many as 30 scribes per studio" ("cleffer," "scribe" = songwriter; "flicker factory" = movie studio). A 1948 Associated Press article called Livingston and Evans "probably the only successful songwriters with steady jobs."

The *Billboard* piece went on to explain that the main reason for the change was that studios were drastically cutting back on musicals. One "pic company exec" was quoted as saying that his company, which had once produced twenty musicals in a year, was now down to two or three. "While in the past," the article explained, "movie makers could grind out a series of n.s.g.* pix held together by a couple of tunes, movie-goers today expect lavish, Technicolor productions with top-name thesps and top tunes. Hence, rather than produce a number of second-rate musicals, studios will concentrate . . . on a few first-class productions. Average cost of a Class musical is $2,500,000."

Starting in the late forties, when Hollywood did make a "class musical," less and less frequently did it contain original songs. Instead, it was usually either a vehicle for *old* songs (*An American in Paris*, *Singin' in the Rain*, *The Band Wagon*) or a film version of a Broadway hit.

A 1947 *Detroit News* article assessing the Oscar-nominated songs termed them "comparatively second rate. . . . In past years it has been a mad scamper because Broadway had drawn all the top Tin Pan Alley boys into the fold. Now, with the gradual decline of musicals, they appear to be heading back to Broadway." Appearances in this case were not deceiving. In 1943, Richard Rodgers had joined with a new lyricist partner, Oscar Hammerstein II, and the Broadway show they wrote together that year, *Oklahoma!*, was a monumental hit that reinvented the American musical. They followed that with the equally splendid *Carousel* (1945) and *South Pacific* (1949), which cumulatively staked Broadway's renewed claim as the center of great American popular

---

*Variety slang for "not so good."

music. (All three were adapted by Hollywood.) Rodgers's work with Hammerstein was just as good as that with Lorenz Hart (who died just months after the opening of *Oklahoma!*), but it was very different in flavor. Rodgers–Hart songs are jazz-inflected and New York to the core. A Rodgers and Hammerstein score generally breaks down into three categories:

- Lyrical love songs, redolent more of operetta than nightclub, like "People Will Say We're in Love," "If I Loved You," "Younger Than Springtime," and "Some Enchanted Evening."

- Comic or character-based set pieces, like "I Cain't Say No," "The Surrey with the Fringe on Top," and "I'm Gonna Wash That Man Right outa My Hair."

- Ensemble or inspirational numbers. In the team's early shows, these songs tended to be rousing, with a strong regional flavor, as in "Oklahoma!," "This Was a Real Nice Clambake," and "June Is Bustin' Out All Over." As time progressed, they became more overtly didactic or sentimental: "You'll Never Walk Alone," "You've Got to Be Carefully Taught," and the culmination in the following decade, "Climb Ev'ry Mountain."

The other surviving titans of popular song, the words-and-music men Irving Berlin and Cole Porter, went back and forth between the coasts, doing superlative work on both of them. Each of them scored 1948 films—Porter's *The Pirate* and Berlin's *Easter Parade*—for the Arthur Freed Unit at Metro-Goldwyn-Mayer Studios. MGM was the last holdout, continuing to produce "class" musicals until the stream finally trickled out with *Gigi* in 1958. The only other producer who made a significant number of original musicals in the fifties was Walt Disney, with such animated films as *Cinderella* (1950), *Peter Pan* (1953), and *Lady and the Tramp* (1955).

Berlin and Porter each wrote their greatest Broadway show in the late forties: *Annie Get Your Gun* and *Kiss Me, Kate*, respectively. (Berlin took over *Annie* from Jerome Kern, who died as he was about to begin work on the score.) The post-*Oklahoma!* 1940s musical was an impressive cultural object. The esteemed émigré composer Kurt Weill had made Broadway his home base, and high-art figures like Leonard Bernstein, Morton Gould, and Marc Blitzstein wrote shows during the decade. A new team, composer Frederick Loewe and lyricist Alan Jay Lerner, had a brilliant debut in 1947 with *Brigadoon*. Broadway work offered the prospect of a level of creative control that would have been a pipe dream in Hollywood. So why wouldn't the top movie songwriters decide to reverse the westward trip they made about a decade earlier? We have already seen that Arthur Schwartz came back to New York. So did Harold Arlen and Johnny Mercer with *St. Louis Woman* (1946); Burton Lane and Yip Harburg with *Finian's Rainbow* (1947); Jule Styne with *High Button Shoes* (1947; lyrics by Sammy Cahn) and *Gentlemen Prefer Blondes* (1949; lyrics by Leo Robin); and Frank Loesser with *Where's Charley?* (1948).

Interviewed by Max Wilk for his 1973 book *They're Playing Our Song*, Jule Styne recalled, "I began to hate California. . . . I saw fellows around me who were big when I came to California and in just a short span of three or four years they were getting less and less. Fellas like Harry Warren. I saw them dismissing him."

Styne got hold of a Dramatists Guild of America standard contract for Broadway writers and composers and was gobsmacked by the idea, so counter to the Hollywood ethos, "that what I write *has* to be played unless *I* decide to rewrite it." After *High Button Shoes*, he said, he realized that the Hollywood pattern of writing a song for a particular performer in a particular picture was limiting. "It took me a long time to break away, but finally I said, 'When Dick Rodgers writes a song, he doesn't know who's going to sing it yet. Somebody along the way, but it's for *everybody*.'" Styne, along with Loesser and Rodgers and Hammerstein, would eventually become a producer as well as a writer of musicals.

In comparison with the frothy confections that predominated before the war, Broadway was producing a higher-quality product in which songs, script, and character were integrated. That had implications for music. Now hits would occasionally emerge, but generally speaking, songs that were tailored for the characters who sang them at a particular moment had no life outside the show. Some years later an aspiring lyricist, Sheldon Harnick, was talking to Styne about trying to find spots for songs that could become popular and still make sense in the larger piece. "Jule, to my surprise, said, 'Forget it,'" Harnick recalled. "'That day is past. We don't write now hoping that they'll be pop songs. Write for the show, write for the character and the situation.'"

Once again following Rodgers and Hammerstein's lead, most of the standout stand-alone songs that did emerge—"Almost Like Being in Love" from *Brigadoon*, "They Say It's Wonderful" from *Annie Get Your Gun*, "So in Love" from *Kiss Me, Kate*, "How Are Things in Glocca Morra?" from *Finian's Rainbow*—represented a change from the prewar era, when the Broadway tunes of Porter, Gershwin, Rodgers and Hart, and even Kern had a jazz quality. These new ballads hailed back to the earlier tradition of operetta; one could imagine Jeanette MacDonald and Nelson Eddy essaying their soaring melodic lines. Jazz bands and small combos could and sometimes did take them on, but it was hardly a natural fit.

For songwriters unable or unwilling to try their hand on Broadway, hanging around Hollywood was an option. The studios would occasionally throw out some work, and if you were on the level of a Jimmy McHugh, you could live off your royalties and lead a life of sunny leisure and country-club schmoozing. Ira Gershwin started to write again a few years after his brother's death and teamed with Arthur Schwartz on Broadway for *Park Avenue* in 1946. But after the show's relatively poor performance, he put down his pencil and, with one notable exception, spent the remaining four decades of his life writing occasional essays and enjoying a life of Beverly Hills leisure. The exception was "The Man That Got Away" and the rest of the exceptional score he and Arlen wrote for the 1954 film *A Star Is Born*.

The one first-rank writer who stayed in Hollywood and stayed busy, at least for a while, was—despite the "dismissal" perceived by Jule Styne—Harry Warren, who had become too much a creature of California to leave. For MGM, Warren scored the eminently classy *The Harvey Girls* (1946), *Summer Holiday* (1948), and *The Barkleys of Broadway* (1949), which reunited Fred Astaire and Ginger Rogers after a decade apart. But his contract with the studio ended in 1952, after which he did such work for hire as "Zing a Little Zong" for Crosby in 1952, "That's Amore" for the 1953 Dean Martin–Jerry Lewis film *The Caddy*, and, in 1957, the title song for *An Affair to Remember*, a number-seventeen record for Vic Damone.

Jimmy Van Heusen had some Broadway success. But California always called to him. He and Johnny Burke kept doing movie work for Hope or Crosby, or Hope and Crosby together, in yet another *Road* picture. (In the final iteration, *The Road to Hong Kong*, Hope's character is given Van Heusen's real name, Chester Babcock.) Van Heusen would reemerge in the late fifties with an exciting final chapter to his career, but for the moment his writing was not up to previous form. "The *Road* pictures symbolized the life span of a whole profession," Wilfrid Sheed wrote. "The Hollywood songwriters had entered the war a short while before as fresh and bouncy as the annual New Year baby, and they were already leaving it as old men and has-beens, their best work behind them."

V

What Happened
to the Music?
1946–1954

The Sinatra phase had ended. And there was nothing happening,
except modern and progressive jazz. Stan Kenton and Dave
Brubeck, and, of course, bop. It was wide open and we offered
a simple beat that the kids could dance to.

• Bill Haley

When jazz and popular music lose all contact with one another,
they both degenerate into pretentiousness, chaos, and absurdity.

• Dave Gelly

The postwar years saw broad shifts in the kinds of music Americans wanted to, or could afford to, listen to. Price controls in the United States had ended in 1946; living costs jumped, and going out for an evening to hear live music became an investment. People didn't have much time or inclination, either; they had missed out on a lot during the war, socially and vocationally, and now was the time to catch up. Americans began marrying in record numbers in 1943, and the presence of one or more small children around the house was yet another reason not to go dancing. Even at home, swing wasn't what people wanted to listen to anymore. These sounds had been around for a long time, and young people—not known for musical fealty—were in the mood for something new. In 1945, major networks dropped twelve big bands from their regular radio shows. Nor were the economics of live performance favorable to the bands. Ballrooms closed or cut their opening hours, and bands' fees dropped dramatically, while their (by definition) big payrolls stayed big and travel costs nudged upward. In a matter of weeks in December 1946, a startling number of bandleaders dissolved their groups: Benny Goodman, Woody Herman, Harry James, Tommy Dorsey, Les Brown, Jack Teagarden, Benny Carter, Ina Ray Hutton, and Alvino Rey.

That meant Rey's trombonist, Johnny Mandel, was out of work. "We were playing to empty ballrooms," Mandel recalled, "because the jitterbugs never came back from the war. The kids who used to dance to the bands before the war, they had no thought for tomorrow. When they went to war, they went through all kinds of hell. The ones that made it back, they wanted to go on with their lives, and jitterbugging wasn't part of it. They married those girls they used to jitterbug with, they were spending all their money on babysitters, on building houses, and nobody was dancing."

Whatever the reasons, the era was definitely over. For a dozen years—roughly 1934 through 1946—for the only time in American history, the most popular music in the country was high-quality jazz, and a staple of that music was good and great songs. Now the center of jazz was no longer holding. Two contentious groups were left at the margins, neither one especially interested in the products of Tin Pan Alley, Broadway, or Hollywood. The first faction hailed the music and performers of New Orleans and Chicago from the 1920s and earlier—which they called "trad," for "traditional"—and asserted that nothing that had come afterward was authentic jazz, or worth listening to. One early success for trad enthusiasts was the discovery in 1943 of venerable trumpeter Bunk Johnson, working in Louisiana's rice fields. He was sent out on a national tour that included a San Francisco concert that *Time* called "the most historic jam session in the annals of jazz." The early forties were a propitious time for these revivalists both because the war effort had claimed so many musicians and because the AFM strike had turned off the flow of new instrumental material. At Decca, Milt Gabler, whose enthusiasm for classic jazz was reflected in his Commodore Music Shop, headed a new label for the music, and other labels took similar action. (This aesthetic found staunch advocates in England, including the poet Philip Larkin, the novelist Kingsley Amis, and the writer and vocalist George Melly, who continued channeling Bessie Smith and Jelly Roll Morton in his performances into the 2000s. One notable U.S. proponent was the young Turkish immigrant Ahmet Ertegun, later to start the Atlantic record label. By now, the main expression of trad is in Woody Allen's performances on clarinet and the soundtracks of his films.)

The trad proponents—many of whom yoked their cause to vigorous left-wing politics—raised hackles from the start, notably among the second group, who sniffed at swing. This contingent wanted jazz to look ahead, not back; they called the trad camp "moldy figs." (The term was coined by Leonard Feather in his book *The Jazz Years: Earwitness to an Era*.) A West Coast bandleader named Stan Kenton refused to play music for his audience to dance to; he wanted them to *listen*. He talked of jazz as a new classical music and later said it should never have been "mixed up with popular music." Meanwhile, on the East Coast, young musicians like Charlie Parker and Dizzy Gillespie were creating bold new sounds at epic jam sessions at Minton's Playhouse in Harlem and other venues. It was hard to dance to this stuff—

eventually dubbed "bebop"—or hum it, for that matter. Tin Pan Alley not surprisingly turned up its nose. Reviewing a Gillespie concert in 1948, *Billboard* sniffed that the music was

> different only in that its purpose seems to be to create as uninhibited and unorthodox a product as the human ear can tolerate. Melody as such is totally eliminated from the scheme of things, with full emphasis falling to awkward (and at times, painful) harmonic combinations, soloists favoring unconventional intervals in jumping from one note to the next which is worked against a background of untamed rhythmic torrents.

Louis Armstrong—who didn't need rediscovering but benefited from the New Orleans revival—complained about bop, which he called "that pipe dream music, that whole modern malice." He warmed to the theme: "So you get all them weird chords that don't mean nothing, and first people get curious about it just because it's new, but soon they get tired of it because it's really no good and you got no melody to remember and no beat to dance to."

Boppers, for their part, thought the handkerchief-waving, grinning Armstrong was an Uncle Tom, and sometimes said so out loud. But the music was just as bad to them as Armstrong's obsequious antics. One modern-jazz arranger commented, "We're tired of that old New Orleans beat-beat, I-got-the-blues pap." Bop may have had the cool factor, but it didn't have anything close to the popularity that had been enjoyed by the big bands. And that would be increasingly true—of bebop, post-bop, and, in fact, every variety of modern jazz. To be sure, there were occasional exceptions, as releases by Dave Brubeck, Miles Davis, or Stan Getz intermittently struck a nerve with the public in the fifties and sixties. But at the end of the twentieth century, jazz was a niche market, its records accounting for less than 5 percent of total sales.

Back in the forties, what the two warring camps shared was a disdain for big bands, both the swing and the sweet. They weren't interested in following regimented arrangements, they didn't want to play music for people to dance to, and performance and expression, rather than songs, was at the heart of their enterprise. Some big bands kept plugging along as the forties ended and the fifties began, but with very occasional and intermittently successful exceptions—Stan Kenton, Duke Ellington, Count Basie, Woody Herman (who started up a new band, known as the Second Herd, in 1947)—they veered heavily toward the sweet. A year after the war ended, *Life* noted, "If the songs a country sings are any indication of its mood, the U.S. last week was lolling in an amorous, sentimental daze. On dance floors and radios were heard such plaintive queries as 'Why don't you surrender?' and such pleas as 'Linger in my arms a little longer, baby.'" In a 1949 *Billboard* poll, well over three-quarters of college students said their favorite kind of music was sweet; swing was second, while just over 1 percent voted for "Progressive Jazz, barely beating out 'Corn.'" Some college promoters put a "three-ballads-out-of-four" clause into orchestras' contracts; *Billboard* reported that "Cornell University, in addition to asking for the slow dance music proviso, forced an agency to include a clause which would prohibit the ork [orchestra] from smoking on the bandstand." A William Morris Agency music booker was quoted in a 1947 newspaper article titled "Swing Has Swung": "Ballroom operators complain that the kids walk off the floor when the music gets hot. Kids haven't got so much money to throw around these days. When a fellow pays a couple of bucks to take his best girl dancing, he wants to hear music that makes her want to cuddle up a little closer, not swing."

The writer of the article, Don Dornbrook, described changes some bands had made:

> Raymond Scott, who rose to musical fame on an unconventional note with such original pieces as "Huckleberry Duck," has changed to a more saccharin style. So have Charlie Barnet, Sonny Durham, Jimmy Dorsey, Boyd Raeburn, and Charlie Ventura. . . .
>
> But for the true hepcat, the man who has added insult to injury is Earl "Father" Hines. For the last nine months, this prince of the jazz piano has been fronting a sweet band. That's almost enough to make a swing fan take to smoking reefers.

According to Dornbrook, "A 21 year old upstart had a lot to do with pointing up the change in dance music preference. He is Elliot Lawrence, a University of Pennsylvania graduate who likes to wear purple plaid jackets, yellow monogrammed shirts and flowered ties. Last fall he played homecoming dances at nine universities." Lawrence had gone out on the road in 1944, right after graduating from Penn, and right before the big-band era had screeched to a halt. He grew up in Philadelphia with an inordinately talented and forward-thinking saxophone player named Gerry Mulligan, and after Mulligan joined the Lawrence band, the leader divided his shows in two. "We had a section for bebop and Mulligan, and a section for ballads," Lawrence said in 2011. But, he said, "the kids wanted ballads to dance to," and by the time Dornbrook's article appeared, the band was 100 percent sweet. In a 1947 *Billboard* poll of college students' band preferences, "sweet-with-a-beat Elliot Lawrence" was named "most promising." Lawrence's yellow shirts and flowered ties didn't hurt, nor did the figure he cut on the bandstand: he was voted one of America's most eligible bachelors by *Look* magazine in 1949. Still, expenses kept going up and revenues down. "Stan Kenton talked to me and said, 'You have to stay in,'" Lawrence recalled. "He said that we were a dying breed. Woody Herman stayed—he loved to tour. But for me, it was hell. I did nine years of it, and that was enough." He put away his baton in 1953. (Lawrence began a career providing music for radio and television and ultimately Broadway, where he was the musical director of *Bye Bye Birdie* and *How to Succeed in Business Without Really Trying*. He was the musical director and conductor for every Tony Award telecast from 1965 through 2011.)

In an uncanny process, jazz was being surgically removed from popular music. Popular music, for its part, didn't seem to mind. With 350 million records sold, 1946 was the biggest year for the industry ever. The figure climbed to 375 million the following year. The records may have been flying off the shelf, yet the fact remained that they weren't very good. The writer Wilfrid Sheed's parents were British, but he spent his childhood in the United States and developed a passion for the great popular songs. He was away during the war, and when he returned in 1947, at the age of sixteen, he was struck that "the Hit Parade . . . seemed to show no variety at all. One day, for instance, it seemed as if the whole city of New York had conspired to play the exact same record out of every door and window I passed, a dental drill of a song called 'Near You' that apparently had the power to keep itself playing indefinitely." "Near You" was written by a Nashville bandleader named Francis Craig, and his recording of the tune had a repeating left-hand piano line that could indeed bring to mind a throbbing drill. The independent Bullet label had released it as the B side of a number called "Red Rose." But it was "Near You" that got picked up on radio stations throughout the South, spread to the rest of the country, and ultimately reached number one on the *Billboard* charts. It stayed there for seventeen weeks. The song's closest rivals that year, both charting in multiple recordings, were equally insipid tunes that shared a soporific tempo and (in most versions) a heavy string arrangement: the 1913 Tin Pan Alley standard "Peg o' My Heart" and "Mam'selle," which appeared in the 1946 film *The Razor's Edge*. Frank Sinatra, who as host of *Your Hit Parade* was forced to sing all three songs, singled out "Near You" as especially "decadent" and "bloodless."

Sheed observed:

> And just like that, the magical coincidence of quality and popularity was over, the music in the public square is nowhere near the best music anymore. Listening to a program recently of the top pop hits from 1940 to 1955, I was startled all over again at how sharp the break was at the end of World War II, as if the bad stuff had been waiting for its cue. And perhaps it had, because several of the new hits seemed to depend on the latest gimmickry and special effects, to celebrate technology more than music. The kid at the piano syncopating everything had died in the war and been replaced by his country cousin.

"Country" is right: during the postwar years, ASCAP writers, the major record companies, and national audiences finally came fully on board with the folk, quasi-folk, western, and hillbilly sounds that BMI had introduced at the beginning of the decade. The most successful record of 1948 was Dinah Shore's version of Livingston and Evans's faux-western ditty "Buttons and Bows." (Shore was from Tennessee, Patti Page from Oklahoma, and Rosemary Clooney from Kentucky, so all three could convincingly put across homespun.) Number one in

Founded in 1914, ASCAP collected payments for songwriters and exemplified the professionalization of what had been a disorganized trade. Some of the founders and early members (from left): Gene Buck, Victor Herbert, John Philip Sousa, Harry B. Smith, Jerome Kern, Irving Berlin, George W. Meyer, Irving Bibo, and Otto Harbach.

Irving Berlin and George Gershwin, both Jewish New Yorkers, propelled the American popular song to new and unimagined popularity and musical distinction.

In the Great American Songbook era (roughly 1925–1950), songwriters were almost always photographed at the piano. Cole Porter wrote both the words and the music, but there was usually a division of labor.

Richard Rodgers (left) and Lorenz Hart.

Jerome Kern and the lyricist Dorothy Fields—
the only woman to crack the boys' club of American songwriting.

The composer Harry
Warren (left) and his
lyricist partner Al Dubin
went to Hollywood early
and provided songs for
the great Warner Bros.
musicals of the 1930s.

Harold Arlen (left) and Johnny Mercer.

Arthur Schwartz, in
a 1933 portrait by
Carl Van Vechten.

A younger generation of songwriters who came along in the early 1940s was deeply influenced by jazz and found success writing for Hollywood. Left: Composer Jule Styne (left) and lyricist Sammy Cahn. Below: Jimmy Van Heusen (left) and Johnny Burke, who became known as Bing Crosby's personal songwriting team. Van Heusen and Cahn would fruitfully team up in the 1950s.

Duke Ellington often composed melodies with the help of players in his splendid orchestra. Sometimes he even gave them credit.

Jay Livingston (at the piano) and Ray Evans were University of Pennsylvania graduates who struggled for years before getting staff songwriting jobs at Paramount Pictures. The first of their three Academy Awards was for "Buttons and Bows," sung by Bob Hope.

From the middle 1930s to the late 1940s, big bands were the primary delivery system for popular music. The biggest band of all was Glenn Miller's, here at a 1939 engagement at the Pennsylvania Hotel in New York City. Miller is the right-hand trombonist with glasses; girl singer Marion Hutton waits patiently for her chorus.

Frank Sinatra—captured by photographer William "PoPsie" Randolph during a 1943 concert with Jan Savitt at the keyboards—was the first ex–band singer to create a sensation as a solo artist.

Nat "King" Cole, who started out leading a jazz trio, and Billie Holiday (with guitarist Jimmy McLin at a 1939 Commodore Records session) were masters at bringing out the jazz rhythms and harmonies that lay at the foundation of the Great American Songbook.

1949 was a slightly more authentic western tune, Vaughn Monroe and His Orchestra's "Riders in the Sky (A Cowboy Legend)," in which a cowboy has a vision of a herd of cattle being chased by the spirits of a group of damned cowboys, one of whom warns him about being doomed to join them, "trying to catch the devil's herd across these endless skies." A guitarist with the Monroe band, Bucky Pizzarelli, recalled some sixty years later that an RCA Victor A&R man brought Monroe the tune while the band was on the road in Chicago. "Our arranger, Don Costa, wrote the arrangements in pencil on the bus," Pizzarelli said. "We went to a studio in the Wrigley Building with a small group, some singers, maybe a couple of trumpets. Don Costa borrowed a guitar, and he was on the session with me. The next night we played in Detroit. We had to play the song three times—the people went bananas. Something grabbed the audience. I saw it happen." The song was number one on the charts for twelve straight weeks.

Another notable country hit that year was a Capitol novelty number called "Slipping Around." It was notable because it was a duet between a bona fide country-western singer (Jimmy Wakely) and Margaret Whiting, the daughter of veteran Hollywood songwriter Richard Whiting ("Hooray for Hollywood"), who was a former big-band singer with impeccable pop credentials.

Interviewed by a California newspaper in 1950, Jay Livingston and Ray Evans mentioned "Slipping Around" as an example of the way genres seemed to be cross-pollinating, and pointed to some currently popular songs with an oddly old-fashioned flavor. One was Teresa Brewer's "Music! Music! Music!," which, though written the previous year, begins, "Put another nickel in, in the Nickelodeon." Another was "Johnson Rag," which was composed during the ragtime craze of the 1910s; Jack Lawrence had added some lyrics in 1940, and now it was a hit in four separate recordings. Both songs had a kind of ersatz 1920s feel, which was referred to as "Dixieland": in essence a watered-down, self-consciously white floater-hat version of the New Orleans jazz championed by the moldy figs. "It's a throwback," Jay told the reporter. "People are trying to forget the H-Bomb. History goes around in circles. Music does the same thing. Musicians got so progressive with bebop, they had to start over. Most people can't understand it. It's just noise."

At the time of the interview, Patti Page's recording of another country tune, Pee Wee King's "The Tennessee Waltz," with her trademark multitracked vocals, hadn't yet become a nationwide sensation. When it did, *The New York Times* called it the "bellwether song of the folk music trend" and said that it threatened "to unseat the Alley's own favorite—Irving Berlin's 'White Christmas'—as the top popular tune of our time." That didn't happen, but Page's record was the top seller of 1950, with nine weeks at number one, and cover versions by everyone from Spike Jones to Guy Lombardo. Nearly as popular in 1950 was a version of "Good Night, Irene" created by the arranger Gordon Jenkins and Pete Seeger's folk group the Weavers, whom Jenkins, the music director at Decca Records, had discovered during an engagement at New York's Village Vanguard. The African-American folksinger Huddie "Lead Belly" Ledbetter had written "Irene" and first recorded it in 1933. The B side of the record was "Tzena Tzena Tzena," a rousing folk song from Israel, just two years into independence; its lyrics, in Jenkins's translation, exhorted listeners to "Come and dance the Hora." Improbably, it reached number two on the pop charts.

"Tzena" and "Irene" represented another kind of music making its way into the national consciousness. The phrase "folk music" dated from the nineteenth century, and traditionally had been used in reference to the songs of folk from countries other than the United States. Carl Sandburg's 1927 anthology *The American Songbag* had put a spotlight on homegrown folk music, and it expanded in the early forties thanks to such diverse and overlapping causes as left-wing enthusiasm, the compositions of Aaron Copland, the success of *Oklahoma!*, the ethnographic and promotional efforts of John and Alan Lomax, and the popularity of such performers as Woody Guthrie, Josh White, Burl Ives, and the Weavers (who had grown out of the earlier, more resolutely political group the Almanac Singers). By 1944, a *New York Times* article noted that American folk music was enjoying "a full-fledged resurgence."

Jo Stafford was from Southern California and started out in Tommy Dorsey's band as Frank Sinatra's counterpart, the girl vocalist. However, her mother came from rural Tennessee and had sung her to sleep as a girl with down-home ballads. In the late forties, Stafford included songs like "Barbara Allen" and "Black Is the Color of My True Love's Hair" on her weekly NBC show. In 1948 she released a three-disk album, *American Folk Songs*, with orchestrations by her future husband, Paul Weston, the music director at Capitol Records. Intriguing as the popularity of this material was, it did not augur especially well for songwriters, since a folk song's songwriter was, theoretically, the folk themselves, or at best some anonymous long-deceased creator.

Interviewed in 1948 by the jazz journal *Metronome*, Patti Page was somewhat apologetic about her material. "But," she said, "there are more people that aren't hip than those that are, so you've got to please those that aren't. You've got to please the people who get up at eight o'clock in the morning." In another interview, she expanded on the theme:

Great songs aren't being written as often as they were 10 or 15 years ago. And when a great song does come along, it doesn't sell.

I guess the reason may be that years ago, the people who bought records were interested in a better quality of song. They enjoyed music and were of all ages. Today the record buying public is mostly composed of the younger people and their interests aren't especially musical when they buy a record.

Page wasn't the only vocalist bemused by the downturn in the quality of songs. Frank Sinatra told jazz writer George T. Simon, "I've been looking for wonderful pieces of music in the popular music vein, what they call Tin Pan Alley songs. Outside of show tunes, you can't find a thing."

Billy Eckstine, a black singer who'd started out with big bands and broke through in the late forties and early fifties with ballads like "A Cottage for Sale," "I Apologize," and "My Foolish Heart," wrote an article for *Down Beat* complaining about current songwriters, who, he said, "just hack out songs for the sake of making a living. They sit around and think up a gimmick a day. They're looking for sounds instead of ideas."

Variety concurred, calling the 1948 crop of songs "tripe" and ascribing the poor state of the business not to the musicians' union strike but to "bad songs on the disks. Tin Pan Alley could use new blood. How long can the writers who have built and sustained the valuable catalogs hold it up?"

What was the precise nature of the tripe? Arnold Shaw was a failed songwriter who entered Tin Pan Alley on the business side in 1945 and over the next two decades had a variety of jobs: song plugger, publicist, A&R man. After that he wrote several books about popular music, and in one of them he provided a knowing assessment of what Tin Pan Alley "lived on" at mid-century:

> Ballads, i.e., romantic songs; rhythm tunes, considered lightweight, like "I'm Looking Over a Four Leaf Clover" or "Cruising Down the River," and novelty songs like "I Tawt I Taw a Puddy Tat" or "Papa Loves Mambo"—these were either overnight smashes or bombs. Ballads, the mainstay of the business, took one of several simplistic directions: a declaration of undying love ("I'm Yours"), an appeal for love ("My Heart Cries for You"), or a troubled query ("Undecided"). As in the movies, happy endings were preferred.

Shaw didn't mention seasonal songs, but they were a definite commodity, especially when it came to the big kahuna of seasons. The trailblazer was Crosby's record of Berlin's "White Christmas," which annually made the top ten from 1942 through 1949 and topped out at number thirteen the next two years. The example was impossible for songwriters, publishers, and A&R men to ignore, and they made the postwar years the heyday of the holiday novelty number, producing scores of contenders each year. The most direct imitation of Berlin was "Blue Christmas," a country-and-western hit for Ernest Tubb in 1950 and for Elvis Presley seven years after that. But it turned out that the most successful Christmas records tended to have two common qualities: catchy, upbeat melodies and imagined unlikely scenarios for anthropomorphized yuletide characters. "Frosty the Snowman" was a triumph in 1950 for the cowboy turned mainstream singer Gene Autry, and "I Saw Mommy Kissing Santa Claus" for thirteen-year-old Jimmy Boyd in 1952. The biggest Christmas song of all came about with Johnny Marks's "Rudolph, the Red-Nosed Reindeer." Gene

Autry's recording, released by Columbia just before Mitch Miller's arrival at the label, shot to number one and had impressive legs.

In 1950, Paramount was putting together a Bob Hope movie called *The Lemon Drop Kid*; based on a Damon Runyon story, it was an obvious attempt to capitalize on the popularity of Frank Loesser's Broadway hit *Guys and Dolls*. It was set in New York at Christmas, and the studio asked Livingston and Evans for a holiday number. Ever the efficient and compliant craftsmen—and aware that their contract was up for renewal in a brutal time for studio songwriters—they produced a simple but memorable song called "Tinkle Bells," about the Salvation Army workers on busy city streets. When Jay told his wife about it, she said, "Are you out of your mind? Do you know what the word 'tinkle' means to most people?" The boys kept the melody and changed the title to "Silver Bells." Bing Crosby and Carol Richards's recording, released before the film, was so popular that the studio called Hope and costar Marilyn Maxwell into the studio to reshoot a more elaborate production number. Hope made "Silver Bells" his Christmas theme, performing it every year on his holiday television special. The website devoted to Ray Evans's legacy website lists 224 recordings of the song, from Clay Aiken through Stevie Wonder. And, yes, their contract was renewed.

Another postwar holiday hit was "The Christmas Song," which is sometimes known by its opening line, "Chestnuts roasting on an open fire." Mel Tormé and Bob Wells had written it back in 1944, and it shared some of the wartime melancholy of Berlin's own chestnut and "Have Yourself a Merry Little Christmas." The first recording was by the King Cole Trio, a jazz combo consisting of guitar, bass, and Nat King Cole on piano. The sharp-eared Johnny Mercer signed the group after cofounding Capitol Records, and the group produced jump jazz of the highest order, often featuring Cole's intimate, precise, and swinging vocals. Through 1946, the group charted with a half-dozen numbers, including "Straighten Up and Fly Right" and "(Get Your Kicks on) Route 66." But they didn't crack the top ten until they replaced swing with sentiment. That word was part of the title of their first big hit, "(I Love You) For Sentimental Reasons," which was number one for six consecutive weeks in the fall of 1946. "The Christmas Song" was originally recorded with just the trio. But Cole, shrewd about the market, insisted on a new session, with strings and a harp. That version became a perennial classic.

Cole's change in material and approach was greeted with horror by jazz stalwarts, who revered his piano chops. In an interview with a jazz writer, Cole countered, "For years we did nothing but play for musicians and other 'hip' people. We practically starved to death. When we *did* click, it wasn't on the strength of the good jazz. . . . We clicked with the pop songs, pretty ballads and novelty stuff. You know that. Wouldn't we have been crazy if we'd turned right around after getting a break and started playing pure jazz again? We would have lost the crowd right away."

Billy Eckstine, who had started out as a vocalist with Earl Hines and, in his own band, had helped launch the careers of bebop pioneers Charlie Parker, Miles Davis, and Dizzy Gillespie, faced similar complaints about the parallel move he made to smooth ballads. But he was even less apologetic than Cole, acidly commenting: "Some creeps said I 'forsook' jazz in order to be commercial. So I saw one of those creeps, a jazz critic, and I said, 'What are you, mad at me because I want to take care of my family? . . . You want me to wind up in a goddamn hotel room with a bottle of gin in my pocket and a needle in my arm, and let them discover me laying there? Then I'll be an immortal, I guess, to you.'"

In 1948, Cole had an even bigger hit. At a club date one night, an unusual man approached Cole's manager with the sheet music for a song he'd written. The fellow was a sort of proto-hippie—he had a full beard and shoulder-length blond hair, went around in a robe and sandals, lived under the Hollywood sign, and had adopted the name eden ahbez (he was born George Aberle)—and his composition was a minor-key aphoristic fable called "Nature Boy." Cole loved it, and his haunting *lentissimo* recording, backed by strings, a harp, and flute, shot to number one and stayed there for eight weeks.

The slowed-down tempo and intimations of intimacy put Cole in company with the other popular singers of the moment, but his light, restrained, almost conversational approach differentiated him from his male counterparts, almost all of whom were Italian-American: Perry Como, Tony Bennett, Mario Lanza, Frankie Laine, Vic Damone, Al Martino, Julius La Rosa, and Dean Martin. (Sinatra, even operating at considerably less than the height of his powers, was in another category.) In Arnold Shaw's description, this cohort engaged in "a pasta of Neapolitan, bel canto, pseudooperatic singing. The accompaniment, a gentle undercurrent of swirling strings, woolen woodwinds, and light rhythm."

Cole had two more monster hits in him, and the first was in fact a faux-Italian ballad by Jay Livingston and Ray Evans. Paramount had assigned them to write the title song for a 1950 Alan Ladd picture, set in Italy during World War II, to be called *After Midnight*. Those words—"After Midnight"—were both the opening phrase and the title of the song. But when the name of the movie was changed at the last minute to *Captain Carey, U.S.A.*, Livingston and Evans convinced the studio to use another set of lyrics Ray had written, with the refrain "Mona Lisa." Paramount logically offered the song to Sinatra, Como, and Damone, all of whom turned it down. Cole liked it. His Capitol recording was at number one for eight straight weeks—the same as

"Nature Boy"—and helped Livingston and Evans win their second Academy Award for Best Original Song. The following year, Cole had a ballad that was nearly as successful. The opening lines—"They try to tell us we're too young"—may have been the first iteration of a theme that would become a staple of the early rock-and-roll era. Not coincidentally, "Mona Lisa" and "Too Young" were arranged by (though not credited to) the same person, a former third trombonist in the Tommy Dorsey band named Nelson Riddle.

In 1956, Capitol Records moved its headquarters into a new, circular office tower in Hollywood. It became known as the House That Nat Built.

A t mid-century, music publishers were by all means still in the game. They still got ASCAP and BMI payouts, still split the mechanical royalties on a record with the writer or writers. So they still sought out potential hit songs and, among the ones they bought, decided which ones should get the most strenuous promotional effort. In 1950, Arnold Shaw published a semi-scholarly essay, in the form of a lexicon, called *Lingo of Tin-Pan Alley*. His definition of "Number One plug" gives a good sense of how the pubberies saw their role in creating a hit:

> Crux, essence and heart of popular music business. A Number One plug is a song to which a publisher gives concentrated, extended and affluent treatment. He works to have all major record companies record it; entire plugging staff works to secure performances; and complete apparatus, all personnel, and all offices are geared to action on the one song. Number One plug refers also to the treatment of process, which takes about 26 weeks from the time a pro copy is made to the

moment when the song is laid to rest, a tired process of tonal nausea. Process involves an outlay of $10,000 to $35,000, most of it spent for plugger's salaries and romance. In the days before radio, major publishers worked on as few as 2 Number One plugs a year. Now, songs die faster and overhead is too great to allow for such extended concentration. Four to six Number One plugs a year, depending on the success they achieve, is now common with most major publishers. . . . With established writers, the interest is not in publication of a song but in a #1 plug. A writer is fortunate if he succeeds in averaging a plug song a year—and not all #1 plugs are hits.

The entry gives a sense of a changing industry, but the changes were even more profound than Shaw suggests. Sheet music sales had become less and less relevant in the total picture, and the power of publishers plummeted concurrently. In 1953, *Variety* editor Abel Green quoted "a veteran on Tin Pan Alley" as griping: "Everybody but the music publisher, who used to be pretty good at that, nowadays picks songs. And don't tell me that in the final analysis the public really picks 'em. We . . . used to have a pretty good concept of quality and value in songs that we published. . . . Today, we don't dare publish a song until some artist perhaps likes it, or when the whim of an A&R genius decides it should be done. . . . A record should be a by-product of publishing; not the sparkplug of songwriting and publishing."

The triumph of record over song took a long time coming, and was linked to changes in radio and copyright law. In the prewar period, live performances were more common on the radio than records. One reason is that FCC rules required a legalistic announcement to be made whenever a recording was played, leading to a perceived stigma and much mockery. In a rather vague implied threat, the words "Not Licensed for Radio Broadcast" were often printed on record labels.

In 1935, sweet bandleader Fred Waring tried to give this some legal backbone—and advance the sense that a performer had ownership of his or her recorded performance—by suing Philadelphia radio station WDAS. Waring won a judgment in the Pennsylvania supreme court in 1937, the majority opinion noting: "A musical composition in itself is an incomplete work; the written page evidences only one of the creative acts which are necessary for its enjoyment; it is the performer who must consummate the work by transforming it into sound." This idea would eventually be considered a self-evident truth and constitute an underpinning of an era when listeners cared more about singers and bands than songs. But in the short term, Waring and Paul Whiteman, who filed a similar suit in New York, lost. Whiteman's case came before the Second Circuit Court of Appeals in 1940, and the court found that a recorded performance had no copyright protection. Judge Learned Hand's opinion characterized performances captured on records as "chattel" and said that restricting their use (by a radio station or anyone else) after sale would be "contrary to the whole policy of the Copyright Act and of the Constitution." In other words, the "Not Licensed for Radio Broadcast" labels had no legal standing.

The strike by James Petrillo's American Federation of Musicians slowed recorded music's march to dominance. But the strike ended, in 1944, when all the major record companies agreed to the principle of paying royalties for performances. Very soon afterward recorded music became the main staple of radio programming and, as a result, the center of the popular music universe. The station or network employee who selected and introduced records to play on the air was known as a "disk jockey," a term first coined by *Variety* (of course) in 1941. The labels found that disk jockey (soon shortened to "DJ" or "deejay") programs, far from hurting record sales, helped them. The most successful early deejay was Martin Block, an announcer for New

York's WNEW, who had started spinning records to fill the time between news bulletins on the Lindbergh kidnapping trial in 1935. He expanded the concept to a program called *Make Believe Ballroom*, borrowing the name and concept from a West Coast announcer, Al Jarvis. The heyday for both Block and his progeny didn't emerge till the end of the Petrillo Ban, the end of the war, and the end of shortages of vinyl and shellac. By 1946, Block was so popular that WNEW built him an actual ballroom, "complete with chandelier, red-velvet chair and black linoleum on the floor."

The deejay was mainly a local phenomenon (the networks relied heavily on soap operas and other serials), and in fact, during the forties, the focus of radio music dramatically shifted from network to local. There were 813 AM stations in 1940, and 2,127 in 1949, and virtually all the new ones were small, independent operations that filled the bulk of their broadcast day with local deejays spinning records.

In 1946, Roy Kohn was a song plugger for a publisher called Mood Music. One day his boss had an idea for him: drive from New York to Boston and stop at radio stations along the way to pass out copies of a Tony Martin record of one of their songs. "As I got to the outskirts of Bridgeport," Kohn recalled, "I saw an antenna on top of a hill. I found the road and went up to the radio station WICC. I got to the door, and since it was open, I just walked in with the Tony Martin record. I got to the control room/studio and the guy on the air called me. His name was Bob Crane, who later moved to KNX in Hollywood, and then years later, starred on television in *Hogan's Heroes*. Bob told me I was the first song plugger to give him a record to play on the air."

The plugging process, haphazard at that early moment, quickly became codified as the industry collectively shifted toward a single goal:

getting a record into a deejay's hands and getting him to play it. The process began when a publisher or his plugger took the elevator to a record company A&R man's office. Because so much was decided there, writes Philip H. Ennis, the place was "hated by the majority of the traditionally oriented publishers and feared by the song pluggers." It was a dismal numbers game. Music historian Russell Sanjek estimates that about two hundred new songs were offered each week by publishers, and another hundred by songwriters, of which fewer than a dozen got any real attention. And even if a song was taken on, it had only about a one-in-twenty chance of making it to the charts.

Once songs were recorded, they were turned over to the labels' substantial plugging departments, which were dedicated to getting disks into jockeys' hands. That was good business, because the evidence was growing that a deejay could single-handedly create a hit. In 1948, Al Collins was a jock in Salt Lake City; he specialized in jazz, hence his nickname, "Jazzbo." One day he got a copy of a record called "I'm Looking Over a Four Leaf Clover" from the sweet bandleader Art Mooney, along with a personal note from Mooney. Unaware that the song was a fairly corny novelty number from 1927, Collins put the record on for a spin during his *Jazzbo Jamboree* show. "As it twanged its way through its three minutes, Collins' ears got redder and redder," recounted author Arnold Passman. "Incensed that he, a jazz jock, would be sent such as song, Collins continued to spin it, giving it a different title every time in protest." He ended up playing it for three and a half hours. Unaccountably, the record became a hit in Salt Lake, and then the country—number one on the charts for five weeks and charting in five additional versions. Two other deejays famously broke records in the late forties, both with songs that were decades old. Chicago's Eddie Hubbard launched a version of "Peg o' My Heart" by the novelty group the Harmonicats, and, even more remarkably, Kurt Webster, of Charlotte, North Carolina, played Ted Weems's original 1933 recording of "Heartaches" into the second most popular song of 1947, right behind "Near You."

The power of these new forces in the business was quickly understood; *Variety* described the rise and reign of the disk jockeys as "a postwar show business phenomenon as revolutionary as the atomic bomb." In hearings before the House of Representatives in 1948, a lawyer for Petrillo's AFM—not pleased with any development that limited live performances—brought up the ostensibly scandalous fact that an unnamed deejay had made $185,000 the previous year. *Billboard* responded that "the disc jockey, in our opinion, plays an important role in the sale of phonograph records. In fact, he plays just about the most important role, having supplanted the jukeboxes as the makers of hits. These hundreds of disc jockeys on the various radio stations have brought recorded music to the homes of people who were never reached by the jukes."

A young graduate student named Philip Ennis, hired by BMI to prepare material to defend against the Arthur Schwartz lawsuit, did an in-depth study of the phenomenon and discovered that it was mainly taking place far away from the Brill Building. "It was believed . . . that the city was isolated from the main action," Ennis wrote later. "'You can't make a hit in New York anymore,' was the insistently repeated statement. I didn't know then why this was the case, but I quickly learned that the industry was willing to go wherever the hits were made. Every Sunday evening the flights from LaGuardia to the Midwest and to the West Coast were filled with song pluggers and record company men flying to visit disk jockeys from Pittsburgh to Seattle, from Detroit to Phoenix."

Howie Richmond started his own publishing company in 1949

and went a bit against the grain, specializing in novelty and specialty numbers instead of the staple of the trade, ballads. "Ballads take a long time to develop," he told *Billboard* years later. "You can get novelty songs started quickly." One way Richmond tried to do so was by airmailing a copy of each new release to some three hundred especially influential deejays. He estimated that he spent half his working day on the phone talking to jocks, and an additional sixteen hours on weekends. His methods paid off: in just four years his company had big hits with "Music! Music! Music!"; Phil Harris's massively successful novelty "The Thing"; "A Guy Is a Guy"; "I Believe"; and the Weavers' double-sided hit, their cover of "Good Night, Irene" and "Tzena Tzena Tzena."

Two days after "Tzena Tzena Tzena" was released, another version of the song, by "Mitch Miller and his Orchestra & Chorus," came out; it eventually climbed to number three. For Miller the recording was characteristic in at least two respects. First, it showed his alacrity in regard to cover records. When a label bought exclusive rights to a particular song, that implied a guarantee that no other company would even see the words or music until the record was released. But after that, all bets were off, and if it smelled like a hit, a half-dozen or more competing versions went in the works. The Beard's speed earned him another nickname—"Cut 'em, press 'em, ship 'em" Miller.

The Chorus was front and center in his "Tzena"—prefiguring the wildly successful "Sing Along with Mitch" albums that started coming out in the late fifties—but there were other notable elements: handclaps, tambourine, accordion, and, improbably, the French horn. As such, the record illustrated a second Miller trademark. "Oddly enough for a man of such musical ability, Miller . . . achieved his power through the use of gimmicks," observed George Frazier in a *Vogue* article on the music business. The Beard had expanded the traditional role of the A&R man beyond just signing artists and selecting their songs. He was involved in every aspect of the recording process, from orchestration and arrangements to setting the sound levels; beyond that, he was the first music man (the term "producer" hadn't yet been adopted by the industry) to think of recordings in terms of production values, or sound effects. Miller told Will Friedwald: "What makes you want to dig in your pocket and buy a record? It's got to be something you want to play over and over again. You look for qualities to make somebody buy it. I was trying to put stuff in records that would tighten the picture for the listener."

One of his most famous pieces of "stuff" was on "Mule Train," put out by Frankie Laine in 1949, when both he and Miller were at Mercury. The record tried to simulate the feel of a real wagon train through the use of an echo chamber (essentially invented by Miller), assorted shouts and grunts, and two wood blocks, which simulated the sound of a cracking whip. Paul Weston, then music director at Capitol Records, made a thinly veiled swipe at his Columbia competitor in a *Down Beat* interview that came out when the song was riding the charts: "Whatever became of music? . . . Arrangements and interpretations have become so big that they're bigger than the music. You've got to snap whips and crack bones to get attention now . . . we're not getting good new songs these days. I don't think anything has been written in the last few years that has a chance of becoming a standard, nothing that can compare with the wonderful tunes that were being turned out in the '30s."

That hardly stopped the Beard, who at Columbia only added new tricks to his bag. He backed up "Come On-a My House" with a sort of barrelhouse harpsichord, and amplified the same instrument on "Delicado," a 1952 number-one hit by Percy Faith. (Faith, one of Miller's go-to guys through the fifties, was a Canadian conductor and arranger who, like his boss, came from a classical music background, and was a pioneer of the "semi-classical" genre, also known as "easy listening." "Delicado" was one of Jack Lawrence's international specials, in which he gave English lyrics to a Brazilian song.) Miller was a pioneer of over-dubbing, first at Mercury with Patti Page, whose close-harmony "duets" with herself became her trademark. Less successful was his decision to have bagpipes accompany Dinah Shore on a song called "The Scottish Samba." The recording enraged one DJ so much that he took the record off the turntable and broke it on the air. Miller's own choral version of "The Yellow Rose of Texas," which knocked "Rock Around the Clock" off the number-one spot in the charts in 1955, had a relentless snare drum. It found a target in Stan Freberg's satirical version, in which Freberg complains that the "snare drum covered up the tra-la-las" and finally can't take it anymore:

> HOLD ON! HOLD ON! Hold on, you smart-aleck Yankee
>   drummer, you!
> You can cover up "yellow" and you can cover up "rose,"
>   buddy buddy,
> But don't you cover up TEXAS!
> Or I'll stick your head through that cotton-pickin' snare drum
> And secede from the band, so help me Mitch Miller I will!

Donald Clarke, in his book *The Rise and Fall of Popular Music*, has a nice description of the not altogether disastrous way the Beard diminished popular music:

Miller had too much power and not enough taste. . . . Miller was as responsible as anyone for turning pop music into jingles, and it was on his watch that pop records began to sound like self-conscious productions rather than straight recordings of musical events. . . . Still, live pop music seemed to be dead by Miller's time and, as jingles went, Miller's jolly records had more personality than most. His own instrumental "Oriental Polka" was a wacky twittering tune for woodwinds doubled by a marimba. Percy Faith's "Funny Fellow" was a slowish, cock-eyed samba with a cheerful, noisy rhythm section and a piccolo carrying the tune, to test the speaker on your "hi-fi" record player; in the middle of the arrangement the band laid out and the tune was carried by a solo bassoon, and the band's "funny fellow" made you chuckle.

It wasn't just Miller. All sorts of musicians and producers were becoming intrigued with unusual sounds, and the public was responding. Anton Karas, a Viennese zither player, scored *The Third Man*, a 1949 film directed by Carol Reed; his instrumental rendition of the film's bouncy Middle European theme, released by London Records, was number one on the charts for eleven weeks in 1950, as was Guy Lombardo's version, which replaced the zither with a more domesticated guitar and trumpets. (Four other versions also charted in 1950, including two with unfortunate lyrics by Walter Lord, which speak of a distant dream that "seems to glimmer when you hear The Third Man Theme.")

Les Paul was a Wisconsin native who'd started off a country guitarist and then turned to jazz, successfully accompanying Bing Crosby, the Andrews Sisters, and Nat Cole. In the late forties, Paul cultivated his remarkable aptitude for engineering. He pioneered the solid-body electric guitar and, encouraged by Crosby, built his own recording studio in his Los Angeles backyard. The critic Jon Pareles recounts:

> There he experimented with recording techniques, using them to create not realistic replicas of a performance but electronically enhanced fabrications. Toying with his mother's old Victrola had shown him that changing the speed of a recording could alter both pitch and timbre. He could record at half-speed and replay the results at normal speed, creating the illusion of superhuman agility. He altered instrumental textures through microphone positioning and reverberation. Technology and studio effects, he realized, were instruments themselves.
>
> He also noticed that by playing along with previous recordings, he could become a one-man ensemble. As early as his 1948 hit "Lover," he made elaborate, multilayered recordings, using two acetate disc machines, which demanded that each layer of music be captured in a single take.

Paul and his wife, the singer Mary Ford, started recording for Capitol in 1950; on most of their productions, multiple layers of Ford's vocals blended with Paul's breakneck guitar runs and electronic effects. With Ford and by himself, he put out twenty-seven records that reached the *Billboard* charts through 1953, most strikingly "How High the Moon," which sounded as if four Fords were singing and Paul's guitar had been speeded up to quadruple time. It was number one on the charts for nine consecutive weeks in 1951.

The voice could be its own special effect. Crosby had established the crooning prototype, and Sinatra worked his own variations on it, but Frankie Laine's records with Miller, first at Mercury and then at

· · · 137 · · ·

Columbia, introduced a new register to male vocals: the shout. It proved capable of expressing more, or at least different, emotions than pop music had been thought capable of. Sometimes the emotion descended into sentimentality. Ervin Drake and three other songwriters put together a lachrymose hymn called "I Believe" that begins, "I believe for every drop of rain that falls, a flower grows." After that, it actually gets more sentimental. At a 1953 session, Miller backed Laine's exerted vocals mainly with a gospel choir whose strains reverberated in Columbia's fabled recording studio on East Thirtieth Street in New York. The song went to number two on the charts and sold more than 20 million copies in dozens of recordings.

In 1952, an A&R man from Columbia's subsidiary Okeh, which specialized in rhythm and blues, discovered a young singer named Johnnie Ray at a Detroit nightclub. Ray's first record, a raucous blues called "Whiskey and Gin," led some listeners to conclude he was black and/or female, though in fact he was a white native of rural Oregon with a rather high-pitched voice and an emotive delivery of the sort traditionally linked with African-American vocalists. The record did well enough to attract Miller's attention, and he produced Ray's next release, "Cry." In rendering the song, Ray stretched out syllables, moaned, and actually appeared to sob; in live performances, he would pound on the piano and writhe on the bench. The record was released in November 1951 and by the following April had sold two million units. That month, *New York Times* critic Howard Taubman wrote an article attempting to explain the phenomenon to the paper's middle-aged, middlebrow readers. "It's easy to laugh at Johnnie Ray, the newest wonder among popular singers, just as it is a comforting self-indulgence to feel thoroughly superior to the vast audience which, in a matter of months, has lifted him from obscurity to dominance," Taubman began. He could not completely shed his condescension, but he correctly sensed that Ray was something more than a novelty. "If one may hazard a guess," he concluded, "one would suspect that this young man's style speaks for young people beset by fears and doubts in a difficult time. His pain may be their pain. His wailing and writhing may reflect their secret impulses."

True to his comment about snapping whips and cracking bones, Paul Weston didn't go in for special effects, but he also contributed to the general movement toward production over song in popular music. Weston was an arranger for Tommy Dorsey from 1935 till 1943, when he joined Capitol Records as music director. The following year he put out under his own name *Music for Dreaming*, a two-disk album of smooth, string-heavy orchestral versions of standards. He followed it up with *Music for Memories*, *Music for Romancing*, and, in 1950, *Music for the Fireside*. Weston's son, Tim, defined the sound: "Take a jazz-tinged band, add strings. It's the ambience of a get-together." *Coronet* magazine gave the sound a name, in 1950 dubbing Weston "the master of mood music." That final two-word phrase had traditionally been used to refer generally to the background music in films or radio dramas. It was now a genre, but would have to wait for technological developments over the next several years to fully come into its own.

Mitch Miller's apparent attention to all aspects of a recording *other* than the song may not seem so odd when you consider where he was coming from, and where popular music had gone. A child prodigy on the piano, he had studied oboe at the Eastman School of Music in Rochester, the city of his birth, and graduated in the same class as Alec Wilder and Goddard Lieberson, who would become president of Columbia Records and bring Miller to the company. As a professional oboist, Miller played with the Budapest String Quartet and under the batons of Leopold Stokowski and Igor Stravinsky. The latter professed to be struck by his "finest musicianship combined with technical perfection together with the rare human qualities of sensibility, dignity, and modesty." The composer Virgil Thomson called him "an absolutely first-rate oboist—one of the two or three great ones at that time in the world." He was in the orchestra accompanying George Gershwin's concert tour as a pianist, and he was in the pit when Gershwin's *Porgy and Bess* opened on Broadway in 1935. Miller was a member of CBS's house symphony orchestra from 1936 to 1947 and as such was a member of "Ramon Raquello and His Orchestra"—the fictional combo heard in Orson Welles's 1938 *War of the Worlds* radio hoax.

In a 1953 *New Yorker* profile, Robert Rice commented on Miller's "deep lack of interest in—in fact, almost a contempt for—popular music." The implication was that his respect was saved for the classics. "Popular songs and singers are only more or less marketable commodities to him," Rice went on. "His appraisal of them is quite unaffected by prejudice or emotion, since he regards them all as negligible from an artistic point of view." Johnny Mandel summed up his sense of Miller's operating aesthetic: "Mitch used to say, 'If I hated it, it would be a hit.'" "I wouldn't buy that stuff for myself," Miller told *Time* magazine in 1951, referring to the hits he produced at Columbia. "There's no real artistic satisfaction in this job. I satisfy my musical ego elsewhere."

Performers and musicians who came out of jazz, broadly speaking, and who did not view popular music as artistically negligible chafed at Miller's approach. Mandel told Will Friedwald, "I think Mitch Miller set the music business back thirty or forty years, which is inexcusable for somebody who was as great a musician as he was." Bandleader Elliot Lawrence said simply, "I liked Mitch as a person, but his taste was horrendous." Tony Bennett, a young singer from Astoria, Queens, had been signed by Miller and had huge success in the early fifties under his direction, but wasn't happy with the material presented to him—for example, country singer Hank Williams's "Cold, Cold Heart," which was about as far from Queens as you could get (naturally, it was a BMI tune). However, the fact that Bennett's record reached number one on the charts in the summer of 1951 and stayed there for six weeks couldn't exactly be ignored. "Mitch had a knack for finding these snappy little novelty tunes," Bennett recalled in his autobiography, *The Good Life*. "I wasn't interested in singing that type of song. Yet Mitch kept trying to push these kinds of tunes on me, and as much as we liked each other, there was always tension between us. I wanted to sing the great songs, songs that I felt really mattered. . . . Fortunately, Mitch and I came to an understanding. We were still doing four tunes per recording session at that time, so we worked out a deal. He picked two songs and I picked two songs."

At one point, Miller hired Johnny Mandel to arrange a Doris Day album. "I loved Doris, she was a wonderful singer and girl," Mandel recalled. "But she was constantly doing terrible material. When I was working on the album, Mitch Miller came in like a general and said to me, 'Kid, you're about to make a lot of money. I'm gonna teach you to write like Ray Conniff.'" Conniff was a former big-band trombonist who emerged as an arranger for Columbia in the mid-fifties. His specialty was (wordless) choral backing vocals, and he was so successful on Don Cherry's "Band of Gold" and other songs that in 1957 Miller let him start putting out mood music albums under his own name.

"And I said, 'Mitch, it's been wonderful meeting you,' and I'm out the door," Mandel said. "I apologized to Doris, and I haven't seen her since. She was one of the really great singers that were totally trashed."

Rosemary Clooney balked when Miller presented her with "Come

On-a My House," which had been concocted by the playwright William Saroyan and songwriter Ross Bagdasarian (later the creator of Alvin and the Chipmunks) on a cross-country drive. She recalled in her auto-biography: "I thought the lyric ranged from incoherent to just plain silly, I thought the tune sounded more like a drunken chant than an historic folk art form, and I hated the gimmicky arrangement: It was orchestrated for jazzed-up harpsichord, of all things, with a kind of calypso rhythm." She told Miller: "I don't think so." "Know what I think?" he replied. "I think you'll show up because otherwise you will be fired."

Miller's relationship with Sinatra was chilly from the moment the Beard arrived at Columbia. At that point Sinatra was not only under contract but in debt to the label, which had advanced him $100,000. He was finding it hard to pay up because his career was at its nadir, the bobby-soxer screams of the 1940s a distant and nearly indistinct memory. Miller emptied his full bag of tricks to get Sinatra a hit record, but, with occasional exceptions like a 1950 cover version of "Good Night, Irene," which peaked at number five, his sides didn't sell. Sinatra, never known for his graciousness when things weren't going well, privately and publicly demeaned Miller and his "repertoire" choices, including this exchange with an Atlantic City disk jockey about the folksy lullaby "Good Night, Irene":

DJ: Hey, that's a nice tune.
Sinatra: You wanna bet? *(pauses)* Naw, it's really cute.
DJ: You oughta do a lot of songs like that.
Sinatra: Don't hold your breath!

Sinatra would crack the top ten only one more time at Columbia, with a swinging 1951 number called "Castle Rock." The ever-resourceful Ervin Drake, together with his partner Jimmy Shirl, had put words to an instrumental by the jazz saxophonist Al Sears, including the lines "We rocked to romance to the Castle Rock" and—years before Bill Haley—"rock-around-the-clock." It's not often mentioned as one of the first rock-and-roll numbers, but it belongs in the conversation.

Eventually, Sinatra went to *Billboard* with his complaints about Columbia, the magazine reporting: "Chief beef hinges on Sinatra's claim he isn't getting a fair shake on song material. Sinatra has waged a long-smoldering feud with Mitch Miller." "Do I still think it's hard to find a decent new pop tune these days?" the singer rhetorically asked in a 1953 *Down Beat* interview. "Man, it's worse than ever. These trick songs are coming out of my ears. . . . I think it's all part of a cycle—including the echo chambers and the other gimmicks—that will exhaust itself." In later years, Sinatra would accelerate his attack, claiming that the Beard forced him to record "Mama Will Bark" and other dreck. In interviews through the 2000s, Miller always countered that neither he nor the label could force Sinatra to record anything— that the singer had right of refusal on song selection and moreover that his career was in such bad shape at the time that he was willing to try anything, even "Mama Will Bark." Sinatra, Miller commented in the 1980s, "was trying to find a scapegoat for the dip in his career."

And Sinatra did indeed turn down some songs. At one session Miller presented him with "My Heart Cries for You" and "The Roving Kind." The former had been adapted by Carl Sigman and Percy Faith from an eighteenth-century French melody, and Howie Richmond had concocted the latter from an old British sea shanty called "The Pirate Ship." Sinatra opined that both were just too corny to put on wax. Miller had the musicians, technicians, and studio already booked, so he brought in a young singer named Albert Cernik to perform the numbers. Cernik did a creditable job, but the name had to go. Miller said, "My name is 'Mitchell' and you seem a nice 'guy,' so we'll call you Guy Mitchell." "The Roving Kind" climbed to number four on the charts and "My Heart Cries for You" to number two. Mitchell went on to have four more top-ten hits for Columbia in the next two years.

Columbia finally dropped Sinatra in 1952. At his last session, the singer, who was possibly the least twangy human being in America, recorded a twangy Percy Faith–Dick Manning number called "Tennessee Newsboy." Miller had hired a steel guitar player named Wesley "Speedy" West, who, according to Paul Weston, "was known for making the guitar sound like a chicken. Frank sang the vocal, and Mitch rushed out into the studio, and everybody thought he was going to congratulate Frank for getting through. . . . Instead, he rushed right past Frank, and embraced Speedy West, because he'd made a good chicken noise on the guitar. Frank was disgusted."

In 1956, a House of Representatives subcommittee held hearings on the issue of possible monopoly in the broadcast industry. One day the chairman, Emanuel Celler, read into the record a telegram he had received from Sinatra. It was basically a complaint about Mitch Miller, expressed with a Damon Runyon faux formality. Sinatra claimed:

Before Mr. Miller's arrival at Columbia Records, I found myself enjoying a freedom of selection of material—a freedom which I may modestly say resulted in a modicum of success for me. Suddenly Mr. Miller by design or coincidence began to present many, many inferior songs all curiously bearing the BMI label. I, on my own behalf, to protect my career then and for the future, engaged Mr. Miller in a series of discussions concerning the merits of the said material against my own choice which by coincidence in each case was from the catalog of ASCAP. If you will pardon the expression, Mr. Congressman, I refused to beat my creative head against the wall. The point is before Mr. Miller's advent on the scene I had a successful recording career which quickly went into a decline.

The next day Celler remarked from the chair, "That is the trouble with a situation like this, when you put a telegram in the record you get a telegram in reply." The reason for his remark was that he had received a sworn affidavit from one Mitchell Miller, asserting "[Sinatra's] charges against me are false. . . . The source of music, whether it be ASCAP, BMI, or another, is immaterial to my choices of songs." Miller went on:

I have caused a search to be made of the files of Columbia Records with respect to the history of Frank Sinatra's activities at Columbia Records from the time I went with Columbia Records in February 1950 until Sinatra left Columbia Records after his last recording there in September 1952. The results of that search are summarized as follows: The first 12 songs which Sinatra recorded with me at Columbia were ASCAP songs. His first BMI song of my tenure was not recorded until June 28, 1950. It was Good Night, Irene, and was a great hit. In the next 13 months Sinatra recorded 28 more ASCAP songs and 1 song in the public domain, and no BMI songs. Not until July 19, 1951, did he record another BMI song—Castle Rock. It also was a hit song. Sinatra's total recordings during the 31 months we worked together at Columbia Records were 57 songs for single-record release, of which 51 were ASCAP, 5 were BMI, and 1 was in the public domain. Of the 51 ASCAP songs which he recorded during that period, 11 were published by music publishing firms in which Sinatra had a substantial interest.

I have caused a check to be made of the public information about

Sinatra's recordings during the period since he left Columbia Records. His first great hit at Capitol Records in that period was the beautiful song, Young at Heart, a BMI song. In less than 4 years at Capitol, he has recorded a total of 49 songs which were released on single records; of these, at least 10 were BMI songs.

Miller won that particular rhetorical battle, but he lost the war. Although he outlived Sinatra, Rosemary Clooney, and virtually all the singers he recorded except Tony Bennett, they and their advocates among critics and journalists seized the narrative of the 1950s and shaped it into a story of Mitch versus the American Songbook. Miller didn't help his cause by the career move he leaned into in 1958 with his LP *Sing Along with Mitch*. The disk featured Mitch and his male chorale, "the Gang," performing hearty and straightforward renditions of old-fashioned tunes like "Down by the Old Mill Stream" (1910) and "By the Light of the Silvery Moon" (1909). It was comfort food for the generation who didn't take to rock and roll or modern jazz; the record went to number one on the *Billboard* album charts and stayed there for eight weeks. Over the next four years Miller released seventeen more sing-along albums, fourteen of which hit the top ten. He parlayed that success into a television series called, naturally, *Sing Along with Mitch*, which ran on NBC from 1961 to 1964.

With the demands of the television show—and the inescapable fact that Miller's sort of music was no longer capable of generating hit singles—he eased into a consultant's role at Columbia. In 1965 he moved to MCA Records, also as a consultant, but that didn't take up much time. For the remaining years of his long life (he died in 2010, just after his ninety-ninth birthday), he would occasionally serve as guest conductor for orchestras around the country, and periodically

give interviews that were alternately rueful, defensive, and defiant—
and almost always got around to Sinatra.

In one, Miller told author Charles L. Granata that, for a talk show
he'd hosted on CBS Radio back in the late fifties,

I'd go out to Las Vegas and do a lot of interviews, and I got to know
Joe E. Lewis. So, this one time, I see him in the lobby of the Sands at
about two or three in the morning. He said, "Look, Mitch. Frank is
with Jack Entratter [who managed the Sands]. Come on over and say
hello." I said, "No, I'm not interested." Now, Joe's a little loaded, and
he grabs me. So, we go over, and Joe says, "I brought Mitch over. Why
don't you shake hands." And Frank, who was half-loaded himself,
said, "Get lost, creep."

VI

....

Brill Building Boys,
and Girl
1950–1955

An office building at 1619 Broadway was constructed in 1931 and soon after became known as the place where, in the words of the writer A. J. Liebling, "the small-scale amusement industry nests like a tramp pigeon." By the dawn of the 1950s, a young songwriter at the time, Dick Adler, later recalled, "the Brill Building *was* Tin Pan Alley. It was the hub of the music business. If you were in the business, that's where you camped out. When you had something to peddle, you went from floor to floor, and you knocked on doors, and if they'd open, you'd say, 'I've got something great to show you!' And if you were lucky, they listened. And if it was a normal day, and you were unknown, they didn't." There was a particular method to the door-to-door rounds. An older songwriter named Al Hoffman—whose credits ranged from "I Apologize" (1931) through the wartime novelty phenomenon "Mairzy Doats" (cowritten with Ervin Drake's brother Milton) all the way up to a 1950 collaboration with Bob Merrill, "If I Knew You Were Comin' I'd've Baked a Cake"—took young Norman

Gimbel under his wing and explained to him how you should take the elevator to the top of the Brill and work your way down. Gimbel eventually got a job as an office boy at a music publisher, and with Hoffman wrote "A Mighty Pretty Waltz," recorded in 1952 by Bill Monroe and the Bluegrass Boys. The irony that the Brooklyn-born Gimbel and the Minsk-born Hoffman were collaborating on this country confection didn't trouble the younger man. "The honesty of country music appealed to me," he said. (In 1954, Gimbel joined forces with composer Larry Coleman and fellow lyricist Joe Darion on "Ricochet Romance," a proto-rock-and-roll song that was a hit for Teresa Brewer, and two years after that wrote lyrics for "Canadian Sunset," a top-ten record for Andy Williams.)

The more successful writers had their own offices, but that sounds more respectable than the reality. "The offices were so small that there was just enough room for a desk, an old upright piano, and an air conditioner that didn't work in a window you could never open," recalled another guy just starting out, Burt Bacharach. "When you finished a song, you would take it to a publisher and play it. If the publisher liked it, he would say, 'Go make a demo.' The publisher would pay for the demo and then it would be up to him to peddle the song to an artist who would record it. Some publishers knew a good song when they heard one, and some had no idea."

The cleffers who patrolled the Brill Building's halls had specific demographic characteristics. The older ones—Hoffman, Al Stillman, Ervin and Milton Drake, Johnny Marks, Sidney Lippman, John Jacob Loeb, Bob Hilliard, Mack David and his kid brother Hal, Buddy Kaye, Bob Merrill, Dick Manning—were of Livingston and Evans's generation but, due to circumstance, temperament, or, frankly, level of talent, hadn't made it out to Hollywood during the period when one still *could* make it in Hollywood. (This group did get the occasional one-off movie assignment. For Disney's 1950 *Cinderella*, Mack David, Hoffman, and the West Coast–based Jerry Livingston—no relation to Jay—wrote "A Dream Is a Wish Your Heart Makes" and "Bibbidi-Bobbidi-Boo," which was nominated for the Academy Award for Best Original Song. It lost to Livingston and Evans's "Mona Lisa.") Broadway, having turned into a fairly stratospheric songwriting club, wasn't an option for them. So they were tethered to the Brill Building, in a perennial change-partners-and-write-with-me effort to hit with a concept and a song.

Dick Adler was twenty-nine years old in 1950—the same age as Merrill and lyricist Hal David. However, in addition to being a rather slow developer, he'd been in the Army during the war, as had Sheldon Harnick, born in 1924. The two of them belonged with a rather remarkable cohort of younger songwriters, all born within a five-year span:

1926 Larry Holofcener, Carolyn Leigh, Jerry Ross, Phil Springer

1927 Norman Gimbel, John Kander

1928 Morris "Moose" Charlap, Burt Bacharach, Jerry Bock, Charles Strouse, Fred Ebb

1929 Cy Coleman

1930 Stephen Sondheim

It is a striking list. All Jewish, twelve out of thirteen male, most born and raised in New York. All but Springer eventually found their way to the Broadway stage, but, with a single exception, that idea wasn't under active consideration by any of them in 1950. The exception was Sondheim, who through a quirk of circumstance in his teenage years had become a protégé and a ward of sorts to Oscar Hammerstein II, and who was determined to one day join his mentor on Broadway. Sondheim graduated from Williams College in 1950, moved to the couch in his mother's apartment, studied musical theory with Milton Babbitt, did odd jobs to keep the wolf away, and embarked on an apprenticeship in the musical theater. Two years later an assignment to write the score for a musical called *Saturday Night* appeared to conclude the apprenticeship. But the producers never raised enough money, and he didn't debut on Broadway until 1957, when he provided the lyrics to Leonard Bernstein's score of *West Side Story*. Sondheim, who always aspired to create both music and lyrics, and did so starting with *A Funny Thing Happened on the Way to the Forum* in 1962, is more or less the opposite of a Tin Pan Alley cleffer. There is no recorded instance of his attempting to write a hit song, and he has always regarded the success of his one composition to appear on the charts, "Send In the Clowns" (from *A Little Night Music*, 1973), with bemusement. But in two of his shows, *Follies* (1971) and *Merrily We Roll Along* (1981), he had reason to construct deliberately old-fashioned pop songs, and emerged with the splendid neo-standards "Broadway Baby," "Not a Day Goes By," and "Good Thing Going." The last, in particular, sounds as if it could have been written by Jimmy Van Heusen in 1946. Sondheim, in any case, felt a kinship with his cohort, memorably displayed in the late-fifties scenes of *Merrily*. He has observed that in writing that show "I was trying to roll myself back to my exuberant early days, to recapture the combination of sophistication and idealism that I'd shared with Hal Prince, Mary Rodgers, Jerry Bock and Sheldon Harnick, John Kander and Fred Ebb, and the rest of us show business supplicants, all stripped back to our innocence."

Sondheim, in common with Bacharach, Strouse, Coleman, and Kander, had a significant musical education. That distinguished them from the older group of composers, and, in fact, from most of their peers. Over the years, writes author Philip Ennis, "the nature of musical literacy changed. New York publishers could no longer impose the standard of competency in reading and writing music on composers or performers as a prerequisite to participation." Indeed, Bacharach, who was a skilled jazz pianist and had studied with the classical composers Darius Milhaud, Henry Cowell, and Bohuslav Martinů, couldn't manage to find any success at the Brill Building in the early fifties. He earned his keep as an accompanist and conductor for performers like Vic Damone, Steve Lawrence, and the Ames Brothers, a vocal quartet from Malden, Massachusetts, whose lead singer—brother Ed—would go on to a solo career and costar in the 1960s TV series *Daniel Boone* as Daniel's Indian sidekick. The brothers had a huge hit in 1953 with "You, You, You," the numbing inanity of whose melody was matched only by the repetitive banality of its lyrics. (Opening stanza: "You, you, you / I'm in love with you, you, you / I could be so true, true, true / To someone like you, you, you.") Bacharach would listen to demos and play the sheet music of songs submitted for the Ames Brothers' consideration, most of which took "You, You, You" as a model. Repetition was the most obvious quality to emulate, as in such subsequent 1953 records as "My Love, My Love" (Joni James), "Hold Me, Thrill Me, Kiss Me" (Karen Chandler), "Love Me, Love Me" (Bobby Wayne), and "Baby, Baby, Baby" (Teresa Brewer, who had previously scored with "Music! Music! Music!"). It occurred to Bacharach that he could go back to the Brill Building and churn out five of those a day. But it didn't work. He went a year and a half without selling anything. Carolyn Leigh said she wasn't even interested in *trying* to write a song with him; when he played a demo for Connie Francis, she picked up the needle after eight bars. "It looked simple," Bacharach later recalled. "But writing something simple that sounded maybe a little derivative, or accessible, was not so easy or acceptable to me."

It was another throwback to the pre–golden age Tin Pan Alley, the sense that songs were just material. Tunes and lyrics were simple and formulaic, and success was a matter of luck, romance (up to and including payola), and serendipity—coming out with an approach or gimmick that tickled the public's fancy at just the right time.

Dick Adler was no Burt Bacharach. Although his father, Clarence, was a noted concert pianist, Dick, in a somewhat self-defeating act of rebellion, eschewed the instrument and all musical training. That proved awkward when he decided to become a songwriter, but he seemed to solve the problem by following the example of his friend Bob Merrill, the composer of "The Doggie in the Window" and "Mambo Italiano," picking out his melodies on a toy xylophone. Clarence Adler had introduced his son to the only one of his piano students who wrote popular music, Phil Springer, and Springer and Dick teamed up on a couple of minor successes in 1950—the countryish "Teasin'" and an "answer song" to "Good Night, Irene" called "Please Say Goodnight to the Guy, Irene" (the lyric went on: "and let me get some sleep"), which Adler claimed would eventually sell 750,000 records. A long dry spell followed, however, and he hoped that he could turn things around by working with a new partner, an even younger man named Jerry Ross, who had come out of the Yiddish theater, where he'd been billed as "the boy star."*

Adler was prone to giving himself compositional challenges— writing a song about the rain, about hands, about the distance between

*Springer went on to cowrite a couple of hits, notably "Midnight Gambler" for Frankie Laine, "Santa Baby" for Eartha Kitt, and "(How Little It Matters) How Little We Know" (lyrics by Carolyn Leigh) for Sinatra. At one point, an aspiring lyric writer named Fred Ebb came to see him. Ebb later recalled that Springer said, "If I would work with him every day from nine to five, regular office hours, he would literally teach me to write songs—and so I did." The partnership lasted about a year, and Ebb eventually joined forces with another young writer, John Kander. They had a one-off hit in 1963 for Barbra Streisand, "My Coloring Book," and then began writing for the stage.

two people, and so forth. One day he took the xylophone, a pencil, and some paper into a room in his apartment for what he described as "the ultimate." He closed the door and told himself he wouldn't leave until he'd written a song about something that happened in the bathroom.

Time passed. Then more time passed. Then the radiator started to hiss. Within a few minutes Adler had plunked out a melody and written the words to a rhythm number he called "Steam Heat." ("The radiator's hissin', / Still I need your kissin' . . .") For the next few days he worked on the song with Ross. The pair managed to get an appointment with Mitch Miller, then in his last weeks at Mercury Records. After they played "Steam Heat" for the Beard, he said he wouldn't be able to take it on. But he thought there was something to the song. "Save it for a show," he said.

That notion increasingly made sense to Adler, who had grown up enamored of Broadway musicals and, before the war, acted with the Group Theater. Broadway had it all over Tin Pan Alley in terms of artistry and prestige. And so he was excited, at about the same time as the failure with "Steam Heat," when Manie Sachs, Miller's predecessor at Columbia Records, offered to set up a meeting with Frank Loesser. After the war, Loesser had returned to Hollywood for a peacetime stint that was brief but long enough for him to write both music and lyrics for a group of first-rate songs: "(I'd Like to Get You on a) Slow Boat to China," "I Wish I Didn't Love You So," "What Are You Doing New Year's Eve?," and "Baby, It's Cold Outside," which won the 1949 Academy Award for Best Original Song.* Then he reinvented himself. In 1949, George Abbott, still the prince of Broadway a decade after he met Livingston and Evans, had written the book for a proposed

---

*Loesser had actually written "Baby" back in 1944 and was famous for performing the duet at parties with his wife, Lynn. In 1948 he sold it to MGM for use in an Esther Williams movie, *Neptune's Daughter*.

musical based on a Victorian farce, *Charley's Aunt*, and had lined up Ray Bolger to star. He and the producers, Ernest H. Martin and Cy Feuer, asked Loesser to write the lyrics for the show, to be called *Where's Charley?* That appealed to Loesser, who had never really cottoned either to the California climate or the Hollywood ethos. "Writers out there were stymied in what they could do," said his widow, Jo Sullivan Loesser, "because you were under contract and they would tell you to write two songs for this movie and another for that one. It didn't matter if it was from your inner soul or what have you, you had to write a song."

The plan was for Harold Arlen to write the score, but Arlen was unavailable. Loesser got the job, the production was a hit, and that led to another music-and-lyrics assignment for Feuer and Martin: an adaptation of Damon Runyon's comical fables about the New York underworld. The production that resulted, *Guys and Dolls*, was one of the greatest theatrical successes of all time, both commercially and artistically. Best of all was Loesser's score, which represented the apogee of twentieth-century American theatrical songwriting. His songs were integral to character and story—from the inspired opener, "Fugue for Tin Horns," through the comic tours de force "Sit Down, You're Rocking the Boat," "Take Back Your Mink," and "Adelaide's Lament," through the finale, "Marry the Man Today." Those and other numbers served their purpose so well that they really couldn't be divorced from the show, but other *Guys and Dolls* songs proved strong enough to stand on their own. "If I Were a Bell" has become a vocal and jazz standard; "I'll Know" is a ballad worthy of Rodgers and Hammerstein; the less well-known "My Time of Day" is a haunting, minor-key tone poem; and Frank Sinatra turned "Luck Be a Lady" into a nightclub show-stopper.

Guys and Dolls would go on to sweep the 1951 Tony Awards and run for 1,200 performances. Loesser used his success, in part, to become a cheerleader, idea man, and mentor for songwriters. He wanted, in Jo Sullivan Loesser's words, to "improve the breed." In 1951 he advised his Hollywood friend Meredith Willson to write a musical based on the memories of his small-town Iowa youth, which he always talked about. Six years later, that germ of an idea had turned into *The Music Man*; Loesser got a production credit. Loesser encouraged a couple of young songwriters, Robert Wright and Chet Forrest, with their idea for a musical based on the compositions of the Russian composer Alexander Borodin. In 1953 the show, *Kismet*, became a Broadway hit as well.

Loesser even agreed to an audience with an eighteen-year-old kid whose mother knew someone who knew him. He sat Jerry Herman down and said, "I want you to play everything you've ever written." The kid played piano and a friend of his from their neighborhood—a girl named Phyllis Newman—sang. When they were finished, Loesser told the boy, "I want you to tell your parents I think you should try songwriting. It's a tough field, but I think you can make it." Then Loesser drew a picture of a train with a caboose and said, "This is what makes a good song. The locomotive has to start it. The caboose has to finish it off. Those are the bookends. Then you fill in different colors for the cars in the middle."

Herman, who would write words and music for *Hello, Dolly!* and many other shows, later recalled, "It was such a graphic, beautiful lesson about how to write a song. It stayed with me forever."

One more story of an audience with Loesser. Dave Frishberg, a St. Paul native and a jazz pianist, had come to New York in 1957, at the age of twenty-four, and immediately began getting work as a sideman. For a year and a half he was the singer Carmen McRae's accompanist. When that gig ended, he realized that because he couldn't sight-read, he was at a disadvantage in picking up work accompanying singers at auditions and rehearsals. He determined to learn to read, and in so doing studied the canon of the Great American Songbook. "I became a song fan . . ." he said later. "I wanted to know everything I could about the people who wrote them, how those people wrote, when, what helped them write." And that process of discovery inspired him to start writing songs himself. "I had a couple friends who were songwriters at the time," he recalled, "and they said, 'These are good. Take them to Frank Loesser.'

> I left them at his office, and one day the office called me to say that Loesser liked my stuff, especially a song called "Wallflower Lonely, Cornflower Blue," and wanted to meet me and talk about songwriting. So I went down there and met with him for an hour or so in his office. He sat there and chain-smoked and so did I. He didn't want to talk about music, he wanted to talk about lyrics. I admired him as a lyric writer, of course, but I was knocked out with his music writing. I thought he was a wonderful, audacious composer and when I tried to talk music with him, he said, "Look, I don't want to talk music. I'm not a musician. I'm a word guy." . . . He was looking at my songs with me, he was giving me this masterful advice. It was wonderful.*

Of course, Loesser's efforts on behalf of other songwriters were not wholly or even mainly disinterested. His years of experience in the industry had taught him how lucrative publishing rights could be. Hoagy

---

*More than fifty years later, Frishberg still remembered Loesser's lyric-writing advice: "He told me that my job as a lyric writer was to grab the listener by the ear and don't let him go. My job was to write a song so that the listener wouldn't be distracted or puzzled. My job is to not let that listener go. He said, 'Make every statement in the lyrics that you're using refer to the concept that's in the title. Don't leave the listener hanging. Keep the listener interested and surprised. If you use colorful language, give the listener a pause, so he can appreciate it and be ready for your next thought. And when you pull off something flashy that you want the listener to remember, to be impressed by, that's when you put in a riff, a couple of bars, a riff. Don't pile climaxes or punchlines right next to each other.'"

Carmichael observed: "Frank always wanted to be Irving Berlin." In the forties he started a company called Susan Music, named after his daughter, to publish his own songs, and in 1950 he hired some of Berlin's lawyers and started a more extensive publishing concern, Frank Music Corp. Loesser secured the rights to *Kismet* and plugged the score so hard that, even before the show opened, thirty-six separate recordings of its songs were released; "Baubles, Bangles and Beads" and "Stranger in Paradise" were the big winners. Frank Music was also in the market for one-off songs, and would have significant successes in the mid-fifties with "Unchained Melody" and "Cry Me a River." Loesser saw writers as students, to some extent, but more so as investments. Dave Frishberg said, "I never got the feeling that he was taking me under his wing. I thought that he saw dollar signs in what I was doing. Not that that's a bad thing. I used to take my songs to that office and they would, quote, publish them—which meant they would take the copyright and put it into their file cabinet."

It was by no means guaranteed that Loesser would be enthusiastic about a songwriter, or even sign him on, as Sheldon Harnick discovered. Harnick had enrolled at Northwestern University near his hometown of Chicago after his World War II service, earning money by playing violin in a sweet band. Inspired by the success of an actress classmate named Charlotte Rae (born Charlotte Lubotsky), he had come to New York and met his hero, Yip Harburg, who advised him to concentrate on lyrics and leave music writing to a collaborator. At one low point Harnick asked a friend who had done choreography for Loesser if she could arrange for a meeting. "She said, 'Sure,'" Harnick recalled. "I called Mr. Loesser, and he said, 'I'm going to California for five weeks. Call me when I get back and you can play for me.' I sweated out those five weeks. I was desperate. Finally I called his office, and his secretary said, 'I'll tell Mr. Loesser you're on the phone.' She came back and said, 'Mr. Loesser knows your work. You don't have to come in.' I was just crushed. Just desolate.'"

In 1951 the young songwriters Richard Adler and Jerry Ross were able to get through the door via the Manie Sachs connection. They played their limited repertoire, and Loesser liked one countryish song, "The Strange Little Girl," enough to offer them a contract: a $500 advance for the song and $50 a week each, against future royalties. Frank Music's efforts led to nine performers recording "Strange Little Girl," including Red Foley, Cowboy Copas, Hank Williams, and Eddy Howard, whose version reached number twenty-eight on the charts. But then "Tennessee Waltz" became a sensation, and that, according to Adler, for the moment satisfied the national demand for country tunes.

Adler and Ross soldiered on. Loesser secured the team a meeting with George Abbott, but Abbott didn't like what he heard enough to proceed with a show. The meeting, and the disappointing result, was repeated the following year. The team did manage to get some jobs writing special material for the young Eddie Fisher, a heartthrob being hyped in some quarters as the next Sinatra (and one of the few male singers who *wasn't* Italian). Talking to Fisher, who had grown up poor and had famously been plucked from obscurity by the venerable entertainer Eddie Cantor, gave Adler an idea. He and Ross produced a sort of Neapolitan bravura ballad called "Rags to Riches." Bypassing Loesser, they brought it directly to Mitch Miller at Columbia. Miller took the song, changing a couple of chords ("something that didn't bother us much," Adler recalled, "because we knew that Mitch suggested a change in almost every song he took"), and produced a record sung by Tony Bennett with "a driving, full-blooded brass choir arrangement by Percy Faith."

At first the record went nowhere. But then, as Adler recounts in his autobiography, he decided to become his own song plugger and personally talk up the record to disk jockeys in half a dozen big cities. The big catch was Bill Randle, number one in Cleveland and one of the most influential DJs in the country. Adler pitched him a wacky idea: play the song on the air six times in a row. Improbably, Randle agreed. The result was reminiscent of what had happened with "I'm Looking Over a Four Leaf Clover" and "Peg o' My Heart." That weekend the song went to number one in Cleveland and eventually hit number one in the country, staying on top of the *Billboard* charts for eight weeks in a row and, according to Adler, selling two million copies.

"Rags to Riches" was Adler and Ross's ticket to a theatrical job: providing most of the music for a revue, *John Murray Anderson's Almanac*, which opened on Broadway in December 1953. (Cy Coleman, Bart Howard, and a young calypso singer named Harry Belafonte also wrote material. The performers included Belafonte, Polly Bergen, Hermione Gingold, Larry Kert, Tina Louise, and Monique Van Vooren.) Revues, a staple of the 1920s, were in the midst of a revival, thanks in large part to the periodic *New Faces* shows produced by Leonard Sillman. His 1952 edition was the most successful of all and helped launch the careers of performers Paul Lynde, Eartha Kitt, and Carol Lawrence. Contributing sketches was a young comedy writer who still called himself "Melvin" Brooks, and contributing music and lyrics was Sheldon Harnick, whose song "Boston Beguine" was a show-stopper for Alice Ghostley. That led to a call to Harnick from someone at the music publishing company Hill & Range, but the audition didn't go well. "I had a portfolio of revue songs and pop songs, and I played them all," Harnick recalled. "They said there were 'too many ideas' in my revue songs. As for my pop songs, they said—and I swear this is true, 'Listen to the crap around, that's what we want.'" That wasn't something he was willing, or in fact able, to do. "I had to recognize for myself that I was not Irving Berlin," he said. "I didn't have the common touch. There are rare writers like Berlin who manage to write songs of common elegance. I knew I didn't have that talent, so I felt that what I could hope for, eventually, was to write something for the theater that would also find popular acceptance."

Harnick kept contributing to revues, including *Two's Company*, with Bette Davis, and *Shoestring Revue* (which introduced Chita Rivera, Dody Goodman, Beatrice Arthur, and Arte Johnson), and made extra money by writing for television and for the big trade shows put on by companies like Buick, the National Biscuit Company, and the Milliken fabric company. ("They made me solvent," he said.) All the while he was waiting for the moment when he could have a Broadway show of his own.

The New York revues were AAA-level farm teams for the Broadway musical. One narrow notch below were the summer revues put on by two mountain resorts, Green Mansions in the Adirondacks and the Tamiment resort in the Poconos. Entertainment at the latter had been presided over for years by Max Liebman; in the early fifties he hired the songwriting team of Jerry Bock and Larry Holofcener straight out of the University of Wisconsin. (Later in the decade, Richard Rodgers's daughter, Mary, and lyricist Marshall Barer would develop the musical *Once Upon a Mattress* at Tamiment.) Sheldon Harnick worked at Green Mansions, as did an aspiring classical composer named Charles Strouse, who, like Mitch Miller and Alec Wilder, had studied at the Eastman School of Music. Until his symphonies were performed, Strouse had been trying to make ends meet by playing the piano in jazz combos and taking on what he remembered as "many humiliating jobs at restaurants where nobody listened to me." Another job had him playing piano at ballet rehearsals for seventy-five cents an hour. "My first split consciously with serious music," he recalled, "was when this guy came up to me at a dance class and said he had a job to write dance music for the revues, and would I be the pianist. I had won a fellow-ship to the MacDowell Colony, I was working on a two-piano sonata and thought to myself, 'Gee that sounds like fun.' A lot of pretty girls." At Green Mansions, Strouse and a lyricist he met there, Lee Adams, started writing songs for the weekly shows, which featured all-new material performed by Carol Burnett, Don Adams, and other young singers and comics. One of their numbers was on the theme of comedy and tragedy; they called it "Put On a Happy Face."

John Murray Anderson's Almanac had only a modest run, but by Adler and Ross's next meeting with Loesser and Abbott, they pos-sessed a theatrical track record. This time, after hearing their dog-and-pony show, Abbott said, "I think you're ready." Not long after that, he hired them to write the score for a musical with the unlikely subject of a strike in a sleepwear factory, due to open in the spring of 1954. The title was going to be *The Pajama Game*, and there ended up being a perfect spot, right at the beginning of the second act, for "Steam Heat."

Carolyn Rosenthal was a Bronx girl who had attended Queens College and NYU and who, in 1951, found herself working as a typist, copywriter, and secretary who "couldn't take dictation." She dreamed of becoming a songwriter and would scribble lyrics in her odd hours. One day she dialed a wrong number and reached a music publisher who agreed to take a look at her work, and liked it enough to sign her to a contract. She affiliated herself with BMI (the only real choice for a writer just starting out), adopted the professional name Carolyn Leigh, and over the next few years had a few songs re-corded, each written with a different composer and none a big seller: a Jo Stafford B side called "Just Because You're You," a rhythm and

blues song that charted for both Lucky Millinder and Rosemary Clooney, and "What Happened to the Music," a Teresa Brewer novelty
song, cowritten with Robert Sadoff and the veteran Nacio Herb Brown,
that decried "all those crazy sound effects" in current pop music.

In 1953 the publisher Tommy Valando hooked Leigh up with yet
another composer, a jazz musician and arranger named Johnny Richards, who'd written a kind of impressionistic, syncopated melody that
needed words. When she got the assignment, she'd just come back
from a visit to her father, who was in the hospital with a heart ailment.
The experience gave her the inspiration to write a lyric called "Young
at Heart." The song was a slight thing, really, but her words had a
lightness and precision that boded well for her future—as well as
some nifty internal rhymes that tipped their hat to the tradition of Ira
Gershwin and Lorenz Hart. ("You can go to extremes with impossible
schemes / You can laugh when your dreams fall apart at the seams.")

Not long after that, Leigh ended her arrangement with Valando to
go freelance. She also had a new, permanent—or as permanent as these
things could be—partner, a young man from Philadelphia. "His name
is 'Moose' (actually, Morris—but he prefers the nickname) Charlap,"
Leigh had written in November to Robert Marks, one of the publishers
who seemed to be falling over each other in pursuit of her. "We've written eight songs in eight weeks and sold every single one—with some
already recorded and others, the Lord willing, scheduled for wax."

Charlap, a native Philadelphian, was a compact five feet, five inches
tall; the nickname "Moose" was ironic. He was not yet twenty-five—
two years younger than Leigh—and was a prodigy of sorts, at that time
ASCAP's youngest member.

Their work together was "a lot of fun," Leigh went on. "Makes real
United States money, too, which never ceases to surprise me. (I still
wonder, when I get a check that I can bank or cash, just why anyone in

his right mind would want to *pay* me for a piece of paper with a few words and hieroglyphics on it that gave my partner and me so much pleasure to create!)"

She heard from all quarters, including Howie Richmond, who had no fewer than seven publishing companies listed on his letterhead. He had been referred to Leigh by George Marlo, who more than two decades back had turned down Jack Lawrence's "Play, Fiddle, Play" and was now on the staff of BMI. "If you are not tied up 'exclusively' with any other publisher," Richmond wrote, "would be most grateful to you for the opportunity to hear any songs you feel are best suited for our type of exploitation. Strongly suggest these be unique, different types of songs, particularly novelties."

Inevitably, Leigh and Charlap's success brought them to the attention of the grand Broadway mentor. The initial connection came through Frank Loesser's wife, Lynn, "who promptly decided that we would be the new protégés of his firm . . . with a new Broadway show in the offing. Whether this will turn out to be more than a lot of talk, I don't know, but it sure makes for happy dreamin'." The Broadway show would come through other channels, but the team did sell a couple of songs to Frank Music Corp.—one, "First Impression," recorded by a talented young singer named Eydie Gormé—and Leigh got a nice note from Loesser himself, who said he was "wonderfully impressed" with her progress and looked forward to the day when she joined ASCAP and could enter into a continuing arrangement with the firm. Yet another encouraging development in yet another medium: she and Charlap were getting steady work writing songs for the variety show Jackie Gleason hosted on CBS television. They were offered a contract with the show, but they turned it down because the deal meant signing on with the Gleason publishing firm.

Things were especially busy on the recording front in late 1953.

That was because James Petrillo was threatening yet another strike by his AFM against the record industry. (The big one of 1942 had been followed by a briefer action six years later.) "The general picture is one of 'make hay while the sun-, etc.,'" Leigh wrote to another publisher. "Victor has been cutting day and night, everything and anything that vaguely resembles a song, and every artist they can pin down long enough to sing a few notes into a mike. Decca and Coral, on the other hand, have announced that neither of them will cut anything for the entire month of December. As for Columbia, well, nobody but The Beard really knows what is happening there, although half of the music business says he's loading up on sides and the other half says he isn't."

Petrillo and the record companies came to an agreement in early January, and soon after that "Young at Heart" found its way to Frank Sinatra, who, cast off by Columbia and the Beard, had just signed a modest contract with Capitol. Leigh and Richards's song was one of his first recordings there, in an elegant strings-with-flute arrangement by Nat Cole's close collaborator Nelson Riddle. Sinatra's voice was back in shape and the song was in his sweet spot. The record was released in February 1954 and reached number two on the charts, Sinatra's biggest success in seven years and the beginning of his comeback as the dominant singer of his era. It made Leigh's name as well. Within a week of the song's release, *Variety* reported, she got calls from seventeen publishers asking her to supply lyrics to melodies they owned.

That spring, Sinatra was filming a movie with Doris Day based on the 1938 film *Four Daughters*. It had no title until the success of Leigh and Richards's song inspired Warner Bros. to name it *Young at Heart*—that, despite the fact that it was a rather bleak story of depression and attempted suicide. For an estimated $15,000, Tommy Valando sold Warners the rights to "unlimited usage" of the tune. At that point, *Billboard* reported, it had sold 350,000 copies—an impressive figure in a supposedly post-sheet-music age. Leigh's share of that, according to a statement from Sunbeam Music in August, was in the neighborhood of $3,500—that is, 1 percent. In addition, there was a quarterly payment from BMI of about $1,200 for radio play, plus her "mechanical" payment for recordings by Sinatra and others—plus her 25 percent share of the Warners payment.

In May 1954, as "Young at Heart" was reaching its peak position on the charts, *The Pajama Game* opened on Broadway. It got rave reviews, ultimately won the Tony Award for Best Musical, and ran for 1,063 performances. Dick Adler and Jerry Ross's songs "Hey There" and "Hernando's Hideaway" became number-one hits, and "Steam Heat," as recorded by Patti Page, reached number eight. The team of Abbott, Adler, Ross, and choreographer Bob Fosse followed up precisely a year later with another huge hit, *Damn Yankees*, which was also named Best Musical and also had a better than 1,000-performance run.

In November 1955, Jerry Ross died from the lung disease that had afflicted him for years. He was twenty-nine. *Variety*, in commemorating his passing, credited him and Adler with paving the way for "the current crop of young songsmiths who have been getting their first crack at the legituner field. (Previously, legit producers had turned for the most part to the old pros for score assignments, leaving newcomers little chance to break into Broadway shows.)"

As examples of "the current crop of young songsmiths," *Variety* mentioned two teams. The first was Jerry Bock and Larry Holofcener, who, having graduated from Tamiment, were preparing a Broadway show called *Mr. Wonderful* for Sammy Davis Jr. The second was Moose Charlap and Carolyn Leigh. Just after the release of "Young at Heart," the actress Mary Martin and her husband and producer, Richard Halliday, were driving on the Merritt Parkway in Connecticut. The song came on the radio. The theme of the lyrics fit in too perfectly with the production the couple was planning, a musical adaptation of *Peter Pan*, with Martin playing the part of Peter. The next day Halliday tracked down Leigh and phoned her in her apartment. As she told a New York newspaper:

"He said, 'Are you busy now?' He should have seen me—in my robe, drinking a cup of coffee. He said that he and Miss Martin had heard my song the night before, and right away Mary had said that she wanted whoever wrote those lyrics to do the music for her new show, 'Peter Pan.'

"Naturally, I thought somebody was kidding. That sort of thing just doesn't happen. So I arranged to call him back at his office, and I did and it was him all right."

She and Charlap wrote a couple of songs on spec and had a meeting with Martin, Halliday, and the director, Jerome Robbins, a well-respected choreographer who had worked both in ballet and on Broadway, where he was a George Abbott protégé. He and Abbott had ended up codirecting *The Pajama Game*; *Peter Pan* would be his first solo credit. Leigh, who had seen only one Broadway musical in her life, was nervous. She sang one of her lines to Robbins: "If I can live a life of crime, and still be home by dinnertime." That got a nod of approval from him, and the team was hired.

As work on the show continued, Robbins would develop some reservations about Leigh's lyrics, based on his sense of her as a creature of Tin Pan Alley rather than the stage. He confided to Edwin Lester, Martin and Halliday's coproducer, that he was concerned about "the tendency of Carolyn's to always write toward the hit record rather than the situation of the show. She shies away from using Peter and Wendy's names or specifics that might make the song unusable in general context."

History has answered Robbins's doubts. Leigh and Charlap wrote a half-dozen outstanding songs for the production, which was scheduled to begin its out-of-town tryout in San Francisco in July. None became a hit record, and although Peter's and Wendy's names aren't prominent in any of them, all were true to the characters and the show: "Tender Shepherd," "I've Gotta Crow," "I Won't Grow Up," "I'm Flying," "Hook's Tarantella," and a haunting ballad called "When I Went Home," in which Peter recalls peeking in on his childhood home to find "that somebody else / Was sleeping in my bed." But history can take a long time to make up its mind. At the time of the San Francisco opening, *Variety* was unimpressed with the production as a whole and called the score "dull . . . with lyrics to match." The producers knew something needed to be done, and their answer was to make *Peter Pan* more of a full-fledged musical than the play-with-music it had been. Rather than call on the novices Leigh and Charlap to generate new songs, they brought in a trio of Broadway and Hollywood veterans: Jule Styne for the music and the team of Betty Comden and Adolph Green for the lyrics. They had about a week to add new material for the Los Angeles opening in late August.

It was an awkward situation. Leigh and Charlap were on-site and still part of the team, but there were the three newcomers barricaded behind a closed hotel-room door, from which continually emerged the sounds of typing, singing, and muted conversation. Comden, Green, and Styne ended up being credited with a half-dozen songs of their own. One of them stuck in Leigh's craw. In J. M. Barrie's original book, Peter Pan's realm is called "Never Land"—and, for the sake of cadence, the lovely song the new team came up with had an extra word, "Never *Never* Land." "We were told to stick to the book," Leigh complained to her agent, "and forget about writing Hit Parade songs for the show." Still, almost all of her and Charlap's songs stayed, with the notable exception of "When I Went Home"—even though *Variety*'s review of the Los Angeles premiere had singled it out as "the second act socko number." Martin told Charlap that it had to go because it was "just too sad." (The song has been recorded only once, by Michelle Nicastro, on *Lost in Boston*, a 1994 album featuring notable songs cut from Broadway shows.)

The final version of *Peter Pan* was a happy mix of the two teams' contributions, and by the time the company hit New York, everyone recognized that good things were in store. Moose Charlap told his future wife, the singer Sandy Stewart, that Richard Rodgers dropped in on a rehearsal one day. After listening for a time, he told Charlap, "My boy, you have not written a score, you've written an annuity." The show opened in October to universal raves, including Walter Kerr's in the *New York Herald Tribune*: "It's the way *Peter Pan* always should have been and wasn't."

Peter Pan could have had a long Broadway run, but Lester and Halliday had accepted an offer from NBC to put the production on live television and stipulated that the show would close by the time of the broadcast. It aired on March 7, 1955, and was seen by an estimated 65 million people: "the largest audience," according to *Collier's* magazine, "ever assembled for anything at any time."

Richard Rodgers was right: with multiple TV airings in the future, record sales, and never-ending revivals, *Peter Pan* would be, for all five songwriters, the gift that kept on giving. But for the time being, Leigh's remuneration was relatively modest. She got an advance of $4,000 for her lyrics, against a payment of 1 percent of the box-office take—roughly $500 a week for a twenty-two-week run; her share of the TV rights was $5,000.

And as successful as *Peter Pan* was, it didn't lead to other Broadway offers for Leigh and Charlap—one significant reason being that, as of the show's premiere or shortly afterward, there was no more Leigh and

Charlap. According to the singer Sandy Stewart, who married Charlap in 1957, there was no enmity; the team dissolved because Frank Loesser signed Charlap to develop musicals with lyricist Norman Gimbel, whom he'd signed on to the Frank Music Corp. stable. (That team ultimately reached Broadway in 1958, with a flop called *Whoop-Up*.)

The change didn't slow Leigh down. It was a moment when songwriters assiduously played the field, and no one played it more enthusiastically than she. She had a particular affinity for working with older writers; over a period of just a couple of years, she collaborated with such veterans as Sammy Fain, Harold Spina, and Jerry Livingston, plus one younger man, Larry Coleman.[*]

Most of those composers were affiliated with ASCAP, and as Leigh gained success and experience, her associates in the business knew she was contemplating a switch. Early in 1954, Robert Marks, of his father Edward's BMI publishing firm, mentioned to her his "hope that you haven't gone ASC'HAPPY so that we can still have a hit tune together."

Leigh replied: "No—I haven't yet gone 'ASC'HAPPY' . . . and I don't know that I ever will. But I haven't come to that and many other bridges yet—so quote me not, either way."

As she later described it, what finally brought her to the bridge was the experience of attending BMI's annual banquet to receive a prize for "Young at Heart." She later told a reporter that she looked around at the other award winners: "At least one of them, I knew, hadn't written the songs he was to receive an award for. He was just a blind for the real writer, an ASCAP member reduced to this in order to live. Others weren't even using their real names. And the songs! 'Sh-Boom,' I

---

[*]It may be relevant that Leigh's father died, of a heart ailment, two years after her hospital visit that inspired "Young at Heart."

remember, and 'Shake, Rattle and Roll' were two of those which also received awards. What pride could I have in being in that company? . . .

"Anyway, it may sound crazy, but while I was sitting there waiting for the chairman of the board of BMI to call out my name and present me with an award, I resolved to get out of there."

That may be true, but there were also practical reasons to go to ASCAP. Opportunities like the one held out by Loesser couldn't be pursued so long as she was with BMI. In addition, ASCAP had decreed what *Variety* termed a "nix" on Broadway collaborations between its members and BMI writers. In May 1955, the publication reported that Leigh had "ankled BMI." According to the society's complicated rules, Moose Charlap was slated to get 75 percent of the performance money from *Peter Pan*. "Miss Leigh frankly attributed her pending switch," *Variety* commented, "to the fact that she could no longer find ASCAP writers who will work with her as long as she is a BMI writer."

An ASCAP publisher, Edwin Morris, set Leigh up with Max Liebman, who had taken his Tamiment revue skills to television, most successfully with Sid Caesar's *Your Show of Shows*. Emboldened by the TV success of *Peter Pan* and inspired by the example of *Kismet*, Liebman was in the process of mounting a series of live television musical "spectaculars," including *The Merry Widow*, *Heidi*, and *The Great Waltz*; he hired Leigh to provide lyrics to classic compositions in the public domain. The productions weren't especially successful with the critics or the public, and Leigh grew frustrated. "I am fed up to the roots of my curly locks with dead composers, and want something done about it if I do any more shows for Max," she wrote to Livingston while working on *Marco Polo*. "The music is to be based on the works of Rimsky-Korsakov, who, I discover, outside of 'Scheherazade' [*sic*] (which I don't want to use because it's too obvious) never wrote more than two consecutive notes of melody in his life.

"All I can think of is the day I'll be free to sit down and write some good old-fashioned score-free songs," she went on. "Never thought I'd think this way, but I do. Only scores that can tempt me otherwise are those in shows headed for Broadway."

But there were no Broadway offers on the horizon, and she wasn't too pleased with the prospect of doing high-quality work in the pop music field. It just didn't seem to sell, and that fact was reflected in the melodies that came across her desk. "Every composer I've met recently seems obsessed with the idea that (pardon the expression) crap is commercial," she complained toward the end of 1954. "All of their output sounds like every other song I've ever heard. I'd give my left eye for eight bars of original music."

Things looked even bleaker the next year, when a song called "Rock Around the Clock," recorded by Bill Haley and His Comets and prominently featured in the film *Blackboard Jungle*, shot to number one on the *Hit Parade*, considerably surpassing "Sh-Boom" and "Shake, Rattle and Roll" (Haley's previous hit). A woman from Columbia, Mississippi, named Elma Duncan had written to Leigh asking for advice about becoming a songwriter. The lengthy reply began by noting Duncan's grammatical lapses:

You may very well object, on the grounds that many songs which become popular today are full of grammatical mistakes; but I can only answer that the songs which have lasted and will last as "standards" through the years are not songs of the type written by a few lucky semi-illiterates. This last by no means is an allusion to you. I refer to "rock'n roll" and "freak" songs, from the pens of people hoping to make an easy dollar. The records show that these people make that easy dollar once, and in ninety-nine cases out of a hundred, no more than once.

Leigh still had faith in popular song, though she realized it wasn't an easy road. She told Duncan:

If you have a legitimate talent, have studied and read a great deal and are willing to go on studying and reading for the rest of your life, are financially able to support yourself for at least three to five years, and can in general, cheerfully be able to give up family life, vacations, pride, money—in short, your whole *life*—why then pack and take the first plane to New York. But be prepared to find that all these conditions fulfilled do not necessarily mean success for you. There is an intangible: luck. Without it all you do is to no avail. I have had overwhelmingly large quantities of that intangible. I cannot guarantee you will, but I wish it to you with all my heart.

VII

The Big Beat
1951–1968

Things were pretty sleepy on the Americana music scene in the late '50s and early '60s. Popular radio was sort of at a standstill and filled with empty pleasantries.

• Bob Dylan

Once upon a time a song had melody and rhyme,
And lovely ballads fused to fill the air.
The songs were sweet and lyrical,
And sang about the miracle
Of love in bloom and love beyond despair.
But gone are the June songs,
The how-high-the-moon songs.
And baritones that used to sing romantic airs
Are singing songs more frantic than romantic.
One o'clock, two o'clock, three o'clock, rock.
You gotta sing rock or you go into hock.
Four o'clock, five o'clock, six o'clock, roll.
Throw away your senses and your self-control.
But brother I've got news,
Mr. Cole won't rock and roll!

• "Mr. Cole Won't Rock and Roll," by
Joe Sherman and Noel Sherman

Beyond, or beneath, the mush at the top of the charts, changes were brewing in the early fifties. Hillbilly music had already made its mark, but vigorous and distinctive new honky-tonk voices like Hank Williams, Floyd Tillman, and Lefty Frizzell were emerging. So were all sorts of propulsive "rhythm and blues" sounds (the term was popularized in the late forties when Jerry Wexler, then an editor at *Billboard*, adopted it in place of the traditional "race music") by performers as varied as Louis Jordan, Ike Turner, B.B. King, Charles Brown, Hank Ballard, Muddy Waters, Ruth Brown, the Ravens, the Orioles, the Drifters, and Willie Mae "Big Mama" Thornton, who hit big in 1953 with "Hound Dog," written by two twenty-year-old Jewish kids from Los Angeles, Jerry Leiber and Mike Stoller. All those artists recorded on the hundreds of independent labels that sprang up in the forties and early fifties (with the exception of Jordan, at Decca) and went out over the radio in the country's largest cities. At first, their tracks were mainly played on stations catering to African-Americans, who had taken part in a massive northern urban migration in the years before, during, and after the war. Then hip white deejays picked them up, and their "teenage" listeners, who represented a demographic group of dramatically increasing significance, responded with enthusiasm.* They loved to listen to this music in their cars, on the jukeboxes at their hangouts, or, in due time, on a recent innovation, a portable device called the transistor radio. A lot of the

---

*The adjective "teenage," to refer to someone between thirteen and nineteen, was first noted by the journal *American Speech* in 1935, and the *Oxford English Dictionary*'s first citation for the noun "teenager" is 1941. But both terms took off in the 1950s. During that decade, according to Google Books, their use in American printed sources rose by roughly 600 percent.

· · · 176 · · ·

new music had decidedly mixed parentage, a sense picked up on by a 1953 *Billboard* headline: POP—C.&W.—R.&B.: DEMARCATION LINES ARE GROWING HAZY.

The jock leading the way was Cleveland's Alan Freed, who started his wildly popular *Moondog Show* in 1951 and began promoting touring R&B shows a year later. Rhythm and blues record sales reached an all-time high of $15 million in 1953. In April 1954, *Billboard* announced, TEEN-AGERS DEMAND MUSIC WITH A BEAT, SPUR RHYTHM-BLUES, and noted, "The teen-age tide has swept down the old barriers which kept this music restricted to a segment of the population."

The magazine expanded on the subject in a long article that summer:

> The rhythm and blues market, formerly restricted wholly to a Negro audience, has repeated the move in the pop field, as did country and western music several years ago. About that time, almost any good c.&w. tune was jumped upon by big label pop a.&r. men. . . . Not only have record stores started selling r.&b. where none was sold before, but juke box operators are reporting requests for r.&b. tunes from pop locations which previously detested the low-down, noisy but exciting numbers. . . . One juke box operator who does terrific business selling used juke box records to neighborhood kids claims the first items they ask for are numbers by such artists as Muddy Waters, Willie Mabon and Ruth Brown.

The following year *Billboard* was starting to recognize that "the r.&b. invasion is only part of a larger pattern," one that had brought with it "pain, turmoil and soul-searching. . . . This pattern spells out what has been coming into focus for some years, to wit: The Brill Building, headquarters of the Broadway based publisher, is no longer a tight little isle, and Tin Pan Alley must integrate itself with a larger musical scene if it is to continue its traditional function of song purveyor to the nation."

When that article appeared, Bill Haley's "Rock Around the Clock" was nearing the end of its twenty-four weeks on the charts. The following year, 1956, saw the irrefutable arrival of rock and roll in the form of Elvis Presley and his four number-one releases, led by "Don't Be Cruel" and "Hound Dog."

At first, to the extent they paid any attention to it at all, the elders of Tin Pan Alley dismissed rock—sometimes termed "the Big Beat"—not only as a fad but as a fad that was already fading. As early as March 1955, *Variety* reported that, based on a poll of teenagers, "the popularity of the rock 'n' roll beat in the New York area is slipping." In the fall of 1956, even as Elvis was dominating the charts, ASCAP president Paul Cunningham said, "From this point on, we can expect a revival of good music in the style of the Gershwins, the Kerns and the Rombergs." Clearly, denial was one tack to take. Another was condescension. In a 1956 interview in *Down Beat*, songwriter Johnny Green ("I Cover the Waterfront," "Body and Soul") compared rock and roll to tarragon: a spice that was useful once in a while, but which no one would want as a steady diet. The next year the venerable bandleader Paul Whiteman said that even though it had only about "two words to a lyric," rock was all right "in a pretty simple way." By the end of 1957, rock and roll accounted for forty of the sixty top records, led by Elvis's "All Shook Up," which sold 2.4 million copies. As *Billboard* had to acknowledge in a headline, DEMISE OF R&R JUST SO MUCH WISHFUL THINKING.

The commentary grew more hostile and defensive. Bandleader Bob Crosby told *Music Journal*, "The so-called 'tunes' are monotonous, with a similarity that is often ridiculous." Meredith Willson, composer of *The Music Man*, stepped up the attack: "The people of this country do not have any conception of the evil being done by rock 'n' roll; it is a plague as far reaching as any plague we have ever had. . . . My complaint is that it just isn't music. It's utter garbage and it should not be confused in any way with anything related to music or verse." (One wonders about Willson's reaction, a half-dozen years hence, to the royalty checks he received from the Beatles' rendition of his song "Till There Was You" on their album *Meet the Beatles*.) Frank Sinatra, over whom girls had swooned just a dozen years before, was quoted as saying: "Rock 'n' roll smells phony and false. It is sung, played and written for the most part by cretinous goons and by means of its almost imbecilic reiteration, and sly, lewd, in plain fact, dirty lyrics, and . . . it manages to be the martial music of every sideburned delinquent on the face of the earth."

In response to Elvis—and other overtly sexual performers, like Little Richard, Chuck Berry, Jerry Lee Lewis, and Gene Vincent—the attack expanded from rock and roll's (poor) quality to the affront it represented to public safety, moral standards, and common decency. As deejay-sponsored record hops and live performances of rock and roll grew more common, they were accompanied by the occasional fistfight or act of vandalism, shocking both municipal elders and the industry establishment. After a handful of such incidents in 1956, *Variety* editorialized that rock's "Svengali grip on the teenagers has produced a staggering wave of juvenile violence and mayhem." According to an editorial in *Music Journal*, juvenile delinquents were "definitely influenced in their lawlessness by this throwback to jungle rhythms. Either it actually stirs them to orgies of sex and violence (as its model did for the savages themselves), or they use it as an excuse for the removal of all inhibitions . . . and an incitement to juvenile delinquency."

There was a racial component to all of this, as there is to most important cultural things that happen in America. As *Billboard* had observed, young white people were listening to and buying music made by black people, and when their elders started to pay attention to this music, they couldn't help noticing that some of it was off-color. The suggestiveness in "Sixty Minute Man," "Work with Me, Annie," and its follow-up, "Annie Had a Baby," wasn't so different from Lorenz Hart's "Horizontally speaking, he's at his very best" (from "Bewitched, Bothered and Bewildered") or Cole Porter's "Let's Do It," but then again, in some ways it was very different indeed. In December 1954, the Music Publishers' Protective Association passed a resolution condemning "dirty" songs "as showing bad taste and a disregard for recognized moral standards and conventions." Early in 1955, *Variety* ran a three-part series on "leer-ics." Radio stations around the country dutifully responded. In Houston, the Juvenile Delinquency and Crime Commission created a "Wash-Out-the-Air" subcommittee, which produced a list of twenty-six records they deemed "suggestive, obscene, and characterized by lewd intentions." All the songs were licensed by BMI, all the records were on independent labels, and almost all were by blacks, including Ray Charles ("I Got a Woman"), Clyde McPhatter ("Whatcha Gonna Do Now?"), and Roy Brown ("Good Rockin' Tonight"). All the radio stations in Houston dropped the songs.

The major record companies had a subtler but ultimately more effective way of co-opting the new music. In 1954, an African-American vocal group called the Chords released "Sh-Boom," a record that resembled what the Ink Spots and the Mills Brothers had been doing for a decade or more, with a prominently peppy beat and a moderately honking saxophone solo in the middle. Shortly after it began to climb the pop charts, Mercury released an almost completely identical version of the song, by a Canadian group called the Crew-Cuts; as their name implied, they were white. There was nothing illegal about the practice: under the Copyright Act or 1909 only the text of a song was protected, not the arrangement or interpretation. (Writers of the original songs did get royalties on the cover versions, depending on their publishing contracts.) The Chords' "Sh-Boom" peaked at number five on the charts in 1954; the Crew-Cuts' version was number one for nine weeks in a row. The same thing happened the following year when Georgia Gibbs reproduced LaVern Baker's "Tweedlee Dee" almost note for note. In the years ahead, Little Richard, Chuck Berry, and other black artists repeatedly had their songs—often in cleaned-up versions—appropriated by white singers, most notoriously Pat Boone, who released pale versions of Little Richard's "Long Tall Sally" and "Tutti Frutti."

The arrival of rock and roll coincided with and was connected to some profound long-term changes in popular music, including a new primacy of record labels over publishers and performers over writers, and a centrifugal decentralization of the industry, away from New York. But the music itself wasn't monolithic, and the dominance that rock (broadly defined) would eventually have over pop wasn't anything close to immediate. The same kinds of songs that had done so well in the early fifties—sentimental, soothing, homespun, novel, or possessing some combination of those qualities—continued to be written, recorded, and purchased.

In 1956, Jay Livingston and Ray Evans, now writing movie theme songs almost exclusively, provided a lilting lullaby called "Que Sera, Sera (Whatever Will Be, Will Be)" for Alfred Hitchcock's remake of his 1934 thriller *The Man Who Knew Too Much*. Doris Day sang it at a crucial plot point in the film. According to the website devoted to the work and legacy of Ray Evans, she initially refused to make a record of

"Que Sera" "because she thought it was a children's song. But this was the important song in the picture, so Paramount insisted that she record it. Paul Weston, who was present at the recording session, said that she knocked it off in one take and said, 'That's the last time you'll ever hear that song.'" Day's record ended up being on the charts for twenty-seven weeks, reaching as high as number two. And "Que Sera" won Livingston and Evans their third (and final) Best Original Song Oscar.*

The veteran songwriter Harry Ruby ("Three Little Words," "A Kiss to Build a Dream On"), who, at seventy-one, was three years older than Irving Berlin, wrote a letter to Jay and Ray:

Last Saturday when I heard "THE STREET WHERE YOU LIVE" on the Hit Parade—and another little ditty, entitled: "WHATEVER WILL BE, WILL BE," I wanted to shout. When such songs can be on top, it proves that, as I have always said, the public does not get mad when someone writes a real song—the kind of song that's here to-day and will be here tomorrow. Which reminds me that I have not heard "CEMENT MIXER" lately.

As for the others songs on the same Hit Parade "HOUND DOG," "DON'T BE CRUEL," etc., if you fellers wrote those too, what I said in paragraph one still goes.

---

*Hitchcock called on the team to write a theme song for his 1958 *Vertigo*. Jay recounted years later: "Paramount had told him that people don't know what 'vertigo' means and he wanted us to pacify them by explaining the meaning of 'vertigo' in our lyric." Ever the efficient craftsmen, they wrote the song, with a slight calypso beat and this lyrical opening: "Down to the depths, up to the heights, / Giddy with joy, crazy with fear, these are my nights." After a session that resulted in a demo recording, Jay said, "I decided to test out lyrics to see if [Ray] had explained the meaning of the word, 'vertigo.' Now the singer had rehearsed it about six times by this time, and I asked him if he knew what 'vertigo' means? And he said, 'It's an island in the West Indies, isn't it?'" Although Hitchcock and Paramount wisely decided not to use the song, one recording of it was released, by singer Billy Eckstine.

Livingston and Evans had an even bigger success the next year with an even simpler and more sentimental tune: "Tammy," from the film *Tammy and the Bachelor*. The record by the movie's star, Debbie Reynolds, was number one for six straight weeks, and the song was nominated for an Academy Award, losing to Van Heusen and Cahn's "All the Way." "Tammy" was recorded over the next decade by dozens of singers and orchestras, collectively selling more than 18 million records.

When Reynolds's record was rising high, the boys were interviewed by the *Los Angeles Mirror-News* for an article called "Rock 'n' Roll Termed Gyp." In the course of the short piece, they covered nearly all the standard reactions against the new music. Jay was quoted as saying: "The kids are being short-changed, cheated out of a part of culture. They won't have anything to be nostalgic about. How are they going to be able to look into each other's eyes and sigh, 'They're playing our tune,' when the radio's blaring 'Raunchy'?"

Ray chimed in: "And 10 years from now, who's going to remember a 1958 top hit—'Short Shorts'?"

Jay: "Professional writers can't and won't write rock and roll, so it's being done by the amateurs. In rock and roll, it's the noise on the record that counts, not the music. . . . Formerly, many would go from an interest in pop tunes to an interest in classical music. But where do you go from rock and roll?"*

The same week, *Billboard* extensively quoted one of Jay and Ray's colleagues, Pat Ballard, a fifty-eight-year-old songwriter who had had a couple of hits in 1954 with "Mister Sandman" and "(Oh Baby Mine)

---

*"Short Shorts" was a novelty song by a New Jersey teenage group called the Royal Teens. It was written by their keyboardist, Bob Gaudio, who would go on to be a member of and write most of the songs for the Four Seasons. "Raunchy" was a 1957 instrumental rock-and-roll hit for Bill Justis. George Harrison played the song at his audition for a group that would be called the Beatles.

I Get So Lonely." Ballard issued what the magazine described as "a call to veteran songwriters with prebop hits behind them to write for today's market or retire gracefully."

"It's worldwide, so it's our duty to produce something to entertain," said the cleffer/publisher/producer. "The Juilliard boys destroyed the dance beat with their over-arrangements, so kids naturally have taken to rock 'n' roll, they're starved for a beat. . . . Isn't it ridiculous to call yourself a songwriter if you haven't written anything since 1940? To write what communicates to the youngsters of the world is a privilege, not a bore. Let's get off our fat royalties and work at our profession."

Also that same week in 1958, the nation's disk jockeys held their first annual convention in Kansas City. They had secured Mitch Miller as their keynote speaker, despite the fact that Miller was notoriously unenthusiastic about the most popular disks the jockeys spun. As the titular boss of "popular" music at the label, he couldn't afford to ignore rock and roll, but he was ambivalent about it. Way back in 1951, he had put out Johnnie Ray's "Cry" and "Whiskey and Gin," which he later called "probably the very first rock and roll record." He wrote a perceptive article for *The New York Times Magazine* in April 1955, just as the harbingers of rock were first being felt. He quoted an unnamed "paunchy prophet of doom" as complaining, "Every time I get within earshot of a jukebox, someone is throwing in a coin to hear something called 'Oop Shoop' or 'Sh Boom' or 'Tweedle Dee' or 'Ko Ko Mo.' What does it mean? Doesn't anyone write a nice, simple love song any more?" Miller's answer, in part, was that "nonsense syllables in popular songs could be traced all the way back to Elizabethan times." He referenced two of the biggest hits of the "good old days," the 1920s: "Yes! We Have No Bananas" and "Diga Diga Doo." He suggested that the popularity of rhythm and blues might represent in part "a steady—and

· · · 184 · · ·

healthy—breaking down of color barriers in the United States." His main point was that the pop music of *every* era offended and mystified the older generation, and he concluded: "In twenty years, when Junior has grown into a sedate married man, father and pillar of the community, he will remember 'Ko Ko Mo' wistfully and be distressed no end by the songs *his* son admires."

But the rawness of rock and roll, as it presently emerged, was antithetical to Miller's approach, which emphasized craft, polish, judicious gimmickry, and production values. "Emotion never makes you a hit," he said in an interview in his later years. "I always tell this to singers: Emotion is not something you feel. It's something you make the listener feel. And you have to be very cool and know what you're doing." Elvis Presley was cool and hot at the same time, a combination with which Miller was not familiar, or comfortable. When Elvis was looking to leave Sun Records in Memphis, the Beard made a lowball offer and was blown out of the water by RCA Victor; later he passed on the chance to sign Buddy Holly, a rock-and-roller from Lubbock, Texas, who, unlike Presley, wrote his own songs. The Big Beat had passed Mitch Miller by, and it was drowning out the sound he worked so hard to create. The previous year, Columbia was responsible for only one of the twenty songs to hit number one, "Chances Are," by the young California vocalist Johnny Mathis; indie labels Cadence, Roulette, and Dot each had more.

Miller's talk to the disk jockeys in Kansas City was titled "The Great Abdication"; the abdicators, in his view, were sitting in front of him. The Beard made no attempt to spare their feelings.

To say you've grossly mishandled this great, fat money-maker—radio—would be understating the case. . . . You carefully built yourself into the monarchs of radio and abdicated—abdicated your programming to the corner record shop; to the eight- to fourteen-year-olds; to the pre-shave crowd that makes up 12 [percent] of the country's population and zero percent of its buying power, once you eliminate ponytail ribbons, Popsicles and peanut brittle. Youth must be served—but how about some music for the rest of us?

By that time, the deejays' power was ebbing, thanks to a new format in which the playlist and frequency of play was strictly determined by record sales. The deejay could gab about this or that between songs, but he had no authority to decide which songs to play. The format, called Top 40, had started in the late forties at Gordon McLendon's and Todd Storz's stations in Texas and Nebraska, respectively, but by now had spread all over the country.

Variety reported that the jocks gave Mitch Miller a standing ovation.

Schwartz v. Broadcast Music, Inc., after attracting a flurry of publicity when it was initiated in 1953, crept on at a petty pace, with action limited to pretrial examinations of all parties. When a special master appointed by the court ruled that BMI would be permitted to examine performance cards of more than 200,000 ASCAP songs dating back to 1934, it appeared that the case could quite literally go on forever. Accordingly, the plaintiffs lowered their sights, focusing on structural rather than financial matters. A 1956 *Variety* article characterized the songwriters as "adamant in their demands for complete divorcement of the broadcasting business from the music business. That covers not only the broadcasters' ownership of BMI but the webs' control of disk affiliates and music publishing companies."

They also moved their battle to different venues. One was the press, where they found a vocal ally in *New York Herald Tribune* radio and television columnist John Crosby. There was also favorable coverage (favorable to ASCAP, that is) of the issue in both intellectual and slick magazines. In the upper-middlebrow *Reporter*, Marya Mannes asked "Who Decides What Songs Are Hits?" Her answer was "an army of disc jockeys" who have "reduced perhaps our greatest area of talent— folk music—to the level of 'Hound Dog' and the tonal and vocal jitters of rock and roll."

An article called "The Battle over the Music You Hear," in the wide-circulation monthly *Redbook*, began with a pair of the sort of hectoring questions you might expect from an Anacin commercial, followed by an answer:

Have you, along with millions of other people, noticed a change in popular music in the past few years? Does much of what you hear today strike you as being raucous and hackneyed, with childish, often suggestive lyrics?

If so, you should know that the music on radio and television today does not always reflect the nation's tastes. You should know that you are not being given a full opportunity to hear the best popular music being written, that second-rate songs are being promoted at the expense of those with more imaginative music and lyrics.

The author, Booton Herndon, offered two explanations for this state of affairs. The first was the excessive power of BMI. The second was the widespread practice of "under-the-counter bribes, called 'payolas' in the trade."

The fizzling of the Schwartz suit led the songwriters to conclude that Congress might serve better than the courts as a venue in which to pursue their agenda. They found a willing ally in Representative Emanuel Celler of New York, chairman of the House Judiciary Committee, who in 1956 called subcommittee hearings into supposed monopolistic practices by the networks, one of the main areas of inquiry being their stake in BMI. Russell Sanjek, a longtime employee of BMI but generally a reliable historian, described Celler as "one of ASCAP's best friends" and reported that he "had chosen the broadcasting networks for his ticket to the U.S. Senate." The substantial portion of the hearings that dealt with music was essentially a debate on the merits of *Schwartz v. Broadcast Music*; every witness was closely aligned with one of the two parties.

Scheduled to testify on the first day of the hearings, held at the Foley Square Courthouse in New York, was Billy Rose, a fifty-seven-year-old showman who was notorious for having grabbed writing credit on such antique songs as "Me and My Shadow," "Without a Song," "It Happened in Monterey," and "It's Only a Paper Moon," despite not having contributed a note or word to them. The witness was not in the hearing room and Chairman Celler read into the record a telegram explaining that he was unable to attend because of an urgent meeting about an artist exchange with "Iron Curtain countries." Inspired to expand the metaphor, Rose charged in the telegram that the networks and BMI had set up "an electronic curtain . . . to keep the music of America's best songwriters away from the public." The play on "Iron Curtain" was fighting words in 1956, and when the witness finally showed up the next day, he backed away from the analogy; he also acknowledged that he had been out of the music business "since 1930, nine years before there was a BMI." However, that did not keep Rose from blaming that organization for "rock and roll and the other musical monstrosities which are muddying up the airwaves." He went on:

Not only are most of the BMI songs junk, but in many cases they are obscene junk pretty much on a level with dirty comic magazines. An ASCAP standard like "Love Me and the World Is Mine" has been replaced by "I Beeped When I Shoulda Bopped." A lovely song like Irving Berlin's "Always" has been shunted aside for "Bebopalula, I Love You." It's the current climate on radio and TV which makes Elvis Presley and his animal posturings possible.

When ASCAP's songwriters were permitted to be heard, Al Jolson, Nora Bayes, and Eddie Cantor were all big salesmen of songs. Today it is a set of untalented twitchers and twisters whose appeal is largely to the zootsuiter and the juvenile delinquent.

ASCAP staffers, members, and allies offered variations on Rose's theme. Jack Lawrence—author of "Play, Fiddle, Play" and "All or Nothing at All"—had no objection to the "electronic curtain" idea. What was happening on the radio, he said, resembled what the Communists did when "they managed to jam the airwaves and keep American words of hope away from the freedom-loving peoples behind the Iron Curtain. Now, the networks have adopted this technique of jamming the airwaves with exactly what they feel should and should not be heard."

A statement by Otto Harbach, a songwriter since 1902, a founding member and past president of ASCAP, and still a member of its board of directors, was read into the record:

A few years ago, when I first began to realize the enormity of the conspiracy launched against good music, it occurred to me that the greatest melodies of the past would never have had the chance to reach the public if they were written now instead of then. Would "Smoke Gets in Your Eyes" be allowed by the broadcasters to be heard instead of "Be-Bop-a-Lulu"? Could "Indian Love Call" penetrate the airwaves which are flooded with "Hound Dog"? It is to me a shocking thing that the power of broadcasters has been used to debase popular music.

No doubt some or many of the congressmen didn't like rock and roll any better than Rose or Harbach did. They certainly would have been receptive to testimony that offered a solution to the menaces of both communism *and* juvenile delinquency, and their mastery of the musical scene was not sophisticated. At one point Carl Haverlin of BMI, backing up Mitch Miller's telegram to the committee, noted that of Frank Sinatra's sixty-six recordings under Miller at Columbia, only six were BMI. He proceeded to name them, beginning with "Chattanoogie Shoe Shine Boy." Kenneth Keating, Republican of New York, interjected, "That was a good song."

Mr. Haverlin: Thank you.
Mr. Celler: I don't admire your taste.
Mr. Haverlin: "Good Night, Irene"—
Mr. Keating: That was good, too.
Mr. Haverlin: Thank you, sir.
Mr. Keating: Somebody said BMI was just this boogie-woogie stuff.
Mr. Haverlin: They attempted to say so, but I am not going to comment on their testimony on the record.
Mr. Keating: "Good Night, Irene" was a very good song.
Mr. Haverlin: Thank you, sir.

But the committee was not presented with support for any "conspiracy" or deliberate boycott of ASCAP material by the recording or broadcasting industries. Only a few pieces of substantive evidence were entered into the record. One was a quote from a 1944 article published in the *BMI Bulletin*, a publication sent to broadcasters. "This is a BMI number—meaning it is your own music," it advised. "Be careful of the other side of this disk, it is not a BMI tune."

Even in the unlikely event that the twelve-year-old article was part of a concerted campaign, the committee members weren't given any reason to think that the campaign worked. On the contrary, Haverlin testified that the music played on the radio in 1954 was 71.1 percent ASCAP and 17.6 percent BMI. (The remainder was in the public domain or licensed through other organizations.) ASCAP's advantage was even greater in television, with 78.6 percent compared with 10.4 percent for BMI. The radio networks, he went on, "use a smaller percentage of BMI-licensed music than the thousands of independent stations which are not BMI stockholders and are not affiliated with the networks." For their part, the ASCAP side offered evidence that BMI songs represented some three-quarters of the *Hit Parade*'s top-selling records. But these figures actually damaged ASCAP's case. That is, they demonstrated that consumers were buying the (mostly BMI) records they wanted to hear *despite* a comparative lack of airplay.

BMI's attorneys inserted into the record some fairly powerful testimony from the Schwartz lawsuit, which, they pointedly noted, had been given under oath (unlike congressional testimony). Richard F. Murray, the head of the ASCAP division "which counts performance of music broadcast over the air," gave even more striking numbers than Haverlin had, stating that approximately 85 percent of radio, "well over 95 percent" of television, and nearly 100 percent of motion picture music was ASCAP-licensed. As for the alleged preference for BMI music on the radio, Murray had this exchange with a BMI attorney:

Q. From your reading the program logs, was it your conclusion that
the broadcasters were discriminating against ASCAP music?

A: That, I couldn't deduce.

Q: That was not an inference you ever drew from your analysis of
the logs?

A: To tell you the truth, to this moment I never gave it a thought.

Stanley Adams, the president of ASCAP, said the same thing
during a pretrial examination, monosyllabically:

Q: Can you give us the call letters of any single station which
discriminated against ASCAP music?

A: No.

Q: Do you have any personal knowledge of your own about any acts
of any discrimination against ASCAP music?

A: I do not.

Once the testimony was complete, the subcommittee went against
its chairman and took no action, merely recommending that the Justice
Department undertake a thorough investigation of the music industry.
Variety reported that "despite an apparent attitude of prejudgment
and a sweeping subpoena power . . . the networks acquitted themselves
on virtually every score."

Two years later, almost precisely the same exercise was repeated,
this time in the United States Senate, where George Smathers, Democrat of Florida, had introduced a bill attempting to divorce broadcast
stations and networks from publishing music or making records. Oscar
Hammerstein kicked off the hearings of the Committee on Interstate

and Foreign Commerce, reading the same 1944 "Be careful of the other side of the disk" quote, and adding to the familiar arguments a new fillip. The current roster of popular songs may in fact be popular, he acknowledged, but after their moment in the sun they will disappear from the public consciousness without a trace. "What do you think is going to happen to rock 'n' roll songs," he asked, "and what has happened to the swing songs and the bebop songs and the corny guitar songs that have been played in the last years and have been put up on the top?"

His answer: "They die as soon as the plug stops."

Arthur Schwartz made a return appearance, reporting that his songs hadn't been recorded more often or gotten any more airplay in the two years since his last congressional testimony. Schwartz nearly smacked himself in the forehead at the irony of Mitch Miller's decrying rock and roll in his speech to the disk jockeys: "This is the man who was as instrumental as any single person in the recording industry for recording, promoting, encouraging this same brand of music."

The chairman of the music department at Brown University, Arlan Coolidge, described what he heard over the radio during a recent cross-country car trip: "Although in a general way I had been aware previously of the cheapening of the character of the music and lyrics going over the air, I was shocked by the perpetual blanket of banality encountered hour after hour."

Vance Packard, author of the recent bestseller *The Hidden Persuaders*, testified that rock and roll spoke to "the animal instinct in modern teenagers" with its "raw, savage tone" and "nonsensical" and "lewd" lyrics. He described rock and "hillbilly" as "the cheapest types of music," forced by the broadcasters on an unsuspecting public. As a result, he said, "our airways have been flooded in recent years with whining guitarists, musical riots put to a switchblade beat, ob-

scene lyrics about hugging, squeezing, and rocking all night long."
In response to a question from the chairman of the committee, John
Pastore, Democrat of Rhode Island, Packard testified that his investigations were subsidized by the Songwriters Protective Association—
an organization that was essentially ASCAP minus the publishers, and
was behind the Schwartz suit.

Also testifying was another journalist friendly to the SPA, Booton
Herndon, author of the *Redbook* article "The Battle over the Music
You Hear." "Senators present listened in chill silence," reported *Billboard*, as Herndon made "a gasper of a statement. Herndon termed
songwriters starry-eyed idealists, not interested in money, while the
'very tone of voice' of BMI spokesmen indicated to him that they
'looked on music only as a commodity.' Senators heard him out, waved
him out of the witness chair without question or comment."

The record absorbed letters and telegrams favoring the bill from
such worthies as George Jessel, Harry Ruby, both Groucho and Harpo
Marx, the widows of Sigmund Romberg and Gus Kahn, and Edward
Laska, who had written the lyrics to Jerome Kern's first hit, "How'd
You Like to Spoon with Me," in 1905.

But the overall case was even less effective in the Senate than it had
been two years earlier in the House. Pastore made his own skepticism
clear at the start: "I don't like rock and roll too much as a personal
taste, but there are a lot of people who do. And I don't think it is within
the province of Congress to tell people whether they should listen to
South Pacific, or listen to some rock and roll." Later, when an ASCAP
representative disparaged the current hit "Yakety Yak," Pastore countered philosophically, "My daughter bought it. What are you going to
do about it?"

The country music industry, aided if not actually created by BMI,
had by this time established in Nashville a center of songwriting, pub-

lishing, and recording. Tennessee's Democratic senator Albert Gore (father of the future vice president) read into the record a telegram from Governor Frank Clement stating that Packard's testimony was "a gratuitous insult to thousands of our fellow Tennesseans both in and out of the field of country music." Gore, an amateur country fiddler, added his own opinion that country music expressed the "hopes and aspirations" of the people of his state. "I would not like to see all country music branded intellectually cheap." This was more than Arthur Schwartz could take. "If you attack country music you attack southern womanhood, I see," he remarked to no one in particular.

Possibly the most effective witnesses were a series of country-and-western songwriters and performers, who, with thoughtfulness, dignity, and humor, described how ASCAP for years had presented them with a closed door, while BMI publishers had allowed their songs to be widely heard for the first time.

Gene Autry: "Well, I tried to get into ASCAP as far back as 1930, and could not get an audience, or could not even get in."

Pee Wee King: "I started writing my own material and collaborating with other writers in the 1930s. I, frankly, never even bothered to apply for an ASCAP membership. I did talk about the possibility to some ASCAP writers I know, such as Bobby Gregory and Bob Lamm, a young man on the record 'Near You.' They were so discouraging about the possibility of my getting into ASCAP that I never pursued it further."

The Honorable Jimmie Davis, former governor of Louisiana and the author of "You Are My Sunshine" and other songs: "I . . . found that the welcome mat at the ASCAP door had a way of disappearing for writers engaged in the country and western, folk music, and gospel music field." Davis finally got into ASCAP as a "nonparticipating" member, meaning that he received no payments from the society. "I never succeeded in collecting a single penny from ASCAP for the performance of my music even though it was being extensively played all over the country," he said. "ASCAP was interested in a limited group of writers and a limited kind of music."

The Smathers bill didn't get out of committee.

In December 1959, more than six years after *Schwartz v. Broadcast Music, Inc.* was filed, Federal District Judge Edward Weinfeld ruled in response to the defendants' motion for summary dismissal. He noted the 20,000 pages of testimony that had accumulated thus far, the 11,000 exhibits filling 55,000 pages, and observed, with palpable annoyance, that "the extensive, if not prolific, affidavits and briefs submitted in support of, and in opposition to, the motion, have strayed in a number of instances far and wide from the basic question." Nevertheless, he could cut through the haze enough to make some judgments. The law held that, in order to collect damages, a plaintiff must be directly injured. And, with respect to public performance rights—over the airwaves and in live performance—he found that the party directly hurt by any conspiracy would not be any individual songwriter but the organization that licensed a songwriter's works. "No matter how phrased," Weinfeld wrote of the suit, "it cannot obscure the fact that ASCAP, and not the individual composers, is the direct target of the alleged conspiracy. Any other conclusion flies in the face of reality." And therefore, "with respect to the nondramatic public performance rights, the plaintiffs are without standing to sue." So any losses related to radio airplay—the focus of the vast majority of testimony in the courts and congressional hearings—were suddenly off the table.

Weinfeld allowed the suit to proceed with respect to publishing and recording rights. However, the following March, Sylvester J. Ryan, chief judge of the U.S. District Court of New York, issued a ruling that was about as devastating to Schwartz and his colleagues as a ruling could be, short of dismissal. He limited the damages sought by the thirty-three plaintiffs to the financial losses they could prove they actually suffered as a result of the so-called conspiracy. In other words, in order to win the case, Ira Gershswin would have to prove that he could have earned more from recordings of, say, "I've Got a Crush on You" if the alleged conspiracy hadn't been in place—and show exactly how much more money he would have made! That would seem to be an impossible proposition. But the plaintiffs who were still alive persisted, and the suit dragged on.

In 1959, Nat King Cole was quoted in *Variety* as saying, "We've entered the era of the complete takeover and the payola . . . I know some of these disk jockeys and you can't tell me they like this stuff they're plugging." "Payola," sometimes preceded by the word "the" and sometimes called "payolas," had been recognized as a fact of Tin Pan Alley life basically since forever, though admittedly it had picked up with the postwar rise of the disk jockey and had become an accepted part of the way the legion of independent labels did business. *Billboard* noted in 1952, "The very general method of promoting r.&b. disks is by means of the deejay, and the payola has become standard operating procedure with a number of indies who regard this payment as advertising."

Now, with the Schwartz suit going nowhere and nothing happening in Congress, alleged payola to disk jockeys replaced BMI favoritism as the most popular scapegoat for the perceived decline of popular music. There was no question that some bribery existed in the industry, but it took place on all levels. The transparency of focusing on payments to deejays by small labels didn't escape Jack Gould of *The New York Times*, no rock-and-roll apologist. Gould wrote that the jocks were "relatively small fry when it comes to payoffs" and remarked that the allegations originated "with many of the country's foremost composers—the writers of Broadway and Hollywood hit tunes—who have been dismayed to witness the dominance of rock 'n' roll on the nation's airwaves." To prove that even intense exposure to a bad record couldn't force the public to buy it, four deejays in Norfolk, Virginia, played a song called "Pahalacaka" 320 times in one day and marched outside the station carrying a placard that read, "We want payola too." They made their point, but they were suspended, leaving the station with no one to man the turntables.

Little mentioned was the fact that no federal law existed against commercial bribery of the sort that payola represented. Some states had such statutes, but they had been prosecuted rarely, if at all. Nevertheless, the scandal, such as it was, struck a chord with the public and took on a life of its own. Several deejays in major cities resigned or were fired over payola, most notably Alan Freed, at the time the host of a rock-and-roll program on a New York television station. He was quoted as saying, "What they call payola in the disk-jockey business, they call lobbying in Washington." Dick Clark, whose *American Bandstand* ABC TV show was broadcast over the country from a studio in Philadelphia, agreed to divest himself of all publishing and recording interests and was allowed to stay on the air.

By the end of 1959, the Federal Trade Commission, the Federal Communications Commission, New York City district attorney Frank Hogan, and the House of Representatives Special Subcommittee on Legislative Oversight—which had recently concluded its widely publicized investigation of fixed television quiz shows—had all begun separate payola probes. The House subcommittee began hearings in February and heard from a parade of disk jockeys, most acknowledging some level of payola, rarely amounting to more than a few thousand dollars a year. The jocks frequently added that the payments did not influence their decisions on what records to play. Stan Richards, formerly with Boston's WILD, compared the money he got to "going to school and giving the teacher a better gift than the fellow at the next desk. It seems to be the American way of life." However, Norm Prescott, of WBZ in Boston, was asked by Representative John Bennett if he thought the "junk music, rock and roll stuff" would be played without payola. Prescott replied, "Never get on the air." The final witness was Dick Clark, who, despite evidence that *American Bandstand* consistently favored records in which Clark himself had an interest, consistently denied any ill intent, emerged without a scratch, and continued his fabulously successful career.

The bill Congress ultimately passed did not outlaw payola. Rather, it mandated that if deejays accepted any promotional "consideration," they had to inform the station owner or manager, and it had to be announced on the air.

Reading the testimony at the various congressional hearings, you would get the impression that no music other than rock-and-roll junk was being recorded or made. While it's true that the Big Beat had come to dominate the singles market and as a result the radio, a whole other area of popular music had been claimed by grown-ups.

Television became a significant force in music and much else in 1952, when more liberal FCC policies led to a tripling of the number of stations. Subsequently, every popular singer was a regular "guest" on variety programs, and many—Perry Como, Nat King Cole, and so on—became the "hosts" of their own shows. The TV musical repertoire was a mix of inoffensive current hits, tried-and-true standards, and forgettable special material. "Spectaculars," such as the NBC productions Carolyn Leigh worked on for Max Liebman, initially promised to be a market for high-quality original popular songs, but faded away after a few years of prominence in the middle of the decade. Only a handful of scores produced lasting songs. One was Sammy Cahn and Jimmy Van Heusen's for an adaptation of Thornton Wilder's *Our Town*, in which Frank Sinatra, as the Stage Manager, sang "Love and Marriage," a singsongy piece of conventional wisdom that wasn't up to the best of the writers' work but was a hit for Sinatra and Dinah Shore, as well as the template for the long-running Campbell's advertising campaign "Soup and Sandwich." Two years later, Rodgers and Hammerstein ventured into television with a score for *Cinderella* that included the soon-to-become standards "In My Own Little Corner" and "Do I Love You Because You're Beautiful?"

Development in recording technology had a more significant impact than television. In 1948, two new formats were introduced that had records spin at, respectively, 33⅓ and 45 revolutions per minute. Each had a corporate sponsor (CBS and Columbia Records for the 33⅓, NBC and RCA Victor for the 45), and for a while the two battled it out, but before long they amicably divided up the sonic territory and in so doing put the traditional 78 out of business, except for some children's records and other specialized uses. The 45 took the singles market, and 33⅓ became the format for long-playing records, or LPs. By 1955, seven years after they were introduced, long-playing albums accounted for half of all record revenues.

The dual formats deepened the gap between the kids' stuff on singles (rock and roll, novelty numbers, romantic fluff) and the more grown-up fare on LPs. And what constituted grown-up fare in the mid-to-late 1950s? From the beginning, there was a strong bond between this format and the Broadway stage. The *South Pacific* cast album was the best-selling LP of 1949, 1950, and 1951, and it was followed by records from other musicals, the most successful over the decade being *My Fair Lady*, *West Side Story*, and *The Sound of Music*.

LPs also proved a perfect format for multiple variations on what had traditionally been dubbed "light music," a kind of blend between the sweet big bands and classical symphonies. A pioneer of the genre was a Russian émigré named Andre Kostelanetz, who, with his sixty-five-piece orchestra, had presided over popular radio programs since the 1930s, and who started putting out records for Columbia in 1941. Also popular were onetime piano prodigy Morton Gould and the Canadian conductor Percy Faith, who had a radio show called *The Carnation Contented Hour* and became a trusted member of Mitch Miller's musical staff at Columbia in the fifties.

The stage was set for the arrival of the LP, which had not only a (self-described) long playing time but also the capacity for stereophonic sound and otherwise distinctly higher fidelity than the 78. That is, it allowed you to put on a record, go about your business (whatever your business was), and have appropriate music in the background for a half hour or so—and even longer than that after the invention of the record changer, which allowed the listener to program a stack of disks for a whole evening's entertainment. Paul Weston, the music director at Capitol Records (and former Tommy Dorsey arranger), was an influential figure in this narrative even before the invention of the LP. After the war, he told author Joseph Lanza, "the tunes got slower and slower. Jitterbugging went out, and my albums stepped into the gap." The first such album was 1945's *Music for Dreaming*, followed by *Music for Memories*, *Music for Romancing*, *Music for the Fireside*, and *Music for Reflection*. In 1950, *Coronet* magazine, coining a phrase, dubbed him "the Master of Mood Music." Weston, with his strong jazz credentials, was ambivalent about the designation. He commented that a "reliance on strings without the jazz feel I brought even to my ballads was the reason the term 'elevator music' came to symbolize most of the later mood music attempts."

Lanza is the foremost chronicler and appreciator of this multi-faceted genre, and in his book on it—unapologetically titled *Elevator Music*—he provides a useful catalog of its common properties: "Slower, more hypnotic time signatures; massed strings treated with echo-reverberation; background vocals that sounded more angelic (or, in some cases, demonic) than human; and often well-conceived theories about music's utilitarian function."

An impressive assortment of practitioners followed Weston. One of the most successful was the television comedian Jackie Gleason, who in 1952 attached his name to a Capitol album called *Music for Lovers Only*, featuring dozens of strings and a single trumpet, played by the former Glenn Miller sideman Bobby Hackett. It is unclear how much Gleason contributed to the arrangements or the recording sessions. According to his biographer William A. Henry III, his musical directions were along the lines of saying he wanted something "like the sound of pissing off a high bridge into a teacup." Gleason probably had more of a hand in the steamy cover art of the album (which would become as much of a hallmark of this genre as of mass-market paperbacks) and the general hubba-hubba air of the enterprise. "It's five a.m.," he reflected, "and you see her body outlined through her dress by the streetlight, and you get that 'Mmmmmm, I want to come' feeling."

Whoever was responsible in what measure, the formula worked. *Music for Lovers Only* sold 500,000 copies and kicked off a series of more than forty Gleason LPs through the decade, cumulatively selling more than 120 million copies. His best year was 1954, when he was responsible for four of the ten top-selling LPs.

Gould, Faith, Kostelanetz, and Mantovani (a native of Italy who at a young age dropped his first name, Annunzio, and whose Decca LPs showed a deep belief in the seemingly magical power of a great many strings) all had classical credentials. In contrast, the Massachusettsan

Ray Conniff was a big-band trombonist before and after World War II. Once the big-band era ended, he found himself working for $30 a week as a pick-and-shovel laborer. He decided to conduct a study of exactly what made a hit record. He later recalled: "There was always a pattern in the background. You could call it a ghost tune behind the apparent one. And there was another pattern, a pattern of tempo. All I can see is that it's a sort of pulsing. The average person likes to hear a pulsation, not obvious, but reassuringly there in the background." Conniff took this discovery to Mitch Miller, who took him on as an engineer and arranger. For Don Cherry's 1955 song "Band of Gold," he hired background singers for the date and—crucially—had them sing nonsense syllables, not words. "Band of Gold" went to number five on the charts. The next year, Columbia signed Conniff to create his first LP, 'S Wonderful, which he recorded with eighteen musicians and eight wordless singers. It was in the Cashbox top album chart for thirty-eight weeks. Through 1965, Conniff had twenty-eight more albums on the charts.

Virtuoso keyboard playing constituted a whole separate mood-music category, as seen in the triumphs of the semi-classical Liberace, the team of Ferrante and Teicher, and Roger Williams, who in 1955 released "Autumn Leaves," the only instrumental to reach number one on the Billboard charts. ("Autumn Leaves" was a French song to which Johnny Mercer had given English lyrics in 1947.) Pianists with serious jazz credentials, including George Shearing, Erroll Garner, Dick Hyman, and Peter Nero, made frequent and successful sorties into the mood-music world.

In 1947, an arranger and orchestra leader named Les Baxter released a 78-rpm album called Music out of the Moon, and thus inaugurated a subgenre that simulated the sounds of tropical jungles and distant planets. Baxter's most successful disciples were Arthur Lyman and Martin Denny, a California pianist who in the mid-fifties incorporated birdcalls and Latin rhythms to the music his combo played during their continuing gig at a Hawaii bar. In 1957, Denny put out an album called *Exotica*, which finally gave this genre its name. It reached the top of the *Billboard* charts in 1959 and stayed there for five weeks.

Clearly, mood music was multifaceted. Possibly the only two traits its various manifestations shared were a sense that it could be played in the background and an indifference to the value of songs.

As the 1950s drew to a close, most of the former big-band singers who had broken through as solo artists a decade before were having a tough time of it. Frank Sinatra and Tony Bennett made out the best, but other middle-aged male singers had little luck, especially on the singles charts. The cohort consisted of Bennett and Sinatra's Italian *paesani* Perry Como, Vic Damone, Julius La Rosa, Frankie Laine, Jerry Vale, Al Martino, and Dean Martin, as well as the variously ethnic Andy Williams (Norwegian), the young Jack Jones (the WASP son of the movie star Allan Jones), Steve Lawrence and Eddie Fisher (Jewish), and Sammy Davis Jr. (Jewish *and* black). These crooners' success came mainly via polished middle-of-the-road LPs composed of show tunes, movie themes, and the occasional rock-and-roll hit whose rough edges could be smoothed away.

The smoothest of them all, Nat King Cole, who had enjoyed such great success in the early fifties, managed only two top-ten records in the second half of the decade, both with rock overtones. "Send for Me" was a mildly propulsive twelve-bar blues, and "Looking Back," which *Billboard* termed a "rockaballad," had that emerging subgenre's char-

acteristic backing triplets. But, as the singer announced in a number
he was featuring in his nightclub act, he balked at being asked "to
throw away your senses and your self-control." Briefly put: "Mr. Cole
won't rock and roll."

Bearing some striking similarities to Cole was a new young singer,
Johnny Mathis, whom George Avakian, the head of popular albums
at Columbia and the label's in-house jazz specialist, had discovered
in 1955. Upon hearing Mathis in a club in his native San Francisco,
Avakian wired back to the home office: "Have found phenomenal
19 year old boy who could go all the way. Send blank contracts." On
Mathis's debut album for the label, Avakian presented him as a sort of
male Sarah Vaughan, working with such jazz stalwarts as John Lewis
and Gil Evans on standards like "Prelude to a Kiss" and "It Might
as Well Be Spring." When the album sold poorly, Mathis was put in
Mitch Miller's stable. Their first collaboration was a contemporary
ballad, "Wonderful! Wonderful!," with one of Ray Conniff's trademark string- and voice-heavy arrangements. It made the charts, and
the Mathis–Miller team followed it up with two more ballads (by Brill
Building stalwarts Al Stillman and Robert Allen), two more Conniff
charts, and a production that emphasized the feathery, trembling quality of the young vocalist's tenor, giving him a bit of the sound of a
one-man doo-wop group. The first single, "It's Not for Me to Say,"
went to number five and the second, "Chances Are," to the top spot. In
1958, Columbia released an LP called *Johnny's Greatest Hits*, despite the fact that Mathis had not really been recording long enough to
have an album's worth of hits. It was the first use of that now familiar
phrase for an album title, and it was number one on the *Cashbox* charts
for sixteen weeks.

Young women made up the bulk of the single-buying market, and even singers older than Mathis could occasionally pass muster as heart-throbs. The thrushes—the onetime girl singers—did not have that advantage. Peggy Lee, Margaret Whiting, Doris Day, Jo Stafford, and Rosemary Clooney among them charted only two records post-1956, Day's "Everybody Loves a Lover" and Lee's "Fever." Columbia and Mitch Miller dropped Clooney in 1958. The following summer she was playing her hometown Kentucky State Fair and was taken aback to read the headline FABIAN, NEW TO MUSIC, HELPS STIR INTEREST IN FAIR'S CLOONEY SHOW. (The reference was to a good-looking Philadelphia youth born Fabiano Forte, a wholly fabricated teen idol, who was to open for Clooney.) At that moment, Clooney later said, she realized "the rock wave was cresting, about to break."

The ever-prescient Arnold Shaw summed the situation up in an article for *Harper's* in May 1959: "What we have been witnessing is the demise of an entire generation of artists, specifically those who appealed to public taste from the end of World War II until 1954."

Livingston and Evans had written for those artists, of course, but may have felt that their Hollywood sinecure protected them from the troubling changes in popular music. It didn't. "Tammy," in 1958, was the last significant song of theirs to feature a Livingston melody. In notes prepared for an "And Then I Wrote" act they performed on cruise ships a couple of decades later, the boys described experiencing, in the years that followed, a change in the rules of their familiar game.

Ray: The so-called background composers—the men who write the dramatic music to underscore a scene—suddenly insisted on writing all the music in their pictures, including the music for all the songs. And they had enough clout to make this stick. Suddenly there was no more work for songwriters.

Jay: This put the great music writers like Harry Warren, Sammy Fain, Jimmy McHugh, Jimmy Van Heusen, etc. permanently out of business.

Ray: But these background composers still needed words to go with their melodies, and in order to survive, we began to write words for melodies that we hadn't written.

The team combined to produce lyrics for movie themes by such composers as Max Steiner, Percy Faith, Neal Hefti, and David Rose. Their most fruitful collaboration was with Henry Mancini, with whom they wrote "In the Arms of Love" (the theme from *What Did You Do in the War, Daddy?*), "Wait Until Dark," and, in 1964, their last Oscar-nominated song, "Dear Heart." They also provided lyrics for several of Mancini's jazz instrumentals from the television series *Peter Gunn*.

Johnny Mercer walked a similar path in Hollywood in these years, with more successful results. With Mancini, he wrote "Moon River," the haunting theme from *Breakfast at Tiffany's*, which won the 1961 Academy Award for Best Original Song and the Grammy Award for Song of the Year; "Days of Wine and Roses," another brilliant composition, which won the Oscar, Mercer's fourth, the following year; and, in 1963, the theme for *Charade*. For *The Americanization of Emily*, Johnny Mandel and Mercer wrote another resonant theme, "Emily."

The situation in Hollywood was a bit more complicated than Ray's account would suggest. In that period, according to the film-music historian Jon Burlingame, "the movie business, and by extension the movie-music business, was in the midst of massive change. Yes, younger composers were coming in and gradually replacing the old guard. Not all of them were great tunesmiths—but the best of them were, just as the older crowd had been. Henry Mancini, John Barry, Lalo Schifrin, Quincy Jones, Johnny Mandel, Burt Bacharach and others were great songwriters as well as great film composers. In addition, studio music departments were considered less important and directors were making their own choices of composer rather than a music-department head making it for them, as had once been the case. And if the composer could write a song that could double as the theme for a movie (as Mancini and others did), why not?"

Whatever the precise sequence of the changes, their results were unambiguous: in the 1960s, Hollywood songwriting pickings got slimmer and slimmer. The convention of the title song barely persisted, mainly because of the potential promotional opportunity of a placement on an Andy Williams or Johnny Mathis LP or, better yet, a Best Original Song Oscar. That prospect lured Norman Gimbel to L.A., where he found that the chance to work with "legitimate musicians" was a booster shot for his career. He teamed up with the Juilliard-trained Charles Fox and other composers on dozens of theme songs for films and television series. He was nominated for three Academy Awards in a five-year period, finally winning in 1980 for the theme from *Norma Rae*, "It Goes Like It Goes," written with David Shire. But by 1967, when Gimbel arrived in Hollywood, title songs had become a vestigial convention, with very little creative juice. Even the most memorable of the late-1960s themes, like "The Windmills of Your Mind" (music by Michel Legrand; lyrics by Alan Bergman and Marilyn Bergman) or "Jean" (music and lyrics by Rod McKuen), had nothing to do with the movies they were featured in (*The Thomas Crown Affair* and *The Prime of Miss Jean Brodie*—or was it the other way around?) and seemed like curious relics from another era.

Meanwhile, the movie musical kept dwindling, as it had for nearly two decades. In 1968, Julie Andrews starred in a big-budget Gertrude Lawrence biopic called *Star!* The film, which combined period songs with a title tune by Van Heusen and Cahn, ran a mind-numbing 175 minutes and was widely seen as having a devastating effect on both Andrews's career and the movie-musical genre.

In the 1960s, only the Walt Disney studio had continued success with musicals, of both the animated and the live-action variety, most of them scored by Richard M. and Robert B. Sherman. Their father, Al, was a Tin Pan Alley pro who had gone out to Hollywood in the very early days and written such perennials as "You've Gotta Be a Football Hero (to Get Along with the Beautiful Girls)" and the Depression-era anthem "Now's the Time to Fall in Love." (Why? Because "Potatoes are cheaper / Tomatoes are cheaper.") Richard and Robert had started out in the late fifties writing mindless rock-and-roll numbers for a Los Angeles BMI-affiliated publisher. One of these songs, "Tall Paul," was covered in 1959 by Annette Funicello, a Disney Mouseketeer on the *Mickey Mouse Club* television program, and eventually earned the brothers a contract with Disney as staff writers. Among the many films they scored was *Mary Poppins*, whose "Chim Chim Cher-ee" beat out "Dear Heart" for the 1964 Best Original Song Oscar. They also wrote "It's a Small World," which is continuously heard during the "It's a Small World" boat rides at Disney theme parks around the world, and has been put forth as the most frequently played song in history.

With Hollywood work ever harder to come by, Livingston and Evans found other markets. *Oh Captain!*, a Broadway musical starring Tony Randall and based on the Alec Guinness film *The Captain's Paradise*, got respectful reviews and ran for 192 performances in 1958. Three years later, another musical, *Let It Ride*, based on the 1930s comedy *Three Men on a Horse*, by Ray's old acquaintance George Abbott, closed after a couple of months. At about the same time, they produced the two Livingston–Evans songs that are still being heard somewhere every day: the themes for the television series *Mister Ed* (it's Jay who sings, "A horse is a horse . . .") and *Bonanza*. (Ray's lyrics—starting "We chased Lady Luck, 'til we finally struck Bonanza / With a gun and a rope and a hat full of hope, planted a family tree"—didn't make it onto the air.)

At the dawn of the new decade of the 1960s, those who wished rock and roll would go back to where it came from found some reasons to be hopeful. Many of the major players had abruptly left the metaphorical building. Elvis himself certainly had: as of 1958, he was in the Army for a two-year stint. Little Richard found God and gave up secular music. Jerry Lee Lewis and Chuck Berry both got caught up in scandals that took them away from performing and recording. In February 1959, Buddy Holly, Ritchie Valens, and another rocker died in a plane crash. (A decade later, folksinger Don McLean's "American Pie" would describe this as "the day the music died.") Dick Clark emerged from the payola hearings more powerful than ever, while Alan Freed found himself without a job or a platform. This reversal of fortune was reflected in the output of performers like Connie Francis, Brenda Lee, Paul Anka, Frankie Avalon, the Everly Brothers, the Four Seasons, Ricky Nelson, and the three Bobbys—Rydell, Vinton, and Vee. Their sound was palpably sweeter than the first rock-and-roll wave's transgressive Big Beat.

By 1960, albums had surpassed singles in overall sales and accounted for about three-quarters of revenues in the industry. Though Mitch Miller and Columbia were tanking on the singles charts, the label had over the decade developed a successful five-pronged approach to LPs: classical, jazz, country and western, original-cast recordings of

Broadway musicals, and easy-listening pop concoctions, perpetrated by singers like Mathis and Williams and orchestras like Percy Faith's and Ray Conniff's. In the wake of the payola investigations and revelations, these tracks got airplay on some radio stations that were changing their formats from rock and roll to softer sounds. That trend inspired Miller to look ahead to a golden age of "good" disk jockeys. "Instead of fearing payola and being burdened by the rock 'n' roll drivel," he proclaimed, "they are truly more program minded." *Variety*, getting with the wishful-thinking program, ran an article with the headline MUSIC BIZ'S CLASSY COMEBACK, reporting that "the wheel" was "starting to turn in favor of the pro songwriter" and record companies were "in full flight from the rock, the roll, the big beat and the teen tunes." Another great technological hope arrived in the form of the FM radio band. A New York broadcast executive predicted in 1961 that FM would "knock rock 'n' roll out of the musical box" by featuring "good pops, show scores, and long-hair music."

Potentially heartening as well was a flock of crew-cut, chinos-clad young men and long-haired, fresh-faced young women wielding guitars and banjos and singing various kinds of authentic and ersatz folk songs. They were the cleaned-up, apolitical progeny of Lead Belly, the Weavers, and Harry Belafonte, a Harlem native of West Indian descent whose calypso songs took the charts and the country by storm in 1957. The most successful group was the Kingston Trio, out of the Bay Area in California, who took their name from the town mentioned in Belafonte's "Jamaica Farewell," made it to number one late in 1958 with "Tom Dooley," and in 1961 recorded "It Was a Very Good Year," a sort of new-old song composed by Ervin Drake, as opportunistic as ever. When Frank Sinatra heard the cut, he determined to record the song himself. His 1965 version won a Grammy Award for Best Vocal Performance, Male, and was, along with "I Believe," one of the two big hits of Drake's career.

Could these wholesome lads be the next Elvises and Jerry Lees? Before that question could be answered, a slightly scruffier type, a Woody Guthrie acolyte from Minnesota who called himself Bob Dylan, signed with Columbia. The year was 1961. Significantly, Dylan inked his pact not in Mitch Miller's office but in John Hammond's, he of the famously fine-tuned ears. (The previous year, Hammond brought on an eighteen-year-old singer named Aretha Franklin.) A subsequent Columbia act, Loudon Wainwright III, would address Dylan in a song called "Talkin' New Bob Dylan Blues." "You were hipper," he declared, "than Mitch Miller and Johnny Mathis, put together."

In 1962, although he was already deeply involved in the *Sing Along with Mitch* albums and television show, the Beard was still active enough at the label to go to the Newport Folk Festival to check out the talent. The sensation of that year's fest was a young singer and Dylan associate named Joan Baez. "Her clear-lighted voice poured over the 13,000 people collected there and chilled them with surprise," reported *Time* in an article titled "Sibyl with Guitar." "The record company leg-and-fang men closed in. 'Would you like to meet Mitch, baby?' said a representative of Columbia Records, dropping the magic name of Mitch Miller, who is Columbia's top pop artists-and-repertory man when he isn't waving to his mother on TV.

"'Who's Mitch?' said Joan."

Informed, Baez was not impressed. "The girl did not want to be exploited, squeezed and stuffed with cash," wrote *Time*'s anonymous correspondent. Baez signed with Vanguard.

Within a couple of years the Folk Revival came down to earth. Striped-shirts acts like the Kingston Trio and the Limelighters were nudged to the margins, and it turned out that Baez, Dylan—and the Everly Brothers, too, for that matter—were all part of a rock-and-roll fifth column. Whatever sweetness they initially may have displayed was an illusion. Beyond folk, all kinds of harder sounds, most of them based in the electric guitar, were burbling under the surface, ready to come forth. The music historian Albin Zak sees 1963 as the tipping point, with the "greatest ever preponderance of rock and roll records." The year saw thirteen Top 40 hits by the Beach Boys and other Southern California surfer/hot-rod acts, and fifteen from Berry Gordy's Motown Records, near the beginning of its amazing ascent.

Then Beatlemania conquered the cosmos. The band from Liverpool appeared on Ed Sullivan's Sunday night TV show in February 1964, and from that point through May, "I Want to Hold Your Hand," "She Loves You," and "Can't Buy Me Love" occupied the top spot on the charts, successively. Before the end of the year, the Beatles had three more chart-toppers. The 45-rpm records put out by the band were familiar-looking, to be sure. They were black and round, and bore the traditional label stating the name of the song and the songwriters: "Lennon-McCartney." That itself was an interesting twist, out of Jimmy Rodgers and Hank Williams (or Chuck Berry and Buddy Holly), the idea that the people singing the song were the same ones who had written it. But that nicety was lost on the older cleffers and singers. The only sounds their ears could make out were electric guitars, pounding drums, and girls' screams. After the Beatles, the deluge. The charts were suddenly filled, as Tony Bennett put it, with "bands called the Byrds and Paul Revere and the Raiders." Bennett concluded: "I thought the world was losing its mind."

. . .

I t was a truism among the older songwriters that with popular music in the thrall of long-haired rockers and Hollywood changed beyond recognition, the only place in which good work could any longer be done was the musical stage. The truism was true, as far as it went. In 1956 alone, Jule Styne, Frank Loesser, and Leonard Bernstein all had ambitious shows open on Broadway—respectively, *Bells Are Ringing*, *The Most Happy Fella*, and *Candide*. The first two were commercial successes; the last, a succès d'estime. A smash on every level that year was a creation of Alan Jay Lerner and Frederick Loewe, little heard from since *Brigadoon* a decade earlier; the show was *My Fair Lady*, which vies with *Guys and Dolls* as the greatest American musical of all time and which became a national phenomenon. The show ran for five years, and the original-cast album, in the new long-playing format featuring Al Hirschfeld's marionette-themed cover, was an unprecedented success, selling a total of 13 million copies and holding a place of pride in every middle-class American home for a decade. Opening the next year was Meredith Willson's *The Music Man*—an ingenious slice of Americana—and *West Side Story*, Bernstein and Stephen Sondheim's groundbreaking reworking of *Romeo and Juliet* on the streets of Manhattan.

The ambitiousness and frequent brilliance of these shows cut two ways. The songs were not designed to be independent entities, instead serving story, theme, script, and character. The scores leaned less toward the jazz part of the American Songbook tradition and more toward operetta (and even, in the hands of Loesser, Bernstein, and later Sondheim, opera). The shows were major productions, in all senses of the phrase; getting financing, script, score, crew, cast, and production together could take years. The upshot was that much less music hap-

In the early 1950s, pop songs drifted away from the traditional jazz foundation into unexpected new directions. In his 1951 smash hit "Cry," Johnnie Ray displayed the sort of raw emotion that had always remained well below the surface.

The childlike ditty "The Doggie in the Window" sold two million copies for Patti Page in 1953—and engendered no small number of gag publicity shots.

In the early 1950s, Frank Sinatra's recordings—overseen by Columbia Records artist and repertoire chief Mitch Miller, here meeting the singer at LaGuardia Airport in 1952—barely dented the charts.

Tin Pan Alley song pluggers waiting for an audience with Miller, who chose the material for every Columbia popular release and was the first music "producer" in the modern sense.

Old-line songwriters, mystified by the new sounds coming over the airwaves, argued in the courts and before Congress that record companies and radio networks were conspiring against them. Rallying to the cause were (left to right, front row) Steve Allen, Oscar Hammerstein II, Richard Adler, Dorothy Fields, Otto Harbach, Leo Shull, and (back row) Arthur Schwartz, Bob Merrill, Harold Rome, and Stanley Adams.

The Brill Building, at 1619 Broadway, was the hub of
Tin Pan Alley in mid-twentieth-century America.

Frank Loesser—here rehearsing with Marlon Brando, star of the film version of Loesser's *Guys and Dolls*—was a mentor to, role model for, and publisher of many young songwriters in the fifties.

Lyricist Carolyn Leigh (shown with the tools of her trade) and the supremely versatile Ervin Drake tried to negotiate the often difficult new rules of the songwriting game.

Tony Bennett made a deal with Mitch Miller: for every pop single he recorded, he got to lay down a jazz-style track for release on a Columbia LP.

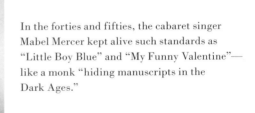

In the forties and fifties, the cabaret singer Mabel Mercer kept alive such standards as "Little Boy Blue" and "My Funny Valentine"— like a monk "hiding manuscripts in the Dark Ages."

Trumpeter Miles Davis made his name with penetrating interpretations of ballads from the American Songbook.

Producer Norman Granz revitalized Ella Fitzgerald's career—and the tradition of classic American popular song—with a series of "Songbook" albums devoted to the great composers.

Arranger Nelson Riddle met Frank Sinatra in a Capitol recording studio in 1953. Magic ensued.

The rock-and-roll explosion created a huge demand for songs, and unprecedented opportunities for young songwriters. The publisher Aldon Music had several married "cleffing" teams on staff, including Gerry Goffin and Carole King, and Barry Mann and Cynthia Weil. Clockwise, King (in hat), Weil, Mann, and Goffin.

The team of Burt Bacharach (at the piano) and Hal David had knocked around the Brill Building for years. But when they teamed up with singer Dionne Warwick in 1962, their music started to soar.

pened on Broadway. In the twenties, 432 musicals opened there; in the thirties, 220; in the forties, 147; in the fifties, 119. The trend showed no sign of reversing and produced an ecology where the creators of musicals were an ever more selective group.

At the very top of the food chain were Irving Berlin, Cole Porter, Harold Arlen, and Rodgers and Hammerstein, who had started this trend with *Oklahoma!* Berlin had a relatively successful musical in 1950, when he was sixty-two, with *Call Me Madam.* Two years later, for the movie *White Christmas*, he wrote his last great song, with the trademark Berlin mix of simplicity and honest emotion: "Count Your Blessings (Instead of Sheep)." But then his production halted until 1962, when *Mr. President* appeared on Broadway. It was a failure and marked the end of Berlin's songwriting life. Porter, three years younger than Berlin, persisted with remarkable discipline, all the more noteworthy since a riding accident he had suffered in the thirties left him increasingly depressed and in pain. In 1956 he wrote the score for *Silk Stockings*, a Broadway musical based on the Garbo film *Ninotchka.* The show was moderately successful, but the still song-oriented craftsman found the new atmosphere difficult. "In today's musical," he observed with a note of frustration, "everything has to be married to something else." Porter's remaining efforts were in other media. For the 1957 film *High Society*, a musical adaptation of the Philip Barry play *The Philadelphia Story*, he wrote several new songs. One of them, "True Love," a duet by stars Bing Crosby and Grace Kelly, reached number three on the charts and inspired Porter's old publisher and supporter, Max Dreyfus, to write him a letter. In his sixty-year career in the business, Dreyfus wrote, "nothing has given me more personal pleasure and gratification than the extraordinary success of your 'True Love.' It is truly a simple, beautiful, tasteful composition worthy of a Franz Schubert." Porter had one more credit before his death, in 1964:

a 1958 production of *Aladdin*, the last big television spectacular, for which he wrote his final song, "Wouldn't It Be Fun?"

Arlen, born in 1905, was the youngest of this group. He concentrated on Broadway during the fifties, first with the Haiti-set *House of Flowers*, a 1954 collaboration with Truman Capote. Wilfrid Sheed, a friend of Arlen's in later years, wrote that *House of Flowers* was "the last musical he had really enjoyed and was still proud of." The production ran for less than half a year and, Sheed wrote, "in a small way, this broke Harold's heart." But Arlen persisted, with another Caribbean-set show in 1957, *Jamaica*, a moderate success, and a 1959 collaboration with Johnny Mercer, *Saratoga*, an outright flop. Arlen was flown out to the West Coast in 1961 to write songs for an animated movie called *Gay Purr-ee*, but felt the assignment was an exception that proved the Hollywood rule. "At the moment, there's nothing to be done for the songwriter here," he told *The New York Times*. "And as for records, they're turned out like waffles." In 1965, Arlen's sixtieth birthday was celebrated by a special edition of *The Bell Telephone Hour* on television and an all-star tribute at New York's recently opened home of classical music, Lincoln Center. Interviewed again by the *Times*, he was again downbeat. "In the past four years, I've written six or seven songs," he said. "But it does not mean anything. They don't get the needed hearing."

The kings of Broadway, Rodgers and Hammerstein, followed two uncharacteristic mid-fifties failures (*Pipe Dream* and *Me and Juliet*) with a 1958 hit, *Flower Drum Song*, and an even bigger one the following year, *The Sound of Music*. Hammerstein died in 1960, while that Mary Martin production was in the first year of its run. One might expect that Rodgers, fifty-eight at the time, would step away from the fray. He certainly had no material needs. Each of his two collaborations— the first with Lorenz Hart, the second with Hammerstein—had produced more great music than any other songwriter's entire output, with the possible exception of Porter and Berlin. But Rodgers was nowhere near ready to call it a day. He wrote both music and lyrics for a 1962 show called *No Strings*, winning the Tony Award for Best Score for a Musical; in 1965, he collaborated with Sondheim on *Do I Hear a Waltz?*

The early sixties were the Indian summer of the post-*Oklahoma!* Broadway musical. You could still hear Rodgers, and Styne, and Frank Loesser, whose 1961 satire, *How to Succeed in Business Without Really Trying*, won the Pulitzer Prize in Drama. Meanwhile, the apprentices of the fifties were reaching their maturity and pairing up with the right partners. Sheldon Harnick and Jerry Bock had their own Pulitzer-winning show with *Fiorello!*, and Carolyn Leigh joined forces with composer Cy Coleman for the Lucille Ball vehicle *Wildcat*, and later the Sid Caesar vehicle *Little Me*.

As he pursued his Broadway dreams, Charles Strouse had taken a job as Frank Loesser's assistant. "I played for Frank because he couldn't play piano," Strouse said. "He used to call me his little colored boy"—a reference to the musical genius whom Irving Berlin, according to legend, kept behind closed doors. "We used to sit up till 2 or 3 in the morning at the piano and he would talk about his life and his feelings about himself," Strouse said. "He always felt that his mother favored his brother [Arthur, a "serious" composer and musician]. He used to sit there saying, 'I'm shit,' and here I am this young kid, who *was* shit, saying, 'Frank, you're wonderful.'"

Strouse, with his classical background, had never been much of a Brill Building guy. "I used to go around with my mother sometimes when I was very young," he said. "We'd wait in the publishers' offices and no one would see me. It was humiliating." But he and lyricist Fred Tobias wrote a number-seven song in 1958 for the Poni-Tails, "Born Too Late," a ballad in the four-chord "fifties progression" that had already become a cliché. Drawing on that experience, he hooked up with lyricist Lee Adams and librettist Michael Stewart—both of them friends and collaborators since Green Mansions days—and created a show about a creative soul, stuck writing moronic rock-and-roll songs like "Ugga Bugga Boo," who falls deep into debt and needs to produce one more hit for an Elvis stand-in named Conrad Birdie. The score included a couple of first-rate songs from Green Mansions—"A Lotta Livin' to Do" and "Put On a Happy Face"—and an ersatz rock-and-roller that wore the fifties progression on its sleeve, "One Last Kiss." Loesser liked the score, Strouse recalls, and offered to have his name put on it—in exchange for "a cut of the action. But our producer couldn't afford that." *Bye Bye Birdie* opened on Broadway in April 1960 and ran for almost two years.

Jerry Herman, who had auditioned for Loesser as a teenager, had his Broadway debut in 1961 as composer and lyricist for a show about the early days of Israel, *Milk and Honey*. (The show would be remembered not as a high artistic moment of musical theater but rather as an epochal success among suburban theater groups.) Sondheim had his first music-and-lyrics credit the following year with *A Funny Thing Happened on the Way to the Forum*. Even the much-maligned Bob Merrill, composer of "Mambo Italiano" and "The Doggie in the Window" and famous for his xylophone, finally achieved some Broadway respect with shows like *Take Me Along* and *Carnival!*

The supernova year, probably, was 1964. Merrill wrote the lyrics to Styne's music for *Funny Girl*, which made Barbra Streisand a star. Bock and Harnick's *Fiddler on the Roof* not only bested *Milk and Honey* in theater group sales but was a masterpiece to boot. Herman's *Hello, Dolly!* was another smash hit, and Louis Armstrong's rendition of the title song knocked the Beatles off the top spot on the *Billboard* charts. But that exclamation point, with its air of trying too hard, perhaps signaled the beginning of the tradition's end. The same creators would continue to put out new shows for some time, but the creative returns were visibly diminishing.

In September 1967, a production called *Hair: The American Tribal Love-Rock Musical* opened off-Broadway at Joseph Papp's Public Theater. It created a sensation (not least because of its first-act closing number, in which the cast stood on stage in the nude) and began a long Broadway run the following spring. Richard Rodgers was presumably bemused by *Hair*, but certainly not enough to stop work on the new musical he was preparing, a retelling of the story of Noah, to be called *Two by Two* and to star Danny Kaye. In the summer of 1968, Rodgers happened to pay a visit to the offices of Columbia Records, which was financing the production. Not long before, Clive Davis, a young Brooklyn native and Harvard Law School graduate, had been appointed head of the label. The reason for Davis's appointment was simple. It had become clear that Columbia's five-headed LP strategy—classical, jazz, country, original-cast recordings, and middle-of-the-road pop—was no longer viable. Rock and roll—now called, simply, "rock"—had conquered the album world, and Columbia finally had to get with the program or die. As one of his first big coups, Davis had just signed to the label a young white blues shouter named Janis Joplin and her band, Big Brother and the Holding Company.

Spotting Richard Rodgers in the hallway that day in 1968, Davis asked if he would mind listening to a Joplin track or two. He recalled in his autobiography, modestly titled *Clive*, that he wanted Rodgers "to hear this new music, to react to it. Perhaps he could make some of its magic known to Broadway. . . . I put on 'Piece of My Heart,'" one of Joplin's most stirring tracks. "After a minute and a half, he motioned me to stop. He said that he just didn't 'understand' it."

After a few minutes, Davis writes, Rodgers "became upset. He shrugged his shoulders and his left arm flailed as he talked. 'If this means I have to change my writing,' he said, 'or that the only way to write a Broadway musical is to write rock songs, then my career is over.'"

Three years later, in 1971, eighteen years after *Schwartz v. BMI* had been filed, a federal judge dismissed the suit, with prejudice. No one took notice, but it was the last bit of punctuation in the last chapter of the Great American Songbook.

VIII

Fly Me to the Moon
1939–1965

The existence of Janis Joplin's "Piece of My Heart" did not in fact signal the end of Richard Rodgers's career. *Two by Two* opened in 1970 and ran for ten months—decent for most people, but, by Rodgers and Hammerstein standards, a failure. In his later years Rodgers survived cancer of the jaw, a heart attack, and a laryngectomy, but did not put down his pen. In 1976 he teamed with Sheldon Harnick for a musical about Henry VIII called *Rex*, which barely stayed open a month; in 1979, working with Martin Charnin, he wrote the score for an adaptation of *I Remember Mama*. Despite the presence of film star Liv Ullmann in the cast, it had a short run, too. It had been a full sixty years since Rodgers and Larry Hart's first song on Broadway, "Any Old Place with You." Rodgers died soon after *Mama* closed, but so monumental was the force of his will, there's no doubt that had he lived on, he would have written even more musicals.

But the world he helped create and represented for so many years was gone and had been for some time. Interviewed by Max Wilk in

1971 and 1972 for his book *They're Playing Our Song*, Rodgers's surviving peers were uniformly retired (willingly or not) and uniformly gloomy about the music they heard around them.

Ira Gershwin: "When you have this influx of country music and that sort of thing, I'm just not interested. Today it's all protesters. Kids protesting against parents, and so forth. And they make a fortune, these protesters. My God, the money they can make!"

Harold Arlen: "I don't know. You can't tell any more. Nobody wants melody. The kids are ignoring it so completely. This is such a percussive era, you know?"

Leo Robin, the lyricist of "Thanks for the Memory," "Easy Living," and the musical *Gentlemen Prefer Blondes*: "I don't think the kids are writing for anyone except themselves. They don't really want to reach anyone else. It's as if they're saying, 'This is a music *for us*. This is our music.'"

The cleffers' gloom was sincere, legitimate, and justifiable. But all was not lost. Even as their professional world had come to an end over the preceding decades, a counternarrative was taking place, not always easy to discern, but present nonetheless. It was a story about the resilience of the standards, and of what they represented. This is no counterfactual history; there is no escaping Elvis Presley, the Beatles, and their aftermath. But certain events that took place in the quarter century before the arrival of the Fab Four led to the reinforcement and permanent establishment of the Great American Songbook.

The rock-and-rollers themselves actually were a part of this story. Fats Domino, a black piano player from New Orleans, had successive hits in 1956 with "Blueberry Hill" (a big-band number from 1940), "When My Dreamboat Comes Home" (1937), and "My Blue Heaven" (1927). In the years that followed, doo-wop groups, taking a cue from Domino, repeatedly drew from the Tin Pan Alley well. Some examples:

- The Marcels: "Blue Moon" (1934), "Summertime" (1935), "You Are My Sunshine" (1939), "Heartaches" (1931), "My Melancholy Baby" (1912).

- The Platters: "Red Sails in the Sunset" (1935), "If I Didn't Care" (written by Jack Lawrence in 1939 and an Ink Spots hit), "Twilight Time" (1944), "Smoke Gets in Your Eyes" (1933), and Livingston and Evans's first big hit from 1947, "To Each His Own."

- Dion and the Belmonts: "In the Still of the Night" (1937), "When You Wish Upon a Star" (from Disney's 1940 *Pinocchio*), "Where or When" (1937).

The Beatles famously absorbed and transformed every conceivable musical influence, and the utility and potency of Tin Pan Alley standards was not lost on them. Among the staples of shows in their formative Liverpool and Hamburg years, besides Meredith Willson's "Till There Was You," were "The Sheik of Araby," "Ain't She Sweet," "Moonlight Bay," and "September in the Rain."

All that was a bit of a sideshow, however. The doo-woppers were in desperate need of songs to sing, and this immense body of work was there for the taking. In taking it, the groups and their producers usually leapfrogged the more melodically and harmonically complex works of the American Songbook's later period, landing on simpler fare, chestnuts that were well suited to their *lentissimo* harmonizing approach. It was material, not much more. The fact that the Marcels had a hit with "Blue Moon" didn't lead any of their listeners to explore Rodgers and Hart's other works.

But those works were indeed being explored. The first citation given by the *Oxford English Dictionary* for "standard," in the relevant sense, is from a 1937 article called "The Slang of Jazz" in the journal *American Speech*: "*Standard*, a number whose popularity has withstood the test of time." Just two years after that, the Oklahoma-born female singer Lee Wiley recorded a series of record albums devoted to selected works of Gershwin, Porter, and Rodgers and Hart. These records may have been the first blip on the public's consciousness that there was such a *thing* as a standard. Admittedly, this was a small slice of the public, as Wiley's disks, produced and released under the auspices of the Liberty Music Shop in Manhattan, were heard only by a select few. In time, though, this idea of an evolving canon of the best American popular songs would prove to have an inescapable logic and power. It grew and persisted even as the annual output of first-rank songs diminished, and especially bore fruit in the careers of jazz-oriented vocalists, such as Wiley, who could interpret both the music and the lyrics of these great compositions. In the later thirties, Billie Holiday, another of John Hammond's finds, recorded exquisitely swinging versions of standard songs for the Brunswick label. These and subsequent recordings, in which Holiday teamed with such jazz artists as Teddy Wilson, Lester Young, Ben Webster, and Johnny Hodges, not only bolstered the standards but did much to establish and popularize the notion of small-group swing. Like Wiley's work, they didn't have a wide audience at the time, but their influence steadily grew, and today they hold places of honor in iTunes, Spotify, and the other universal jukeboxes on which music is heard.

Less well known than Holiday but equally influential was Mabel Mercer, who was born in England in 1900, the daughter of an English showgirl and a black American musician whose identity she never knew. She performed in Paris in the thirties, came to the United States after the outbreak of World War II, and took up residence in the first of a series of New York supper clubs over which she reigned for the next thirty years. In 1942 she recorded her own album for the Liberty Record Shop, a selection of songs from *Porgy and Bess*, accompanied by the pianist Cy Walter—whose precise and swinging renditions, in his own club dates and recordings, would also help keep the standards alive. Will Friedwald writes that Mercer and similar singers were "virtually the only artists to keep performing the great songs of the twenties and thirties into the forties and fifties, like monks hiding manuscripts in the Dark Ages."

Mercer was an astute curator, not only selecting the great songwriters' better-known works but also resurrecting forgotten but deserving compositions. Thus she was known for singing Rodgers and Hart's "My Funny Valentine" and "Little Girl Blue" and also the same team's "Wait Till You See Her," which, Alec Wilder felt, she *made* a standard. Mercer also sought out and performed new songs, usually wistful and bittersweet ones, by a group of writers that formed around her, including Wilder and Cy Walter, whose most enduring composition was "The End of a Love Affair." Bart Howard, an Iowa boy who moved to New York in 1937, when he was twenty-three, eventually became Mercer's accompanist and started writing songs in the manner of his idol, Cole Porter. The Howard ballads "Let Me Love You," "It Was Worth It," and "The First Warm Day in May" became part of Mercer's repertoire. In 1954, in what he later described as a twenty-minute burst of creativity, Howard wrote a haunting song, worthy of Porter, that uncannily prefigured the Space Age. It opened, "Fly me to the moon and let me play among the stars, / Let me see what spring is like on Jupiter and Mars." It was frequently recorded in the years ahead. Eventually, Peggy Lee, who had one of the more successful records, convinced Howard to officially change the title to what most people already thought it was called: "Fly Me to the Moon."

Jerry Herman, still a few years away from *Milk and Honey*, got a job in the mid-fifties as intermission pianist at a club called RSVP, tickling the ivories when Mercer took her breaks. Years later he observed that the singer "never possessed a great voice, but watching her night after night was an extraordinarily valuable course in song interpretation. She acted those wonderful ballads she sang with a fierce passion and intelligence that forced you to listen to every word." All kinds of fans, known and unknown, made it their business to come see Mercer at RSVP. Being a devotee of hers was like being a member of an exclusive club; she became famous for being unknown. One prominent member of the club was Frank Sinatra, who in 1955 was quoted in Walter Winchell's column in the *New York Mirror*: "Everything I learned I owe to Mabel Mercer."

It makes sense that Sinatra was onto Mercer, for he is without question the key figure in this counternarrative. His contributions began in 1953, when everything turned around for him. He had a career-changing movie role in *From Here to Eternity*, for which he would win an Academy Award; his voice returned to form; and he signed with the Los Angeles–based Capitol Records. The executive who brought him to the label was Alan Livingston, the brother of Ray Evans's songwriting partner, Jay Livingston. (Alan Livingston had started out working on children's recordings at Capitol. In that capacity he wrote the song "I Tawt I Taw a Puddy Tat," a top-ten hit for Mel Blanc in 1951, and created the character Bozo the Clown. In 1963 he was instrumental in signing up the Beatles.) Since it had been founded a decade earlier by Johnny Mercer and his partners, Capitol had been known as a performers' label, geared toward bringing out their best. Thus, instead of having to deal with a Mitch Miller–like control freak, Sinatra was assigned the accommodating Voyle Gilmore as producer; the two had a roughly equal (less equal as the years went on) partnership on the selection of songs and their treatment. It was agreed that there would be no whip-cracks or in fact any studio shenanigans. The formula was good songs, a good singer, and good musicians. The final essential member of the team was the young staff arranger Nelson Riddle. Riddle first worked with Sinatra at the singer's second recording session, at which they recorded four tunes, including "I've Got the World on a String," a Harold Arlen–Ted Kohler song from 1932.

Photographer Sid Avery was at the session and later told Riddle's biographer, Peter J. Levinson: "When Frank listened to the playback of the recording, he was really excited about it and said, 'Jesus Christ, I'm back. I'm back, baby, I'm back!'" And he was: even from the first sessions, you could hear that Sinatra and Riddle—and the superb musicians in Capitol's stable, most of them big-band alumni—were creating one of the defining sounds of the 1950s, a sound of swing, wit, artistry, authority, honest feeling, and relaxed precision.

Sinatra's first Capitol album came out in January 1954 and established the pattern: impeccably chosen and performed songs, mostly standards, all following a theme. The first disk was called *Songs for Young Lovers* but the songs were old: two from Rodgers and Hart and the Gershwins, and one each from Porter ("I Get a Kick out of You"), Van Heusen–Burke ("Like Someone in Love"), Hugh Martin–Ralph Blane (one of their *Meet Me in St. Louis* tunes gender-reversed into "The Girl Next Door"), and Matt Dennis–Tom Adair ("Violets for Your Furs").

The record went to number two on the *Billboard* albums chart, and Sinatra's next several records were commercial triumphs as well. They featured Riddle arrangements and were dominated either by ballads or up-tempo numbers. The latter group all had some variation of a particular word in their titles—*Swing Easy!*, *Songs for Swingin' Lovers!*, *A Swingin' Affair!*, *Sinatra's Swingin' Session!!!* The insistent repetition and exclamation points were appropriate, for the albums reinvented and reinvigorated swing, long presumed dead. Riddle dusted off the classic big-band vocabulary and, with his trademark flutes and bass trombones, freshened it up. The traditional band-vocalist balance was turned upside down. A listener's experience of the tracks (and of Sinatra's live performances henceforth) was that the band followed the singer's lead in every way. At first, this was just a matter of his command of the lyrics and the rhythm, but within a couple of years he started to insert at strategic points the vocal equivalent of a brass exclamation—a bark or a *HUH!*—or sometimes an extra syllable or a substitute word that elegantly varied the lyric. Singing "I Won't Dance" on *A Swingin' Affair!*, he replaced a couple of words of lyrics with one of the pieces of in-joke slang he shared with his buddies: "ring-a-ding-ding." He'd subsequently trade "guy" for "cat," or "girl" for "chick," and ultimately have a whole chorus of "doo-be-doo-be-doo" in his 1966 hit "Strangers in the Night." By that time, the device was stale and prone to parody, if not self-parody. But a decade earlier, it was cool.

The swingin' Sinatra spawned such admiring mimics as Sammy Davis Jr., who in 1957 alone put out *Sammy Swings* and *It's All Over but the Swingin'*, and Bobby Darin, whose ring-a-ding-ding update of the Brecht–Weill–Blitzstein "Mack the Knife" was the top hit of 1959. But anyone foolish enough to follow Sinatra's path on the introspective fare was left in the dust. *In the Wee Small Hours*, whose cover showed the melancholy and pensive singer standing under a streetlamp, came out in 1955 and was followed by *No One Cares* and *Only the Lonely*. The repertoire was ballads, most of them standards, but presented in a new and almost revolutionary way. The emotion was real and searing, never sentimental or formulaic. In the era of Jackie Gleason and Mantovani, Sinatra and Riddle created true mood music, a searing brand of 1950s melancholy.

In 1955, Sinatra played songwriting matchmaker, bringing together two of his newly unattached buddies. Lyricist Sammy Cahn had
been working with Jule Styne, but Styne was committed to Broadway
and Cahn to California; Jimmy Van Heusen's longtime partner, Johnny
Burke, was in poor health. Sinatra put Cahn and Van Heusen together
to write the title song for his MGM film *The Tender Trap*, and then
the score for the live television production of Thornton Wilder's *Our
Town*. The team became Sinatra's house songwriters, and the commission brought out good things in the veterans. In particular, their title
songs for a series of theme albums—*Come Fly with Me, Come Dance
with Me!*, and *Ring-a-Ding-Ding!*—achieved what no one had been
able to do over the span of a decade and more: create a new, absolutely
fresh sort of swinging number. Van Heusen's melodies had a syncopated, sprung rhythm to them, and Cahn's lyrics were hip precisely in
the slangy new way Sinatra was defining the quality. "Come Dance
with Me" starts off: "Hey there cutes, put on your dancin' boots and
come dance with me, / Come dance with me, what an evening for some
Terpsichore." (Cahn takes poetic license in subtracting a syllable from
that last word for the sake of the rhyme with "dancing floor.") With
Van Heusen's roller-coaster melody and Billy May's supercharged arrangement, the song took the premise of Berlin's "Cheek to Cheek"—
which was also on the album—and rocketed it twenty-five years into
the present.

Nearly as influential as Sinatra in keeping standard songs alive was
the jazz impresario and independent record producer Norman
Granz. Standards were the backbone of virtually every record he put
out and every concert he promoted—he was the man behind the long-
running, globe-trotting Jazz at the Philharmonic series—in his lengthy

career, which lasted from the early 1940s till the late 1980s. Granz dipped his toe into bebop but mainly specialized in small-group swing, recording such stalwarts as Lester Young, Ben Webster, Coleman Hawkins, Benny Carter, Roy Eldridge, Teddy Wilson, and Art Tatum; he deserves credit for helping to keep the swing tradition alive, too.

Granz discovered Oscar Peterson, a prodigiously talented young Montreal pianist, in 1949, and they remained associated for the rest of both men's careers. In 1952 the two men revived the Lee Wiley notion of focusing on a single composer, with four LPs devoted to highlights from the oeuvres of Porter, Berlin, Gershwin, and Ellington. Granz had grown up loving Fred Astaire—not only Astaire the dancer but Astaire the singer, who in his movies gave definitive first performances of classics by the Gershwins, Berlin, and Jerome Kern and Dorothy Fields. The same year as the Peterson series began, Granz hatched the idea—"for kicks," he said—of putting together a set of LPs in which Astaire, backed by such top jazz players as Peterson, Flip Phillips, Barney Kessel, and Ray Brown, would put on disk a wide range of tunes that had been written for him in plays and films. The final product, a four-LP set called *The Astaire Story*, was hugely influential and sounds as fresh today as it did when it was released more than sixty years ago.

The artist most closely associated with Granz was the immaculate-voiced Ella Fitzgerald. Initially a girl vocalist with the Chick Webb band, Fitzgerald signed with Decca in 1942, and under the guidance of the label's A&R man, Milt Gabler (also Billie Holiday's producer), cut records with a wide variety of the label's musicians, including Louis Armstrong, the Ink Spots, Louis Jordan, and the Mills Brothers. Granz became her manager in 1954 and started a new label, Verve, in large part to showcase her talents. Early in 1956, Verve released *Ella Fitzgerald Sings the Cole Porter Song Book*, a double LP containing thirty-two tracks. It was a revelation—and probably introduced both the term and the concept "songbook" to mean a thoughtful selection of pieces from a given writer or musical genre. William Zinsser later commented, "I thought of jazz and popular song as dwelling in different rooms. Then . . . Ella Fitzgerald broke down the walls." Granz quickly followed up with a Fitzgerald and Louis Armstrong duet album; the repertoire was singing standards and the backup band was Granz's splendid house musicians. The delightful result, *Ella and Louis*, was the top-selling jazz record of the year and led to two follow-up disks.

Over the next eight years, Fitzgerald recorded albums dedicated to the "Songbooks" of Rodgers and Hart, Ellington, Berlin, Kern, Arlen, Mercer, and the Gershwins, the last arranged by Riddle. "I never knew how good our songs were," Ira Gershwin said, "until I heard Ella Fitzgerald sing them." After Fitzgerald's death, Frank Rich of *The New York Times* wrote that the Songbook series "performed a cultural transaction as extraordinary as Elvis's contemporaneous integration of white and African American soul: Here was a black woman popularizing urban songs often written by immigrant Jews to a national audience of predominantly white Christians."

And with that, those songs seemed to be everywhere. Former Stan Kenton singer June Christy leaned heavily on the American Songbook in her influential 1954 LP, *Something Cool*. Mel Tormé, equally cool, released a series of standards-based albums in the mid-fifties and continued to brilliantly till those fields until his death four decades later. Jazz singers Sarah Vaughan and Billy Eckstine teamed up on an Irving Berlin LP in 1957, and Vaughan—who was kind of the anti–Ella Fitzgerald, with her swooping low notes and propensity for improvisation and emotional display, and who had for a decade been confined to uninspiring pop material—did a solo Gershwin disk the following year.

Beverly Kenney, a promising young singer from New Jersey, put out six albums of standards between 1956 and 1960, the year she ended her own life with an overdose of pills. Tony Bennett, ever since making his arrangement with Mitch Miller at Columbia, had never stopped singing standards backed by top jazz musicians; his albums in this vein started in 1955 and have never stopped.

The phenomenon struck more broadly than the performers just mentioned and was a matter not only of taste but of necessity. The L in "LP" stood for "long." This popular new format had a great deal of playing time to fill, and, like the doo-woppers, labels saw the standards as a large body of material for their mainstream singers and easy-listening orchestras to take. In March 1957, *Billboard* ran an article headlined TOO MUCH OF A GOOD THING POSSIBLE WITH THOSE STANDARDS: ABUNDANT RECORD VERSIONS OF OLD SONGS RAISE SATURATION PROBLEMS. The piece, by Bill Simon and Paul Ackerman, gave the example of "Give Me the Simple Life," a Rube Bloom–Harry Ruby composition introduced in a 1946 B movie called *Wake Up and Dream*. When the song was first published, the authors noted, it

had no hit records and was virtually forgotten, except for a few jazz vocalists, until a little over a year ago. In the past year, it has been recorded 15 times, is selling more records, more sheet music and getting more performances than it did in the year it was being plugged.

Many of the obscure tunes, once known only to the East Side café connoisseur crowd, now have become so common as to have lost their chic-ness completely. "The Boy Next Door," which in Tin Pan Alley jargon would be the epitome of "non-commercialism," has 20 recordings. Cole Porter's most sophisticated offerings are found in the homes of even illiterate slobs.

Simon and Ackerman pointed out the seemingly inevitable predicament: "When will the repertoire of so-called 'standard' tunes be exhausted, and, when the market has been saturated with innumerable versions of each, what will the album producers use to fill the grooves?" They noted that some new tunes "are making the grade," mentioning Carolyn Leigh and Johnny Richards's "Young at Heart" and "Cry Me a River." They also credited "café singers" for "commissioning new material and also perpetually hunting for those obscure show gems." But ultimately the problem, they ruefully observed, "may call for more resourcefulness than many of our modern writers and a.&r. men possess."

Any depletion of the song stock was still off in the future; for the time being, there was enough good material for even those who seemed unlikely to put their voices on wax. Chet Baker, an Oklahoma boy whose tenor had even less vibrato than his Miles Davis–influenced trumpet, released *Chet Baker Sings* in 1956. The entire lineup came from the Great American Songbook, from the Kern–DeSylva "Look for the Silver Lining" and the Donaldson–Kahn "My Buddy," written in 1919 and 1922, respectively, up to "I've Never Been in Love Before," from *Guys and Dolls*. In between, Baker essayed tunes by the Gershwins, Rodgers and Hart, Hoagy Carmichael, and Styne and Cahn, plus two by Van Heusen and Burke.

Davis himself had a profound impact on the persistence of standards and what they represented. Moving away from Charlie Parker and Dizzy Gillespie and the bebop virtuosity of his early years, he became associated with what jazz writers called the "Cool School." For Davis, that meant in part emphasis on ballads, which he explored with unsurpassed emotional honesty and intensity. Every one of the albums he put out for Prestige starting in 1951 featured standard songs; *Blue*

Moods, in 1955, consisted of four of them: "Nature Boy," "Alone Together," "There's No You," and "Easy Living." That year George Avakian heard Davis at the Newport Jazz Festival, playing a riveting solo
on Thelonious Monk's composition "'Round Midnight," and determined to sign him to Columbia. "I heard and saw jazz's first modern
superstar," Avakian said in an interview with Marc Myers more than
fifty years later. "What struck me was that Miles was the best ballad
player since Louis Armstrong. I was convinced that his ballad playing
would appeal to the public on a very large scale. . . . It's really Miles'
melodic playing that put him across with the public on a wide scale."

Even Davis's old bebopping colleagues were playing standards,
after a fashion. Many of their best-known songs were based on the harmonic structure—"chord changes," in musicians' parlance—of classic
numbers. Charlie Parker's "Ornithology" came from "How High the
Moon," and "I Got Rhythm" alone launched a thousand bop solos. Ray
Noble wrote "Cherokee" in 1938 as a slow ballad, but Charlie Barnet
speeded it up the following year, and it became an up-tempo jazz staple, ultimately turned into bebop via Parker's "Ko-Ko."

When Bob Dorough got discharged from the Army in 1949, he
moved in with his parents in Amarillo, Texas, and started getting gigs
playing piano in a local club, the Aviatrix. He met a couple of hip older
musicians from the Air Force band who took a shine to him. Dorough
recalled:

> They said, "You ever heard Bird and Diz?"
> I said, "I heard *about 'em*."
> They said, "Oh, come over to the pad tomorrow and we'll play
> some." So they're playing these quintets with Diz and Bird and the
> rhythm section. They'd play "Hot House" and then they'd say, "You

know, that's just 'What Is This Thing Called Love?'" And then "Groovin' High" is just "Whispering," an old, old song.

Dorough moved to New York in 1950 and breathed in deeply; the prime era of bebop was just fading out. On his first album, *Devil May Care*, Dorough played and sang a version of Charlie Parker's "Yardbird Suite," for which he'd written lyrics. He later wrote a bop-flavored song called "Nothing Like You." Miles Davis recorded it, with Dorough's vocal.

One of the most modern of modern jazz musicians, John Coltrane, was a connoisseur of the standards. His biographer, Lewis Porter, suggests that the post-bop saxophonist may have derived the harmonic progression of his 1960 masterpiece "Giant Steps" from Rodgers and Hart's 1937 "Have You Met Miss Jones?" The following year Coltrane put out an album consisting of extended versions of three Songbook chestnuts—Cole Porter's "Ev'ry Time We Say Goodbye" and Gershwin's "Summertime" and "But Not for Me"—and a brand-new standard, Rodgers and Hammerstein's anodyne "My Favorite Things," from *The Sound of Music*. Coltrane's not-very-cheery modal version, with its sheets of saxophone notes, became the closest thing to a hit he ever had. In 1963, Coltrane put out two marvelous standards records, *Ballads* and *John Coltrane and Johnny Hartman*, a collaboration with the soulful singer.

Mabel Mercer wasn't the only club singer devoted to the classic songs. The husband-and-wife team of Jackie Cain and Roy Kral (who played piano as well as sang) debuted at Manhattan's Blue Angel in 1954, offering standards and a recent innovation, based on Ella

Fitzgerald's scat improvisations: songs constructed by putting lyrics to jazz riffs and solos. The influential British-born critic Leonard Feather dubbed it "vocalese" in his 1955 *Encyclopedia of Jazz*. As befitting the club-singer job description, Jackie and Roy also made it a point to seek out new songs. One they put on the map was a lilting ballad, written by Fran Landesman and Tommy Wolf, that imagined the first line of T. S. Eliot's "The Waste Land" from the point of view of a melancholy hipster: "Spring Can Really Hang You Up the Most." In 1959, Landesman and Wolf, who were based in St. Louis, teamed up to write a musical comedy satirizing bohemia, *The Nervous Set*; one of its songs, "The Ballad of the Sad Young Men," became a part of many singers' repertoire as well. Landesman also collaborated with Bob Dorough, notably on "Nothing Like You." Dorough wrote and sang on a dyspeptic Miles holiday tune called "Blue Xmas (to Whom It May Concern)."

Another important figure was a delicate-voiced singer and pianist from upstate New York whose real *and* stage name was Blossom Dearie. In Paris, in the early fifties, she formed a vocal group called the Blue Stars of France, which included Christiane Legrand (the composer Michel Legrand's sister) and Bob Dorough, who had found himself in the city through his job as the music manager for boxer Sugar Ray Robinson, then attempting a career as an entertainer. Norman Granz, passing through in 1956, saw Dearie perform solo and signed her to a Verve recording contract. When she returned to New York, she became a fixture at Julius Monk's Upstairs at the Downstairs club, sometimes sharing the bill with Annie Ross, a Scottish-born singer who would eventually become one-third of Lambert, Hendricks, and Ross, masters of vocalese (most famously, "Twisted," with lyrics by Ross) and probably the best-known singing jazz group of all time. Like Jackie and Roy, Dearie blended the standards with carefully chosen new songs, including "Spring Can Really Hang You Up the Most," which became a signature number.

On July 31, 1957, Sheldon Harnick caught Dearie's show at Upstairs, and one of the numbers she performed impressed him so much that he was inspired to go home and write a letter to its lyricist, Carolyn Leigh:

> As you may know, Blossom Dearie has been performing. "I Walk a Little Faster" there as part of her act. I loved the song the first time I heard it, and after repeated hearings I just felt I had to write you a fan letter . . . not just for that lyric, but for all the ballad lyrics I've ever heard of yours. To me, they are the freshest and most moving ballad lyrics around today.

The composer of "I Walk a Little Faster" was Leigh's new partner, Cy Coleman. Theirs was a volatile partnership that began in 1957 and ended five years later, during the pre-Broadway Philadelphia run of their show *Little Me*, a Sid Caesar vehicle. According to Coleman, Leigh, who had grown more emotional over the years, tried to have director Bob Fosse arrested for cutting a lyric without her permission; for Coleman, that was the last straw. But while the collaboration lasted, it produced smart, precise, up-to-date, honest, haunting, swinging, sexy songs. "It Amazes Me," like "I Walk a Little Faster," was a favorite of Dearie and of Tony Bennett, two performers of impeccable taste; Sinatra, whose ears weren't bad, either, chose "Witchcraft" and "The Best Is Yet to Come" for singles. Who would have thought that such one-off wonders could still emerge from the Brill Building? It was as if the clock had been turned back twenty years.

Another intriguing development was bossa nova, a blend of samba and jazz that emerged in Brazil in the 1950s and came to the United

States in the early sixties via jazz musicians Charlie Byrd, Dave Brubeck, and Stan Getz. In 1963, the enterprising producer Lou Levy, trawling the foreign markets for properties, came across a Brazilian track called "Garota de Ipanema." He tracked down the composers, Antônio Carlos Jobim and Vinícius de Moraes, secured American rights, and commissioned Norman Gimbel, still patrolling the Brill Building, to write English-language lyrics. The saxophonist Stan Getz recorded the song, now called "The Girl from Ipanema," backed by Jobim and another bossa nova songwriter, João Gilberto, with vocals by Gilberto's wife, Astrud. She mangled some of Gimbel's lyrics, singing, for example, "She looks straight ahead, not at *he*" instead of "*me*." Gimbel told *The Wall Street Journal* in an interview marking the fiftieth anniversary of the original song, "I was tearing my hair out when I learned that later." But his pain was eased by the fact that "The Girl from Ipanema" reached number five on the pop charts—no small feat for a jazz recording in 1964, the year of Beatlemania—and won the Grammy for Record of the Year. (Gimbel developed a specialty in putting new lyrics to international songs, including Jobim's "How Insensitive" and "Meditation," Marcos Valle's "Summer Samba," and Michel Legrand's score for the 1964 French film *The Umbrellas of Cherbourg*, which included "Watch What Happens" and the Oscar-nominated "I Will Wait for You.")

Jobim, in a peculiarly South American way, brought cool sophistication back to the pop charts. The pianist Dick Hyman (who was devoted to jazz but made ends meet by backing rock-and-roll records, making electronic easy-listening albums, and playing the piano on *Sing Along with Mitch*) says, "Jobim took over where Cole Porter left off, especially with the medium-tempo things. Some of his songs are very clever. All of them have harmonies that are of interest to jazz guys. And almost all of them have some kind of catchy melody."

Dave Frishberg feels the same way. "When Brazil entered the picture, it was a huge shot in the arm for American music," he says. "Talk about rebirth—it was the Brazilians who introduced that." Frishberg's songwriting career had never gone much of anywhere by virtue of his association with Frank Loesser, and he was concentrating on the piano-playing side of his career. In 1962, he had a job as an accompanist for the nightclub act of singer Dick Haymes and his wife, Fran Jeffries. "Dick asked me to write something for Fran—a cute, sexy piece," Frishberg remembered. He removed "Beulah" from the classic Mae West line "Beulah, peel me a grape" and emerged with a charming jazz-inflected paean to the grammatical indirect object. "Peel Me a Grape" became one of Blossom Dearie's go-to songs, but Frishberg's songwriting career proceeded slowly. "I tried to write for what I perceived was the market," he recalled. "I ended up writing shit, on purpose. I was trying to sound like this writer or that. A few country songs, a few folk songs—that was big at the time. After two or three years of futility, I abandoned that. I began to write songs as if it were 1937. The music that I liked to play, the music I liked to listen to, what the jazz musicians I worked with were playing, was music from the Gershwins, from Porter. I thought to myself, 'If that's the stuff you love so much, that's what you should try to write like. Pretend it's 1937. It's either going to be me or Johnny Mercer who writes this.' Of course, when I said that, I abdicated from the market. But that's when I began to enjoy songwriting more."

In 1964, Frishberg wrote the lyrics for an extremely funny number called "I'm Hip" that would become a minor classic. The composer was Bob Dorough, who on his own was writing words and music for some pungent jazz-influenced songs. Mel Tormé recorded his "Comin' Home, Baby," Carmen McRae his "Devil May Care," and Roy Kral's sister Irene a moody ballad called "Love Came on Stealthy Fingers."

"Not the kind of song that's gonna be played on the jukebox," Dorough said. "It would still be in my trunk were it not for Irene."

Frishberg was somewhat more prolific than Dorough, a friend and frequent collaborator. Over the next twenty-five years he produced a series of sharp and distinctive compositions, several of which became part of Dearie's repertoire. Frishberg's songs aren't quite vocalese, but they are jazz to the core; for the most part, you don't start humming them after a hearing. Some of their flavor can be sensed from their titles: "Blizzard of Lies," "My Attorney Bernie," "Do You Miss New York?," "Quality Time," "You Are There" (lyrics by Frishberg; music by Johnny Mandel), and "Van Lingle Mungo," whose lyrics consist of the names of old-time baseball players. Frishberg's songs in some way represented the end of the jazz-based songwriting tradition: an admirable end, but an end nonetheless.

When he talked to me on the telephone in 2012, from his home in Portland, Oregon, he pulled out a postcard sent to him by Mercer himself, whom he'd met through their mutual friend Dearie. Frishberg estimated the year as 1969 or 1970. He read the card to me, in its entirety: "You are my favorite lyric writer at the moment. Boy, are you uncommercial!!!!"

Epilogue
Do You Believe in Magic?
1957–1965

They're dancin' in Chicago
Down in New Orleans
Up in New York City

> • "Dancing in the Street," by Marvin Gaye,
> Ivy Jo Hunter, and Mickey Stevenson, 1964

When Allen Toussaint was a kid in New Orleans, his mother bought an Emerson record player, on which he thrilled to the sounds of Paul Weston's Orchestra and Edvard Grieg's Piano Concerto in A Minor. In 1948, when he was ten, listening to Benny Goodman's rendition of the Gershwins' tune "Love Walked In," he was knocked out by a solo for two trombones. "That was heaven," he said more than sixty years later, in his Manhattan apartment. It inspired him to create on the family piano his first musical composition, a duet for trombone and trumpet. Not long after that, while still a teenager, the prodigiously talented Toussaint was writing songs and working as a session musician in New Orleans. He even had an album of his own in 1958; one of the songs on it, an instrumental called

"Java," was a big hit for local trumpeter Al Hirt a half-dozen years later. But the record sold next to nothing, and Toussaint concentrated his efforts on session playing, producing, and writing for the local Minit label; his nom de plume on the first batch of songs was Naomi Neville (his mother's maiden name), a necessity because of a publishing contract he'd signed elsewhere. Toussaint turned basic chord progressions into a string of fine and distinctive songs; his secrets were a New Orleans beat that rocked even the ballads, exquisite musical and lyrical grace notes, and renditions by outstanding local artists: Irma Thomas on "It's Raining" and "Ruler of My Heart"; Aaron Neville on "Over You," "Wrong Number," and "Every Day"; Benny Spellman on "Lipstick Traces (on a Cigarette)"; and Ernie K-Doe on "I've Cried My Last Tear." (K-Doe's biggest hit, and the one early Toussaint song to go national, all the way to number one, was hardly exquisite but was pretty funny and very catchy: the novelty tune "Mother-in-Law.")

Allen Toussaint was not a unique case, least of all in his emergence as a songwriter roughly in the year 1960. It was a moment when the tremors of Elvis and the other first-wave rock-and-rollers had quieted, and when it became apparent that a space had been cleared in which a new sort of song could emerge. These compositions had an odd relationship with the American Songbook standards (which most of their writers, like Toussaint, greatly admired). In certain respects, they were very different. Rather than jazz, they came out of folk, country, rhythm and blues, and the blues itself. The beat was right there on the surface, and inescapable. And the harmonic structures were simple, though not always simplistic. "Compared to jazz songs, which are based on 7th chords, the songs of the sixties are very triadic," said jazz pianist Bill Charlap, son of composer Moose Charlap and singer Sandy Stewart. "There's not as much meat on the bones." In keeping with the post-1950 trend, the song was less an independent entity than raw material for a recording; the performance, production, and technology could make up for any lack of refinement or sophistication.

Yet as the decade of the sixties progressed and the kids' compositional discernment and skill evolved, it turned out that through a different route, they could achieve the classic values of melodic and lyrical sophistication, and also bring some new and intriguing qualities to the songwriter's craft. In 2000 the music magazine *Mojo* asked twenty of the most respected working songwriters, including Paul McCartney, Brian Wilson, Jerry Leiber, and Hal David, to give their list of the ten best songs of the twentieth century. It doesn't really prove anything about the quality of the songs that were emerging in the early sixties, but it's at least noteworthy that the aggregated top-ten list included six records released between 1963 and 1965, plus one from 1966.[*]

Another parallel with the older model was institutional. Toussaint and many of his contemporaries were paid small salaries against hoped-for royalties; they punched the clock at a record label or publishing company's offices and put in a regular workday, just like a traditional Tin Pan Alley cleffer. Gone, however, was the old geographical imperative. Far from feeling compelled to leave for New York or Los Angeles, the new writers were nourished by the water and air and cadences of their hometowns. The local idiom usually had a direct or indirect southern lilt, and the songs were in the tradition of rhythm and blues or country and western. Ray Charles once said, "R&B is an adult music about adult matters." The same was true of the best country songs, and the grown-up themes and emotions in both were appreciated more than ever in the era of bubblegum rock and roll. Charles

---

[*]The songs, in order, are: "In My Life" (1965); "(I Can't Get No) Satisfaction" (1965); "Over the Rainbow" (1939); "Here, There and Everywhere" (1966); "The Tracks of My Tears" (1965); "The Times They Are A-Changing" (1963): "Strange Fruit" (1939); "I Can't Make You Love Me" (a song recorded by Bonnie Raitt in 1991); "People Get Ready" (1965); and "You've Lost That Lovin' Feelin'" (1964).

was one of a number of writers and performers who blended country and R&B; all around, all kinds of traditions were swapping juices. In 1958, *Billboard* writer Bob Rolontz observed that rock was "moving closer to pop in style and content, and . . . pop is absorbing the rock and roll beat." The year before, the magazine had coined the term "rocka-ballad" and subsequently applied it to such records as Ritchie Valens's "Donna," the Teddy Bears' "To Know Him Is to Love Him," and the Everly Brothers' "All I Have to Do Is Dream." The subgenre had its own conventions, such as backing triplets and a I-vi-IV-V chord progression (subsequently dubbed "the Fifties Progression"), that would eventually become clichés, but at the beginning they were fresh.

A record company about four hundred miles due north of New Orleans created another extremely tasty new recipe by combining country and R&B, then adding gospel, ending up with a riveting sound that was starting to be called "soul music." The label, Satellite, was based in Memphis and in 1961 changed its name to Stax. House musicians (the house band would later go out on its own as Booker T. and the MGs), singers, and writers all contributed to the distinctive Stax sound. Otis Redding combined the last two roles, making his mark in 1962 with "These Arms of Mine." The song had the same slow tempo of so many thousands of others, but with it a striking emotional rawness and intensity. The one thing dated about this track more than half a century after its release are the backing triplets, but that crutch was gone by 1964, when Redding wrote and released the momentous "Respect" and "I've Been Loving You Too Long."

At the dawn of the 1960s, some ambitious young music men started an enterprise they called Florence Alabama Music Enterprises (FAME)—Florence being one of the four towns collectively known as Muscle Shoals. A lot of creative musicians, singers, and writers, also young, were drawn into FAME's orbit, including two Caucasian Alabamans born Wallace Daniel Pennington and Dewey Lindon Oldham. As Spooner Oldham and Dan Penn, they formed a songwriting team and produced "Wish You Didn't Have to Go," "Let's Do It Over" (a hit for Joe Simon), and "I'm Your Puppet." Arthur Alexander, a stellar Alabama singer-songwriter for FAME, was African-American, but his work had a country feel. (Eventually, top singers, from Aretha Franklin to Paul Simon, would make regular journeys to Muscle Shoals to record with the crack regular session musicians—the Swampers.)

Nashville forms the eastern point of a triangle, with Memphis to the west and Muscle Shoals to the south. Boudleaux and Felice Bryant, a husband-and-wife team, had been working songwriters in Music City since 1950, when that term was coined, but hit their stride at the end of the decade with a string of rockaballad hits for the Everly Brothers, notably "Bye Bye Love," "All I Have to Do Is Dream," and "Devoted to You." In 1960, a twenty-seven-year-old Texas honky-tonk singer and guitar player moved to Nashville, determined to make it as a writer. Willie Nelson had no success at first, but Hank Cochran, the cowriter, with Harlan Howard, of the Patsy Cline hit "I Fall to Pieces," got him a $50-a-week contract with the publishing company he was affiliated with, Pamper Music. Curley Putman, an Alabama native, was working at the time as a song plugger for Tree Records, and would later write such hits as "Green, Green Grass of Home," "My Elusive Dreams," and "D-I-V-O-R-C-E." "Hank and Willie were tuned in," he said. "The sparks were flying off of them." Pamper had a little of the creative ferment of Max Dreyfus's T. B. Harms decades earlier, with a down-home feel. "The office was a house in Goodlettsville [on the outskirts of Nashville]," Cochran recalled in a 1991 interview, "and out back we had turned the garage into a little ol' bitty thing out there where me and Willie and Harlan and all of us wrote out there." Building on the work of—and competing with—other talented young writers and writer-performers such as Johnny Cash, Roger Miller, John D. Loudermilk, Bill Anderson, and the Bryants, Nelson in short order placed "Night Life" with Billy Walker, "Hello Walls" with Faron Young, "Funny How Time Slips Away" with Ray Price, and, most important and successful, "Crazy" with Patsy Cline. In the post–Hank Williams country music world, the idea of a performer singing songs he'd written himself was still so unusual that Nelson highlighted it in the title of his 1962 debut album, . . . *And Then I Wrote.*

It would have been unthinkable for a Jack Lawrence or a Richard Rodgers to get onstage or behind the microphone and sing one of his own songs. The old-time tunesmith was a scriptwriter, fashioning notions and emotions for someone else (a singer/actor) to declaim. But people like Nelson and Redding were following a different path, one blazed by Williams, by bluesmen like Robert Johnson, by Woody Guthrie, by Chuck Berry, and by a bespectacled, guitar-playing, hiccupping kid out of Lubbock, Texas. In 1957 and 1958, before his sudden death, Buddy Holly released a series of infectious self-penned hits—"Peggy Sue," "That'll Be the Day," "Oh, Boy!"—that resonated widely and deeply. The mere act of declaiming your own music and words added some exciting new elements to the musical mix, and would only gain more power with the years. After kvetching to Max Wilk about these kids today, lyricist Leo Robin acknowledged that the youngsters' new model had some points in its favor: "The things they're writing are at least honest expressions of how they feel, in relation to the conditions of their world, and how they react to their own lives and futures. I'm sure you cannot fault these kids for their attitudes. Not the way you could fault some hack Tin Pan Alley songwriter back in 1925 who was writing second-rate mechanical songs about how sweet it would be to be back in dear old Dixie with his dear old mammy or his lovely little tootsie-wootsie baby. Maybe he was doing a professional job, but he was peddling a totally false picture. Today these kids are, at the very least, *honest*."

The idea made economic sense as well. As historian Elijah Wald has observed, "The money one earned from writing and recording even a million-selling single was peanuts compared with what one got for writing and recording every song on a string of million-selling albums. The combination of prestige and wealth was irresistible."

One of the biggest demographic changes of the twentieth century was the northern migration of African-Americans, and its effect on popular song was as great as on any other facet of American life. A key hub was Chicago, where Sam Cooke, born in Mississippi in 1931, moved as a toddler with his family. Cooke started out singing gospel, moved into doo-wop, and released his first single as a solo artist in 1957. It was a tune he had written, "You Send Me," and it shot to number one on the charts. (On the B side was Cooke's version of the George Gershwin–Ira Gershwin–DuBose Heyward "Summertime.") Around the same time, two Chicago guys named Jerry Butler and Curtis Mayfield were singing in a quartet called the Northern Jubilee Gospel Singers. In 1958 they went secular as Jerry Butler and the Impressions; Mayfield, on guitar, was the only instrumentalist. He also proved to be an inspired and prolific songwriter. As the Impressions (Butler left early on to go solo), the group had a string of hits in the early sixties, climaxed in 1965 by Mayfield's gospel-influenced protest song "People Get Ready," number nine on the *Mojo* list of the greatest songs of all time.

An even bigger urban center, as far as music was concerned, was Detroit, where the percentage of black residents increased more than sevenfold between 1920 and 1960, from 4 percent to more than 29

percent. Berry Gordy was born in the city in 1929, to parents who had
come up from Georgia seven years earlier. He returned from serving
in Korea in 1953, spent some time as a professional boxer and a record store manager, then succeeded in placing some songs he'd written
with the singer Jackie Wilson. He began managing a few performers—
notably the Miracles, a local singing group led by William "Smokey"
Robinson—and in 1959 launched his own record label, Tamla, which
would in due time change its name to Motown. As Gordy's vision
turned into reality, the company became less like a traditional label
than an entertainment version of the Chrysler plant whose clock he
had once punched. Gordy's model was the vertically integrated Tin
Pan Alley of 1915, except that he seized control of even more elements
of the process. The company not only issued the records but controlled
all aspects of the recording process, and had under contract artists,
backing musicians (a crackerjack combination known as the Funk
Brothers), and writers. Gordy had very particular ideas about the nature of the songs that would appear on his label. Early on, he paid a
call on Jerry Leiber and Mike Stoller in New York and explained to
them, as Leiber recalled, that "he wanted to make R&B more appealing to whites by softening the sound." Gordy was true to his vision.
Motown records offered a new kind of soul: the sound was unmistakably black yet had a glossier pop sheen than what was coming out of
Memphis or Muscle Shoals. Gordy's roster of prodigiously talented
tunesmiths was led by Robinson, sometimes working alone and sometimes with various collaborators, and two teams: Norman Whitfield
and Barrett Strong, and Lamont Dozier and Brian and Eddie Holland.
(The singers Stevie Wonder and Marvin Gaye eventually became top
songwriters for Motown as well.) Melodically, the classic Motown song
was characterized by an irresistible hook, and lyrically by unlikely
metaphors and a transformation of the vernacular into street poetry:

"Ain't That Peculiar," "I Second That Emotion," "You Beat Me to the Punch," "Can I Get a Witness?," and "I Can't Help Myself." These songs harked back thirty or more years, to when Ira Gershwin and Irving Berlin were doing much the same thing with "Nice Work If You Can Get It" and "Let Yourself Go."

The various teams were primed to compete with each other. Demos of new songs were played at Friday morning meetings, with the best ones assigned to the hottest group or singer of the moment. Things really heated up late in 1964. When Holland-Dozier-Holland wrote "How Sweet It Is (to Be Loved by You)" for Marvin Gaye, Robinson answered with "My Girl" for the Temptations. H-D-H came back with "Nowhere to Run" for Martha and the Vandellas; Robinson's response was "Ooo Baby Baby" for his own group, the Miracles. All astonishing songs, hitting the charts in a four-month span. Just a couple of months later, Robinson and the Miracles recorded what could be the greatest Motown song of all, "The Tracks of My Tears." The writers were capable of turning out first-rate material with incredible speed. One morning Gordy found out that Columbia Records, previous home of the Motown group the Four Tops, was going to rerelease one of the Tops' old records. He instructed his top team at the time, Holland-Dozier-Holland, to produce a response, and by early afternoon they'd come up with "It's the Same Old Song." The track was recorded later the same day; the record was in stores three days later. It reached number five on the charts and became a classic. (The Columbia Four Tops release peaked at number 93.)

I t wasn't that *everything* was happening in the hinterlands. The traditional outposts of New York and Los Angeles were fertile ground for new kinds of songs, too. When last glimpsed, Burt Bacharach was failing miserably as a Brill Building cleffer in the early fifties. In 1956, publisher Eddy Wolpin paired him with the veteran lyricist Hal David. Cue the Hollywood ending? Not so fast. The team's early efforts were undistinguished and, with the exception of "The Story of My Life" for Marty Robbins and "Magic Moments" for Perry Como, unsuccessful. Bacharach spent a couple of years touring the world as Marlene Dietrich's music director. On a stop in Rio de Janeiro, he and the singer would walk in the hills at night and hear drumbeats coming up from the city. "That was the first time I heard the *baion* beat," Bacharach recalled, "where the one is followed by a one-beat pause and then two half-beats."

When he returned to New York in 1961, something clicked—some combination of the sounds he'd absorbed on his travels, his classical training, the lessons he'd learned from modern jazz artists like Charlie Parker and Thelonious Monk, and just being ready to find his voice as a writer. Between 1961 and 1964, Bacharach produced a string of remarkable songs, including "Baby It's You," "Only Love Can Break a Heart," "Wives and Lovers," "I Just Don't Know What to Do with Myself," "A House Is Not a Home," "(There's) Always Something There to Remind Me," "Any Day Now" (which featured the *baion*), and "Make It Easy on Yourself." (Hal David's brother Mack wrote the lyrics for "Baby It's You," Bob Hilliard for "Any Day Now," and Hal David for all the rest.) Chicago's Vee-Jay Records bought the Bacharach–Hal David "Make It Easy on Yourself" for Jerry Butler, and assigned Bacharach himself to produce and conduct the recording session. The experience was a revelation for the composer. "After I did that session," he recalled, "I knew I never wanted to work any other way again, because by actually being in the studio while the record was being cut, I could protect my material and make the song sound the way I had heard it in my head. . . . I could start with a framework and then evolve from that as the musicians heard the song and then played it."

Interviewed by *Billboard* in 1964, Bacharach took pains to convey how much labor he and David (but especially he) put into every composition:

> We take three days to two weeks to compose a song, working separately and together. We hear the song over 400 times in going over it. When we feel it is right and have taught the song to the artist and thoroughly rehearsed the performance, we are up to about 450 listenings. I then go home and plan the arrangement which gives me another 80 listenings. We then do maybe 24 takes in the studio. We listen to the play-backs, re-mix and listen to the acetates. After 1,000 listenings we must force ourselves to listen to the record as if we had just thought of it and were hearing it in completed form for close to the very first time.

The final piece of the puzzle, for Bacharach, came when he met Dionne Warrick, a backup singer on the Drifters' record of his song "Mexican Divorce"; he was struck by her "special kind of grace and elegance." In 1962 she recorded the Bacharach–David "Don't Make Me Over," nailing the rapid pitch changes and the rhythm switch from 12/8 to 6/8. (When the record came out, her name on the label was misspelled "Warwick," and she adopted the new spelling.) She became, literally, the voice of Bacharach and David's music, recording "Walk On By," "Anyone Who Had a Heart," and, by the time the curtain came down on the sixties, more than thirty of their songs. "Dionne could sing that high and she could sing that low," Bacharach marveled. "She could sing that strong and she could sing that loud, yet she could also be soft and delicate. As our musical relationship evolved, I began to see her potential and realized I could take more risks and chances."

Rhythmically, melodically, and harmonically, Bacharach–David songs zig when you expect them to zag. The lyrics are more conventional, but in an unassuming way they stand up to and complement the musical experimentation. The faster numbers show the brand the clearest; a little like Van Heusen and Cahn in the previous decade, Bacharach and David were reinventing and modernizing the upbeat pop song. Overall their music provided, as well as any body of work, a soundtrack for the period.

Bacharach and David started out as Brill Building songwriters, with all that designation entailed, and it's curious that in later years it would commonly be applied to another, younger group of writers, most of whom weren't even based in Brill. This cohort fit in with the traditional Tin Pan Alley–New York–Jewish demographic, with one notable departure: a lot of them were female. Carol Klein was born in Brooklyn in 1942; in high school, inspired by her neighborhood friend Neil Sedaka and the high school math curriculum, she started a band called the Co-Sines. In 1958, ABC-Paramount signed her to a recording contract and changed her name to Carole King. Her parents saw to it that she kept at her studies, and in 1959 she met a fellow Queens College student named Gerry Goffin, who wrote lyrics. They formed a team (and eventually a marriage) and signed on as staff songwriters at Aldon Music; the terms were $1,000 for a year, against royalties. (The main character of *Bye Bye Birdie* owns a publishing company called Almaelou, surely an intentional similarity.) The company had offices at 1650 Broadway, a building peopled mainly by BMI-affiliated publishers, as opposed to the more established ASCAP brands down the block at the Brill Building. It had been formed by a fairly unsuccessful songwriter named Don Kirshner and an Alley veteran named Al Nevins for the express purpose of feeding rock and roll's voracious maw.

Like Motown, the company used competition as a motivational tool. In her memoir, *A Natural Woman*, King wrote that every Aldon team was assigned a cubicle:

> Each was barely big enough to contain an upright piano with a bench, a chair for the lyricist, and a small table with enough room for a legal pad, a pen, an ashtray, and a coffee cup. The proximity of each cubicle to the next added an "echo" factor. While I was playing the song on which Gerry and I were working, we heard only our song. As soon as I stopped playing we could hear the song on which the team in the next cubicle was working. Not surprisingly, with each of us trying to write the follow-up to an artist's current hit, everyone's song sounded similar to everyone else's. But only one would be chosen. Inevitably the insecurity of the writers and the competitive atmosphere fostered by Donnie spurred each team on to greater effort, which resulted in better songs. It wasn't only about writing a great song; it was about *winning*.

Goffin and King won most of the time, turning out a lot of not-always-distinguishable four-chord material recorded with varying degrees of success by Bobby Vee, Gene Pitney, the Everly Brothers, Brenda Lee, James Darren, Steve Lawrence, Dion, and the Cookies, an African-American girl group who recorded a rhythm number of theirs called "Chains." King was still in her teens when she wrote many of these tracks, Goffin was barely out of his, and even the least memorable of their songs had an appealing heartfelt quality, with none of the clock-punching cynicism that the older Brill Building songwriters' youth-market efforts betrayed. And some of their work was piercing, empathic lyrics complementing soulful melodies. That was decidedly true of their first big hit, in which Goffin convincingly spoke with the voice of a teenage girl. The Shirelles took "Will You Love Me Tomorrow" to number one in January 1961 and earned the writers a $10,000 advance from Kirshner. In 1963, for a *male* black singing group, the Drifters, Goffin and King penned the ultimate urban escape song, "Up on the Roof."

Neil Sedaka and his partner, Howard Greenfield, were signed to Aldon, but, by accident rather than design, the company specialized in young husband-and-wife songwriting teams. The first to approximate Goffin and King's success consisted of Cynthia Weil (lyrics) and Barry Mann (music). Weil, who was another one of Frank Loesser's finds, teamed with Mann in 1961. They started out with bubblegum fare but ventured into more ambitious efforts, notably "Uptown" and "On Broadway," the latter a collaboration with rock-and-roll veterans Jerry Leiber and Mike Stoller. These were little symphonies, with distinctive movements, elaborate production, heavy use of strings, and a palpable social awareness.

Leiber and Stoller had moved their operation from L.A. to New York a couple of years earlier, and were working as producers for Ahmet Ertegun and Jerry Wexler's Atlantic Records. For a new incarnation of the Drifters, a veteran doo-wop group, they wrote and produced a series of songs that featured big string arrangements and pulsing Latin rhythms: "There Goes My Baby," "This Magic Moment," "Save the Last Dance for Me." Like Bacharach, Leiber and Stoller had found and fallen in love with *baion*. When the Drifters' lead singer, Ben E. King, left the group in 1960, his first hit was "Spanish Harlem," a Latin-tinged collaboration between Leiber and Stoller and Phil

Spector, an L.A. kid they had taken on as a combination apprentice producer and contract writer. ("He wore his ambition like a topcoat," Leiber said of Spector years later. "It was all over him.") That song hit big and so did the follow-up, which had a Leiber–Stoller–Ben E. King songwriting credit: "Stand by Me."

As the continental crisscrossing of Leiber, Stoller, and Spector suggests, this rebooted, youth-centered Tin Pan Alley was peripatetic. Sam Cooke made his way from Chicago to Los Angeles, where he wrote and recorded such hits as "Bring It on Home to Me," "Another Saturday Night," and "Wonderful World"—the last cowritten with Herb Alpert and Lou Adler, two young L.A. writers and producers who co-managed the surf group Jan and Dean. (Alpert played some trumpet, too.) By that time Spector was back home in L.A., on his way to becoming the central figure on the pop music scene there. Periodically, young New York writers made pilgrimages to work with him, much as Tin Pan Alley tunesmiths had trekked west in the early days of talkies. Jeff Barry and Ellie Greenwich—yet another husband-and-wife team, who were under contract to Lieber and Stoller's publishing company—went out to the coast in 1963 to collaborate with Spector on "Be My Baby," a number-two record for the girl group the Ronettes. The next year, Cynthia Weil and Barry Mann teamed with him on an even bigger hit, the Righteous Brothers' "You've Lost That Lovin' Feelin'." Already, Spector was paying as much attention to production as songwriting, if not more. Mann and Weil went back to New York, and Spector started tinkering with the recording. After a few weeks he played them the finished record, Mann recalled years later. "I yelled over the phone to get Phil's attention: 'Phil, you've got it on the wrong speed.' The song we had written had been about three ticks faster and a tone and a half higher. Phil came on and said, 'Barry, that's the record.'" The original recording ran three minutes and five seconds, the retooled version 3:45. But Spector had 3:05 printed on the label, so deejays would think it was shorter.

Spector wasn't just fussing with tempo. He belabored every aspect of the recording and editing, eventually turning into a somewhat more obsessive and less genial latter-day Mitch Miller. His most famous contribution was the multilayered approach to instrumentation that would become known as "the Wall of Sound." A key element of his work was the Wrecking Crew, a loosely defined group of backing musicians that included Leon Russell on piano, James Burton and Glen Campbell on guitar, Cheryl LaPiere (who usually went by just "Cher") on background vocals, and Hal Blaine—who gave the Crew its name— on drums. The Wrecking Crew would play, usually anonymously, behind virtually every song that came out of Los Angeles in the sixties. Dean Martin used them on his 1964 number one song, "Everybody Loves Somebody." That impressed Frank Sinatra, and, backed by the Crew, he matched his buddy's success with "Something Stupid" and the doo-be-doo-be-doo "Strangers in the Night."

It sure wasn't Ray Evans and Jay Livingston's L.A.—or even Henry Mancini's and Johnny Mandel's. A link between that rapidly fading Hollywood music world and the new reality was Randy Newman. His father was a Los Angeles doctor, but his three uncles were all Hollywood composers and conductors, and he spent a lot of time with them, absorbing all the musical knowledge his brain could hold. Crucially, his mother came from New Orleans, and Randy spent his summers there until he was eleven, absorbing the rhythms and attitudes that permeated the air.

He also took in the mystification and resentment of his uncles and their cohort for the new music. "I have enormous sympathy for the people who knew a lot of chords and arrangements and the depth of their hatred for rock and roll," he said. "They just couldn't comprehend what had happened—all the years of studying and listening to Glenn Miller and Fletcher Henderson. Even Burt Bacharach. My uncle Lionel once joked that all Bacharach songs sounded like the second oboe part."

By the time he entered his freshman year at UCLA, Newman had a job as a staff writer with Metric Music, the publishing wing of the Liberty label. In exchange for $100 a month (increased to $200 after five years), he assigned the publishing rights for everything he produced to the company. (Now, some fifty years later, Newman is starting to get those rights back.) When he finished a song, Wrecking Crew members like Russell, Campbell, and David Gates would put together a demo, and Liberty's Tommy LiPuma would shop it around to singers. Newman wrote for and sometimes with Jackie DeShannon, a midwestern girl who had moved to L.A. in 1960 and quickly earned contracts for both recording and songwriting. (She would find particular success writing for British bands, as she did with the Searchers' "When You Walk in the Room," which led to a brief but fruitful songwriting collaboration with Jimmy Page, later the lead guitarist of Led Zeppelin.) A wide range of artists cut Newman's songs: between 1962 and 1965, there were records by the Fleetwoods, Vic Dana, Erma Franklin (Aretha's older sister cut Newman's "Love Is Blind," as did Lou Rawls), Frankie Laine (one of his father's patients), Irma Thomas, and the Tokens. Much of this early work, while craftsmanlike, had a boilerplate quality. "I was trying to do songs that people would do, but it wasn't where my talents lay," he said. Still, there were occasional glimpses of Newman's distinctive talent, as in "I Don't Want to Hear It Anymore," an aching ballad recorded by Jerry Butler in 1964 and, five years later, by Dusty Springfield for her album *Dusty in Memphis*. A breakthrough was "I Think It's Going to Rain Today," with its elegiac melody, near-recitative bridge, and rueful refrain, "Human kindness is overflowing." The song, included by Judy Collins on her 1966 album *In My Life*, presented the unmistakable Newman songwriting voice, with its pervasive irony, and humor and beauty in the midst of desolation—and its sense of writing for a character, as in a short story.

An even younger writer on the scene was Jimmy Webb, who in 1964, as a seventeen-year-old, moved with his family from Oklahoma to Southern California. The following year his mother died and his father decided to go back to Oklahoma. But Jimmy stayed on to pursue songwriting. He was going to college in San Bernardino and drove up to L.A. every weekend to make the rounds, "carrying my reel-to-reel tapes (in a paper sack)." He'd start with Dick Glasser, a producer at Reprise (the label Sinatra had started in 1961, after leaving Capitol), who, he recalled, was never in a buying mood. "I would go to Warner Bros. and get turned down. Verve, same story. I would hit the studios, Sunset Sound, Western Recorders and storefronts that didn't have names searching in vain for a singer who needed a song." One day, on a whim, he called on Jobete Music, Motown's L.A. publishing arm, and despite his inexperience and skin color, he landed a contract. Webb's tune "This Is Where I Come In" was recorded by one of Motown's rare white acts; better yet, he landed a song called "My Christmas Tree" on the Supremes' 1965 holiday LP. He met and worked with Billy Eckstine and Tony Martin and absorbed the assembly-line songwriting ethos that had been established by Berry Gordy. Webb remembers the rules and instructions: "Put the chorus first. Does it need a bridge or doesn't it? It was more helpful than a high-priced finishing school." The next year Webb met singer and producer Johnny Rivers, whom he described as "a *much* more experienced nineteen-year-old than I was." Rivers signed him to a publishing deal and recorded an utterly original Webb song called "By the Time I Get to Phoenix." Shortly after that, a group on Rivers's label, the Fifth Dimension, cut another Webb song, "Up, Up and Away," with the Wrecking Crew backing up.

One day in 1963, Brian Wilson, the musical leader and main songwriter of a group called the Beach Boys, was driving on a Southern California highway when "Be My Baby" came on the radio. Fifty years later he remembered, "I had to pull over to the side of the road—it blew my mind. It was a shock." At his first opportunity, he bought the Ronettes' single and started analyzing everything on it, determined to reproduce its genius for his own group.

Wilson, his two brothers Dennis and Carl, their cousin Mike Love, and a friend, Al Jardine, had started their band two years earlier. Brian's compositions were derivative, to put it kindly. The thrust of his lyrics can be sensed from the titles of the band's early hits: "Surfin'," "Surfin' Safari," "Surfer Girl," and "Surfin' U.S.A." Except for Brian, none of the boys were very good instrumentalists; the Wrecking Crew were the accompanists on their records, uncredited. The most distinctive thing about the Beach Boys was their sweet, Four Freshmen–influenced harmonies. But after his revelatory moment, Brian Wilson recalled, "I felt like I wanted to try to do something as good as that song." The effort led him, by the end of the year, to compose two classic pieces: "Don't Worry Baby" (which took "Be My Baby" explicitly as its model) and "The Warmth of the Sun" (written the day of John F. Kennedy's assassination). In 1964, '65, and '66, Wilson would expand his songwriting art, putting down on paper the beautiful and utterly distinctive sound that played continuously in his head. The period culminated in a masterpiece, *Pet Sounds*, with such songs as "Caroline,

No," "God Only Knows," and "Don't Talk (Put Your Head on My Shoulder)." Linda Ronstadt covered the last and said, "It has one of the most beautiful arcs of a melody I've ever heard. How can you sing about not talking, about silence? It's paralyzing and galvanizing at the same time."

Whenever Wilson was asked, though, he acknowledged that he had never made a record better than "Be My Baby."

Distilling his yearning into songs, Wilson was a reference point for a particular kind of singer-songwriter who had even earlier models as well: Romantic poets, or, looking yet farther back, medieval troubadours. Most of these young men slung their acoustic guitars on their backs, à la Woody Guthrie, and congregated around Greenwich Village coffeehouses and clubs. Through their use of original material, they began the process of differentiating themselves from earnest Folk Revival acts like the Kingston Trio and Peter, Paul and Mary. The man who drew everyone's attention was Bob Dylan, but among the others crafting impressive and decreasingly generic new songs in the early sixties were Tim Hardin, Fred Neil, Jim McGuinn, Richard Fariña, and John Sebastian, playing "jug band music or rhythm and blues" or the other genres his band, the Lovin' Spoonful, would later memorialize in "Do You Believe in Magic?" One of the first to move from authentic or ersatz folk songs, to political statements, all the way to personal expression, was Paul Simon, a buddy of Carole King's who had once made demos with her at Aldon and had had a minor hit in 1957 with the heavily Everly "Hey, Schoolgirl." The performance on the tune was credited to Tom and Jerry; "Jerry" was Simon's lifelong friend Art Garfunkel. By 1964, Columbia released an album under the boys' real names, *Wednesday Morning, 3AM*. It did so poorly that the duo decided to split up . . . until a Columbia producer had the idea of remixing one of the songs on the LP to a rock-and-roll arrangement. "The Sounds of Silence" went to number one on the charts, and Simon and Garfunkel were back in business.

The moments that appear in retrospect as obvious and profound turning points don't usually seem that way at the time. The Beatles' arrival in America in January 1964, in the form of their single "I Want to Hold Your Hand" and their subsequent performances on *The Ed Sullivan Show*, would appear to be an exception. It escaped no one that the Beatles were amazing. You could glimpse one of the amazing things about them in their knockout performance on *Ed Sullivan*; the more you kept listening to their records, the clearer it was. This was that they had absorbed basically everything that had happened in American popular music over the previous decade. Their cover songs, even now, radiate unmatched hipness and discernment. They covered King and Goffin ("Chains"), Chuck Berry ("Roll Over Beethoven"), Arthur Alexander ("Anna [Go to Him]"), Bacharach–David ("Walk On By"), the Coasters ("Searchin'"), the Miracles ("You've Really Got a Hold on Me"), and on and on. They covered the Coasters ("Young Blood") and they covered Buck Owens, a country singer out of Bakersfield, California ("Act Naturally"). The first song the band ever recorded (when they were still called the Quarrymen) was Buddy Holly's "That'll Be the Day"; when it came time to acquire a new name, their choice was partly a tribute to Holly's band, the Crickets. "The Beatles" won out over "The Foreverly Brothers," which was a contender because they loved the Everlys so much.

In the cover songs, the Beatles told us where they were coming from. But their originals were much more important. They took the tools and ideas of the 1957–1963 American songbook and exploded them in a glorious centrifugal cascade of melody and riveting vocals, with a back beat you couldn't lose. The band's early hits mainly wanted to make the listeners get up, twist, and shout, and that they did. But in 1965 (having absorbed what Bacharach, Dylan, Brian Wilson, the Byrds—a band fronted by Jim McGuinn, now called Roger—and other Yanks were doing, largely in response to *them*), Paul McCartney, John Lennon, and George Harrison came out with a collection of songs the likes of which no writer, or even a trio of them, had ever produced in a year. A partial list:

"Day Tripper," "Drive My Car," "Girl," "Help!," "If I Needed Someone," "I'm Looking Through You," "In My Life," "It's Only Love," "I've Just Seen a Face," "Michelle," "Norwegian Wood (This Bird Has Flown)," "Nowhere Man," "Think for Yourself," "Ticket to Ride," "We Can Work It Out," "The Word," "Yesterday," "You Won't See Me," "You've Got to Hide Your Love Away."

All of a sudden, as Jimmy Webb put it, "everything shifted. Rock and roll had morphed into something much more interesting musically. It was a gift from God to be alive and working in the music business from 1966 to the early 1970s. It's hard to imagine a more fecund atmosphere—the air was pregnant. Record companies were willing to let us do anything we wanted to. It wasn't like Mitch Miller was in the booth."

It's only a slight exaggeration to say that the Beatles' 1965 output set the template for all subsequent pop songs. (If you add their 1966 and 1967 work, the exaggeration recedes nearly to zero.) Lennon's "In My Life" was as confessional and moving as anything by Dylan or the new singer-songwriters already starting to emerge. A host of them were warming up for their entrances: John Prine in Chicago, James Taylor out of Massachusetts, Townes Van Zandt and Guy Clark in

Texas, Jeff Buckley and Jackson Browne in California, Kris Kristofferson in Nashville, and an impressive Canadian contingent comprising Leonard Cohen, Joni Mitchell, and Neil Young. "Norwegian Wood," also a Lennon tune, with its sitar accompaniment and minor-key voicings, suggested pop might fruitfully plant its flag in foreign lands. And if you closed your eyes while listening to McCartney's "Yesterday," you could swear you were listening to a lost classic from the Great American Songbook. Less than a year after that song's release, *Billboard* declared it a "modern standard" and reported that more than 175 versions had already been released, including renditions by Lawrence Welk, Perry Como, Xavier Cugat, and Mantovani.

The final page had been turned on one songbook. Another was just starting to be written.

ACKNOWLEDGMENTS

It's a pleasure to thank the many people who helped this project on its fairly long and winding road to becoming a book. Enthusiasm at the start of the process from Gary Giddins, a writer whose work I greatly respect, was enormously helpful and encouraging. Michael Feinstein, the chief page-turner of the Great American Songbook, gave the book his blessing early on and—equally important—pointed me in the direction of Ervin Drake and of Ray Evans's papers. Later on, two fine writers, Wes Davis and Gary Rosen, read the manuscript and had a lot of helpful ideas and suggestions.

Many other writers, scholars, and authorities generously provided information, encouragement, introductions, and other kinds of assistance: Jon Burlingame, Samuel Freedman, Adam Gopnik, Peter Guralnick, Tad Hershorn, Miles Krueger, John Leland, Jill Lepore, Joyce Maynard, Marc Myers, Mark Rotella, David Suisman, Michael Tisserand, Thomas Vinciguerra, Ed Ward, Joseph Weiss, and Sheila Weller.

I am grateful to the remarkable people who agreed to be interviewed. They are more or less my heroes. Their names are listed on page 267, but I'd like to make mention of two inspiring women who have since passed away: Marian McPartland and Mary Rodgers Guettel. They are among a number of interviewees who are not directly quoted in the book, but whose insights enriched my understanding of themes, people, and periods.

Thanks to friends and colleagues who offered insight and encouragement, and at the very least acted interested: Bruce Beans, Laurie Bernstein, Mark Bowden, John Caskey, Andy Cassel, Richard Davison, Jim Dean, Bruce Dorsey, Henry Fuhrmann, Denis Harper, Martha Hodes, Sam Hughes, John Jebb, Kevin Kerrane, McKay Jenkins, Don Lessem, Donald Mell, Dan Menaker, Elizabeth Mosier, Daniel Okrent, Rachel Pastan, Tom Pauly, Craig Pittman, Dan Rubin, Gene Seymour, Michael Stein, Bill Stempel, Nanette Tobin, and Rick Valelly.

ACKNOWLEDGMENTS

Special appreciation to three couples who put me up (and put up with me) on research trips: Ann Gerhart and Michael Sokolove, in Washington, D.C.; Ann Toler and Thomas Bourgeois, in Los Angeles; and Jana DeHart and John Marchese in New York.

As always, my work was greatly facilitated by the good work of librarians and archivists. Special mention goes to John W. Rumble at the Country Music Hall of Fame, Juliette Appold of the University of Pennsylvania, Jeff Bridgers at the Library of Congress, and Susan Brynteson and Linda Stein of the University of Delaware.

I could have not completed the book without the great work of my assistants Sara Wilson and Maddie Thomas. Research assistance was also provided by Nathan Truman and Lizy Yagoda, and, at the University of Delaware, Emily Arnold, Michael Golden, Hans Howk, Sean Kauffman, Daniel Kolitz, Mary Kate Reilly, and Anna Short.

Linda Ng has been an extraordinary photo researcher and aide. I also want to thank Michael Randolph for his cooperation and his fine work in curating the invaluable photographs of his father, William "PoPsie" Randolph.

Thanks to June Rosenthal Silver, for permission to quote from her sister Carolyn Leigh's papers.

My interest in and knowledge and appreciation of great American songs have been shaped over the years by the writings of Stephen Holden and the late Whitney Balliett, and by the radio programs of Jonathan Schwartz. I have been listening to him for four decades that have flown by as if by magic. Tony Bennett's six-decade dedication to the highest standards in repertoire and performance is an inspiration.

Thanks to Geoffrey Kloske of Riverhead Books, for the jacket, and much else. I am delighted to have had the opportunity to work with the whole Riverhead team, including Caty Gordon, Anna Jardine, Jynne Martin, Claire McGinnis, and Mary Stone. David Chesanow's astute copyediting saved me from error and infelicity.

The namesake of the Stuart Krichevsky Literary Agency and his colleagues, Shana Cohen and Ross Harris, are, in a word, aces.

I often marvel at my good fortune in sharing my life with Gigi Simeone, Lizy Yagoda, and Maria Yagoda. In the words of an underappreciated song by Cy Coleman and Carolyn Leigh, "It amazes me."

NOTES

Record Charts

This book includes frequent references to the ranking of individual records—"number-one record," "top ten," and so on. Unless otherwise indicated, the sources for these are the charts compiled by *Billboard* magazine, as collated in a serious of invaluable books written and edited by Joel Whitburn. The particular books I relied on most were:

The Billboard Book of Top 40 Albums. New York: Billboard, 1987.

The Billboard Book of Top 40 Hits. 8th edition. New York: Billboard, 2004.

Joel Whitburn's Pop Hits, 1940–1954: Compiled from Billboard's *Pop Singles Charts, 1940–1954.* Menomonee Falls, WI: Record Research, 1994.

Interviews

I conducted interviews with the following: Herb Alpert, Roger Angell, Irvin Arthur, Irving Caesar, Barbara Carroll, Bill Charlap, Ervin Drake, Michael Feinstein, Dave Frishberg, Norman Gimbel, Mary Rodgers Guettel, Sheldon Harnick, Dick Hyman, Jack Jones, Elliott Lawrence, Jo Sullivan Loesser, Susan Loesser, Johnny Mandel, Marion McPartland, Peter Nero, Phyllis Newman, Randy Newman, Bucky Pizzarelli, Curly Putman, Linda Ronstadt, Paul Schwartz, June Rosenthal Silver, Sandy Stewart, Charles Strouse, Gay Talese, Allen Toussaint, Jimmy Webb, and Tim Weston. In cases where a quotation is attributed to one of those people and no other source is given, it comes from the author interview.

Abbreviations

Evans. Ray Evans papers, Kislak Center for Special Collections, Rare Books and Manuscripts, University of Pennsylvania.

Leigh. Carolyn Leigh papers, Billy Rose Theatre Division, The New York Public Library.

Celler. U.S. Congress. House Antitrust Subcommittee of the Committee on the Judiciary, House of Representatives, *Monopoly Problems in Regulated Industries.* Part 2, vol. 3, 84th Cong., 2nd sess., 1956.

Pastore. U.S. Congress. Senate Subcommittee on Communications of the Committee on Interstate and Foreign Commerce, Amendment to the Communications Act of 1934 (Prohibiting Radio and Television Stations from Engaging in Music Publishing or Recording Business). 85th Cong., 2nd sess., 1958.

Prologue: Premises, Premises

1   **"Standard tunes, first of all":** "Keith Jarrett: 'I Want the Imperfections to Remain,'" *All Things Considered,* NPR, May 27, 2013, http://www.npr .org/2013/05/27/186505248/keith-jarrett-i-want-the-imperfections-to-remain.

6   **Near the height of the Great American Songbook era:** Duncan MacDougald Jr., "The Popular Music Industry." In Paul F. Lazarsfeld and Frank N. Stanton, *Radio Research 1941,* 66.

8   **Berlin's payments from ASCAP:** Laurence Bergreen, *As Thousands Cheer,* 524. Berlin got $87,000 from ASCAP in 1952 and $101,000 in 1954.

8   **A 1980 *People* magazine interview:** Barbara Rowes, "Johnny Marks Has Made Millions off 'Rudolph,' but the Songwriter Still Says Humbug," *People,* December 22, 1980.

I. Mr. Miller and Mr. Schwartz, 1954

13   **"Like, 'You know, all those songs'":** "Bob Dylan: The Paul Zollo Interview," Americansongwriter.com, https://www.americansongwriter.com/2012/01 /bob-dylan-the-paul-zollo-interview-3/5/.

14   **"wrote with total self-assurance":** Alec Wilder, *American Popular Song,* 313.

14   **Schwartz's father was a lawyer in Moscow:** Author interview with Paul Schwartz.

14   **"cut a suave path":** Jonathan Schwartz, *All in Good Time,* 23.

17   **A year later, some staffers at ASCAP put together figures:** *Pastore,* 88–89.

19   **Interviewed by *Cue* magazine:** Ralph Blumenthal, "Bob Merrill, 74, Composer and Lyricist, Dies," *New York Times,* February 19, 1998.

19   **"Their conclusions were the same as mine":** *Pastore,* 467.

20   **"I took a Broadway show score":** *Celler,* 4200.

21   **"ASCAP has tried to live":** "Justice Dept. Sifts ASCAP Complaints Against BMI," *Billboard,* April 12, 1952.

22   **"While top names like Rodgers & Hammerstein":** "Songsmiths Do Solo on $150,000,000 Suit; Touch Off Music-Radio Discord," *Variety,* November 11, 1953, 50.

22   **"preference to the performance":** *Schwartz v. Broadcast Music, Inc.,* 16 F.R.D., 31, 33 (S.D.N.Y. 1954).

22   **"placing American music in a strait jacket":** Russell Sanjek, *American Popular Music and Its Business*, 402.

22   **"20,000 pages of testimony":** *Schwartz v. Broadcast Music, Inc.*, 180 F. Supp. 322 (S.D.N.Y. 1959).

23   **Miller testified:** *Pastore*, 48.

24   **"Hereafter, more emphasis will be placed":** "New Pop Era Plotted by Col Records: Miller Post Sparks It," *Billboard*, February 11, 1950, 3.

24   **Within a year and a half, the label's pop music sales:** *Time*, "Music: How the Money Rolls In," August 20, 1951.

25   **"looked in the control room":** James Kaplan, *Frank*, 526.

25   **"donned a coonskin hat":** Arnold Shaw, *The Rockin' '50s*, 45.

26   **"There were publishers":** Robert Rice, "The Fractured Oboist," *The New Yorker*, June 6, 1953.

28   **"I thought it over":** *Pastore*, 49.

II. I Get a Kick out of You, 1885–1933

31   **"The word for Dick Rodgers' melodies":** Quoted in William McBrien, *Cole Porter*, 368.

31   **Tin Pan Alley background:** Ben Yagoda, "Lullaby of Tin Pan Alley," *American Heritage*, October/November 1983.

31   **The median total payment Foster received:** David Suisman, *Selling Sounds*, 23.

31   **"In his 1926 autobiography":** Charles K. Harris, *After the Ball*, 57.

32   **His brother the novelist Theodore Dreiser:** Quoted in Gary A. Rosen, *Unfair to Genius*, 12.

32   **"The reader will naturally wonder":** Harris, *After the Ball*, 15.

33   **"Nowadays, the consumption of songs in America":** "How Popular Song Factories Manufacture a Hit," *New York Times*, September 18, 1910.

34   **they generally sold a publisher:** Suisman, *Selling Sounds*, 44.

34   **"With a few notable exceptions":** Quoted ibid., 43.

37   **"I can speak of only one composer":** Alec Wilder, *American Popular Song*, 119–20.

38   **Early-twentieth-century changes:** Suisman, *Selling Sounds*, 319.

39   **A milestone . . . which sold two million records each:** Charles Hamm, *Yesterdays*, 336.

39   **By 1929, more than 105 million records:** Suisman, *Selling Sounds*, 16.

39 **"Previous to 1897 every song":** Paul Whiteman and Mary Margaret McBride, *Jazz*, 171.

39 **"The skill and genius of Tin Pan Alley":** Hamm, *Yesterdays*, 361.

41 **"popular songwriting is the most highly overpaid form":** Quoted in Russell Sanjek, *American Popular Music and Its Business*, 91.

42 **"It is true that music":** Quoted in Suisman, *Selling Sounds*, 173.

42 **About 190,000 radio units:** Ann Douglas, *Terrible Honesty*, 419.

42 **By the mid-1930s, ASCAP was annually collecting:** Hamm, *Yesterdays*, 339.

42 **by means of a complicated classification system:** Sanjek, *American Popular Music and Its Business*, 104.

43 **Jelly Roll Morton and ASCAP:** Howard Reich and William Gaines, "Down and Out in New York," *Chicago Tribune*, December 13, 1999.

43 **"People buy music":** Isaac Goldberg, *Tin Pan Alley*, 308.

44 **Max Dreyfus biography and quotations:** Yagoda, "Lullaby of Tin Pan Alley."

47 **"Important composers and lyricists of that day":** David Ewen, *The Life and Death of Tin Pan Alley*, 296–97.

47 **"was considered radical for this abuse":** Sanjek, *American Popular Music and Its Business*, 91.

47 **In the 1920s in particular, musical comedies:** Ibid., 355.

48 **"were no longer subsistence piece workers":** Rosen, *Unfair to Genius*, 22.

48 **Sigmund Romberg grossed:** Russell Sanjek, *From Print to Plastic*, 16.

48 **"Angry because Dick Trevor has not returned":** Thomas Hischak, *The Oxford Companion to the American Musical*, 411.

49 **Warner Bros. paid the team of Harry Warren and Al Dubin:** Sanjek, *American Popular Music and Its Business*, 153.

50 **"Harlem cabarets, other cabarets":** Edmund Wilson, *The Twenties*, 183. Wilson's references are to Hugo Riesenfeld (the second and third letters of his name were often transposed), a conductor and composer known for elevating jazz to the classical realm; Burton Rascoe, a literary critic; Webster Hall, a Greenwich Village ballroom famous for wild soirees; Vincent Lopez, a popular bandleader; and the burlesque shows offered by the Minsky family at the National Winter Garden theater on Houston Street.

51 **"displacement of beat":** Hamm, *Yesterdays*, 373.

52 **"Syncopation is the soul of every American":** Quoted in Douglas, *Terrible Honesty*, 356.

52 **"Our whole present music":** Gilbert Seldes, *The 7 Lively Arts*, 73.

53   **"In the search for song-pluggers":** Hazel Meyer, *The Gold in Tin Pan Alley*, 50.

53   **"As I breathlessly awaited":** Richard Rodgers, *Musical Stages*, 88.

54   **"Where did *he* get it?":** Quoted in Douglas, *Terrible Honesty*, 358.

55   **"combines slow and fast":** Mark N. Grant, *The Rise and Fall of the Broadway Musical*, 136.

55   **"Love songs":** Will Friedwald, *Stardust Melodies*, 6.

55   **"fast and jazzy":** Ira Gershwin, *Lyrics on Several Occasions*, 111.

56   **"all too often ultra-sentimental":** Kenneth S. Clark, "Why Our Popular Songs Don't Last," *Forum*, March 1934, 171.

57   **"polluting the once-pure air":** Quoted in Jonathan Yardley, *Ring*, 366–67.

III. *Jukebox Saturday Night, 1925–1942*

60   **Here are the songs that reached number one:** Joel Whitburn, *Pop Hits, 1940–1954*, 385–90.

60   **"There is better popular music today":** Abbe Niles, "Ballads, Songs and Snatches," *The Bookman*, April 1928.

60   **"too many" current offerings were "entirely too intricate":** Kenneth S. Clark, "Why Our Popular Songs Don't Last," *Forum*, March 1934, 170–71.

61   **"All those publishers":** Jack Lawrence, *They All Sang My Songs*, 91–92.

62   ***Variety*'s 1970 obituary of Marlo:** *Variety*, February 11, 1970, 63.

64   **"Play, Fiddle, Play" lawsuit:** Gary A. Rosen, *Unfair to Genius*, 6–7.

65   **"The 'sweet' technique":** Abbe Niles, "Ballads, Songs and Snatches," *The Bookman*, June 1928, 422.

66   **"The best white ensembles":** *Fortune*, August 1933, 90.

66   **"a weak sister incapable of holding":** *Music & Rhythm*, August 1941, 10, quoted in Lewis A. Erenberg, *Swingin' the Dream*, 69.

66   **"The stranglehold music publishers had":** John Hammond, *John Hammond on Record*, 142.

67   **The long-forgotten Shep Fields:** William Ruhlmann, *Breaking Records*, 78.

67   **"Hot musicians look down":** E. J. Nicholas and W. L. Werner, "Hot Jazz Jargon," *Vanity Fair*, November 1935, 71–72.

67   **"projected rich, full musical sounds":** George T. Simon, *The Big Bands*, 4.

68   **In an eight-month period in 1941 and 1942:** Peter Townsend, *Pearl Harbor Jazz*, 178.

68   **"Swing fused love songs":** Erenberg, *Swingin' the Dream*, 53.

69   **By 1937, *Variety* estimated:** Russell Sanjek, *American Popular Music and Its Business*, 204.

69   **All the top bands were heard:** Andre Millard, *America on Record*, 172.

69   **an average hit sold about 250,000 copies:** Duncan MacDougald, "The Popular Music Industry," in Paul F. Lazarsfeld and Frank N. Stanton, *Radio Research 1941*, 71.

70   **They consumed about 13 million records:** Millard, *America on Record*, 169.

71   **The most successful group:** Hamm, *Yesterdays*, 384–85.

71   **"When we started out":** Clarissa Start, "Man of Musical World," *St. Louis Post-Dispatch*, August 1, 1940.

74   **"He seems to have":** Johnny Mercer, unpublished memoir. Johnny Mercer Collection, Georgia State University.

75   **"who did not always receive credit":** Terry Teachout, *Duke*, 113.

76   **"It was a great period!":** Max Wilk, *They're Playing Our Song*, 147.

77   **"George died on July 11, 1937":** *Newsweek*, July 15, 1940.

77   **"The harmonic language of Tin Pan Alley":** Hamm, *Yesterdays*, 367.

79   **Livingston and Evans:** Unless otherwise noted, all quotations concerning Livingston and Evans are from scrapbooks, diaries, and correspondence in the Ray Evans Papers at the University of Pennsylvania.

83   **At the beginning of the Depression:** Philip H. Ennis, *The Seventh Stream*, 101.

IV. As Time Goes By, 1941–1948

87   **"do their bit in the present crisis":** "Gene Buck Tells Tin Pan Alley to Pen War Songs," *Variety*, December 1, 1941, 4.

90   **"Old songs and sentimental ballads":** Mike Levin, "Since You Went Away," *Down Beat*, November 1944, 1.

90   **"The trouble, from the viewpoint of America's Ministry of Propaganda":** Abel Green, "New Dance Steps of Martial Spirit May Be Necessary to Cue Songs from Slush into War Channels," *Variety*, October 7, 1942, 2.

90   **"hits me right where it hurts":** Judy Litoff and David Smith, *Since You Went Away: World War II Letters from American Women on the Home Front*, 107.

90   **"so inclined to escape":** *Down Beat*, June 1, 1942, 3.

91   **"I also think Frank showed":** Will Friedwald, *Sinatra!*, 126.

91   **Crosby had once told his in-house lyricist:** James Kaplan, "The King of Ring-a-Ding-Ding," *Movies Rock* (a *Vanity Fair* publication), December 2007.

92   **"In CBS's Manhattan playhouse":** *Time*, July 5, 1943.

92   **"put the kibosh on the big bands":** Friedwald, *Sinatra!*, 127.

94   **"We're going into the open market":** *Down Beat*, April 15, 1942, 12.

95   **"Four- and five- and even seven-voice":** Mel Tormé, *My Singing Teachers*, 161.

95   **"We record like mad":** Milt Gabler, *The Milt Gabler Story*, 12. Unpublished manuscript, Milt Gabler Papers, the Smithsonian Institution.

95   **In 1940, ten of twelve songs:** William Ruhlmann, *Breaking Records*, 169.

96   **All told, that year Como sold:** Russell Sanjek, *American Popular Music and Its Business*, 223.

97   **"I didn't want it to seem":** Quoted in Michael Castellini, "Sit In, Stand Up and Sing Out: Black Gospel Music and the Civil Rights Movement" (master's thesis, Georgia State University, 2013).

97   **"all these Wall Street types":** Will Friedwald, "When He Was 46 It Was a Very Good Year," *Wall Street Journal*, April 2, 2009.

100   **"We got a call from Louis Lipstone":** Gene Lees, *Portrait of Johnny*, 166.

101   **"It was not, as one realizes":** George Frazier, "Jocks, Jukes and Discs," *Variety*, April 9, 1947, 33.

103   **"The historic thing about 'The Paleface'":** "'The Paleface,' Without Bing Crosby and Dot Lamour, Opens at the Paramount," *New York Times*, December 16, 1948.

103   **"Only four studios":** "Budget Cuts Hit Tunesmiths," *Billboard*, November 15, 1947.

104   **"comparatively second rate":** *Detroit News*, February 22, 1947, in *Evans*.

106   **"I began to hate California":** Max Wilk, *They're Playing Our Song*, 158–59.

109   **"The *Road* pictures symbolized":** Wilfrid Sheed, *The House That George Built*, 235–36.

V. What Happened to the Music? 1946–1954

111   **"The Sinatra phase had ended":** Quoted in Arnold Shaw, *The Rockin' '50s*, 142.

111   **"When jazz and popular music lose":** Quoted in Richard Palmer, *Such Deliberate Disguises*, 21.

112 **In 1945, major networks dropped:** Lewis A. Erenberg, *Swingin' the Dream*, 217.

113 **"the most historic jam session in the annals of jazz":** *Time*, May 24, 1943, 63–64.

113 **"mixed up with popular music":** Nat Hentoff and Nat Shapiro, *Hear Me Talkin' to Ya*, 372.

114 **"different only in that its purpose seems to be":** "On the Stand: Dizzy Gillespie," *Billboard*, October 9, 1948.

114 **"So you get all them weird chords":** Quoted in Ernest Borneman, "'Bop Will Kill Business Unless It Kills Itself First'—Louis Armstrong," *Down Beat*, April 7, 1948, 2–3.

114 **"We're tired of that old New Orleans":** Richard Boyer, "BOP," *The New Yorker*, July 3, 1948, 28.

115 **But at the end of the twentieth century:** William Ruhlmann, *Breaking Records*, 99.

115 **"If the songs a country sings":** "Top Song Hits: Sentimental Ballads About Love Are Most Popular in U.S. Today," *Life*, October 21, 1946.

115 **In a 1949 *Billboard* poll:** "11th Annual College Poll," *Billboard*, June 11, 1949.

115 **"Cornell University, in addition":** "Campus Kids' Ork Squawks," *Billboard*, February 14, 1948, 19.

115 **"Ballroom operators complain":** Don Dornbrook, "Swing Has Swung," *Milwaukee Journal*, February 16, 1947, 8.

116 **"sweet-with-a-beat Elliot Lawrence":** "Dinah, Bing, Melchior, Cop Vocal Honors," *Billboard*, August 2, 1947, 38.

117 **"the Hit Parade . . . seemed to show":** Wilfrid Sheed, *The House That George Built*, 244.

118 **"Near You" as especially "decadent" and "bloodless":** "What's Wrong with Music," *Metronome*, April 1948, 16, quoted in Albin Zak, *I Don't Sound Like Nobody*, 87.

118 **"And just like that, the magical coincidence":** Sheed, *The House That George Built*, 244.

120 **"It's a throwback":** *Valley Times*, March 4, 1950. In *Evans*.

120 **"bellwether song of the folk music trend":** Allen Churchill, "Tin Pan Alley's Git-tar Blues," *New York Times*, July 15, 1951, 8.

121 **"a full-fledged resurgence":** Jack Gould, "Comedy and Music," *New York Times*, December 24, 1944, 35.

121 **"But there are more people":** Quoted in Elijah Wald, *How the Beatles Destroyed Rock 'n' Roll*, 154.

NOTES

122 **"Great songs aren't being written"**: *Down Beat*, July 30, 1952, 6, quoted in Zak, *I Don't Sound Like Nobody*, 59.

122 **"I've been looking for wonderful pieces"**: "What's Wrong with Music," *Metronome*, April 1948, 16, quoted in Zak, *I Don't Sound Like Nobody*, 87.

122 **"just hack out songs"**: Quoted in Cary Ginell, *Mr. B*, 125.

122 *Variety* **concurred, calling the 1948 crop of songs**: "Jukes, Jocks, and Disks," *Variety*, August 4, 1948, 34.

123 **what Tin Pan Alley "lived on" at mid-century**: Shaw, *The Rockin' 50s*, 14–15.

124 **"Are you out of your mind?"**: The Ray & Wyn Ritchie Evans Foundation. http://www.rayevans.org/.

124 **224 recordings of the song**: Ibid.

125 **"For years we did nothing but play"**: Frank Stacy, "Nat Cole Talks Back to Critics," *The Capitol*, April 1946.

125 **"Some creeps said"**: Quoted in Ginell, *Mr. B*, 107–8.

126 **"a pasta of Neapolitan, bel canto"**: Shaw, *The Rockin' 50s*, 21.

126 **Paramount logically offered**: Daniel Mark Epstein, *Nat King Cole*, 208.

127 **"Crux, essence and heart"**: Arnold Shaw, *Lingo of Tin-Pan Alley*, 15.

128 **"Everybody but the music publisher"**: Russell Sanjek, *American Popular Music and Its Business*, 329–30. Ellipsis in original.

129 **"A musical composition in itself"**: *Waring v. WDAS Broadcasting Station*, 327 Pa. 433, 441, 194 A. 631, 635 (Pa. 1937), quoted in Zak, *I Don't Sound Like Nobody*, 21.

129 **"chattel"**: *RCA Mfg. Co. v. Whiteman*, 114 F.2d 86, 89 (C.A.2 1940), quoted in Zak, *I Don't Sound Like Nobody*, 24.

130 **"complete with chandelier"**: "Martin Block, Disc Jockey, Dies; Started 'Make-Believe Ballroom,'" *New York Times*, September 20, 1967.

130 **There were 813 AM stations**: Philip H. Ennis, *The Seventh Stream*, 136.

130 **"As I got to the outskirts"**: Roy Kohn, *Songplugger, or How Much Is That Doggie in the Window?*, 19.

131 **"hated by the majority"**: Ennis, *The Seventh Stream*, 120.

131 **two hundred new songs were offered**: Sanjek, *American Popular Music and Its Business*, 236.

131 **one-in-twenty chance**: Ennis, *The Seventh Stream*, 120.

131 **"As it twanged its way":** Arnold Passman, *The Deejays*, 128.

132 **"a postwar show business phenomenon":** Quoted ibid., 123.

132 **"the disc jockey, in our opinion":** "Lo, the Poor Disc Jockey," *Billboard*, February 7, 1948, 36.

132 **"It was believed . . . that the city":** Ennis, *The Seventh Stream*, 12.

133 **"Ballads take a long time to develop":** "Howie Richmond Views Craft of Song," *Billboard*, August 28, 1999, 43.

133 **One way Richmond tried to do so:** Shaw, *The Rockin' '50s*, 65.

133 **His methods paid off:** "Songwriters Hall of Fame 1983 Award & Induction Ceremony." http://www.songwritershalloffame.org/.

133 **"Cut 'em, press 'em, ship 'em":** Sanjek, *American Popular Music and Its Business*, 237.

133 **"Oddly enough for a man of such musical ability":** George Frazier, "Weird Business— Pop Music," *Vogue*, August 1, 1954.

134 **"What makes you want to dig":** Will Friedwald, *Sinatra!*, 178.

134 **"Whatever became of music?":** John S. Wilson, "Weston: What Became of Music?" *Down Beat*, December 30, 1949, 7, quoted in Keir Keightley, "You Keep Coming Back Like a Song."

136 **"Miller had too much power":** Donald Clarke, *The Rise and Fall of Popular Music*, 408.

137 **"There he experimented with recording techniques":** Jon Pareles, "Les Paul, Guitar Innovator, Dies at 94." *New York Times*, August 13, 2009.

138 **The song . . . sold more than 20 million copies:** http://www.songwriters halloffame.org.

138 **"It's easy to laugh at Johnnie Ray":** Howard Taubman, "Cry with Johnnie Ray," *New York Times*, April 27, 1952.

140 **"finest musicianship":** Quoted in Friedwald, *Sinatra!*, 175.

140 **"an absolutely first-rate oboist":** Quoted in Richard Severo, "Mitch Miller, Maestro of the Singalong, Dies at 99," *New York Times*, August 2, 2010.

140 **"deep lack of interest":** Robert Rice, "The Fractured Oboist," *The New Yorker*, June 6, 1953.

140 **"I wouldn't buy that stuff for myself":** "Music: How the Money Rolls In," *Time*, August 20, 1951.

140 **"I think Mitch Miller":** Friedwald, *Sinatra!*, 178.

141 **"Mitch had a knack":** Tony Bennett with Will Friedwald, *The Good Life*, 172–74.

142 **"I thought the lyric ranged":** Rosemary Clooney with Joan Barthel, *Girl Singer*, 74.

142 **"Hey, that's a nice tune":** Friedwald, *Sinatra!*, 188.

143 **"Chief beef hinges on Sinatra's claim":** Ibid., 196.

143 **"Do I still think it's hard":** Nat Hentoff, "Hokey Tunes 'Bug' Frank," *Down Beat*, March 25, 1953.

143 **"was trying to find a scapegoat":** Ted Fox, *In the Groove*, 47.

144 **"My name is 'Mitchell'":** James Kaplan, *Frank*, 476.

144 **"was known for making the guitar sound like a chicken":** Ibid., 527.

144 **"Before Mr. Miller's arrival at Columbia Records":** *Celler*, 4675.

145 **"That is the trouble":** Ibid., 4911.

147 **"I'd go out to Las Vegas":** Charles Granata, *Sessions with Sinatra*, 77.

VI. Brill Building Boys, and Girl, 1950–1955

149 **"the small-scale amusement industry":** A. J. Liebling, *The Jollity Building*, 30.

149 **"the Brill Building *was* Tin Pan Alley":** Richard Adler with Lee Davis, *You Gotta Have Heart*, 7.

150 **"The offices were so small":** Burt Bacharach, *Anyone Who Had a Heart*, 42, 43.

152 **"I was trying to roll myself back":** Stephen Sondheim, *Finishing the Hat*, 381.

153 **"the nature of musical literacy changed":** Phillip Ennis, *The Seventh Stream*, 41.

153 **"It looked simple":** Paul Zollo, *Songwriters*, 200.

154 **"If I would work with him every day":** Jackson R. Bryer and Richard A. Davison, *The Art of the American Musical*, 97.

155 **"Steam Heat" origin:** Adler with Davis, *You Gotta Have Heart*, 10–11.

157 **"I want you to play everything":** Jerry Herman, *Showtune*, 19. The meeting was in 1951.

158 **"I became a song fan":** Phillip D. Atteberry, "A Conversation with Dave Frishberg," *Mississippi Rag*, April 1996.

159 **"Frank always wanted to be":** Thomas Laurence Riis, *Frank Loesser*, 234.

159 **thirty-six separate recordings of its songs:** Ibid., 238.

160 **"something that didn't bother us much":** Adler with Davis, *You Gotta Have Heart*, 30.

163 **"couldn't take dictation":** C. Gerald Fraser, "Carolyn Leigh, Lyricist for 'Peter Pan,' Dies," *New York Times*, November 21, 1983.

163 **One day she dialed a wrong number:** *Leigh.*

164 **she'd just come back from a visit to her father:** Author interview with June Rosenthal Silver.

164 **"His name is 'Moose'":** Carolyn Leigh to Robert Marks, December 28, 1953. This and the following quotations from Leigh (hereafter CL) correspondence are from *Leigh.*

165 **"If you are not tied up":** Howard Richmond to CL, August 24, 1953.

165 **"who promptly decided":** CL to Robert Marks, December 28, 1953.

166 **"The general picture":** CL to Charlie Adams, undated.

166 **she got calls from seventeen publishers:** *Variety*, March 3, 1954.

166 **it had sold 350,000 copies:** "'Young at Heart' Title of New Warner Flick," *Billboard*, June 12, 1954, 18.

167 **Leigh's share of that:** Statement from Sunbeam Music, August 15, 1954. *Leigh.* "Standard royalty" for writers at the time was three cents a copy.

167 **"the current crop of young songsmiths":** "Jerry Ross (& Adler), B'way's Cleffing 'Boy Wonder,' Dies at 29," *Variety*, November 16, 1955, 49.

167 **The song came on the radio:** Mary Martin, *My Heart Belongs*, 205.

168 **"He said, 'Are you busy now?'":** New York *World-Telegram and Sun*, October 4, 1954.

168 **"If I can live a life of crime":** "On Peter Pan," *The Journal of the Society of Stage Directors and Choreographers*, June 1982.

168 **"the tendency of Carolyn's to always write":** Deborah Jowitt, *Jerome Robbins*, 245.

169 **"dull . . . with lyrics to match":** "Legit Tryout," *Variety*, July 21, 1954, 3.

169 **"We were told":** CL to Harry Kalcheim, William Morris Agency, August 8, 1954.

170 **"the second act socko number":** "Plays Out of Town," *Variety*, July 21, 1954, 50.

170 **"just too sad":** Author interview with Sandy Stewart.

170 **"My boy, you have not written a score":** Ibid.

170 **"the largest audience":** *Collier's*, May 27, 1955.

171 **"hope that you haven't gone":** Robert Marks to CL, March 15, 1954.

171 **"No—I haven't yet gone":** CL to Marks, March 17, 1954.

171 **"At least one of them":** Booton Herndon, "The Battle over the Music You Hear," *Redbook*, December 1957, 91.

172 **"ankled BMI":** *Variety*, May 18, 1955.

172 **"I am fed up":** CL to Jerry Livingston, January 10, 1956.

173 **"Every composer I've met":** CL to Harold and Edith Spina, November 7, 1954.

173 **"You may very well object":** CL to Elma Duncan, October 19, 1955.

VII. The Big Beat, 1951–1968

175 **"Things were pretty sleepy":** Bob Dylan, *Chronicles: Volume One*, 5.

177 **a 1953 *Billboard* headline:** Bob Rolontz, "Pop—C.&W.—R.&B.: Demarcation Lines Are Growing Hazy," *Billboard*, September 12, 1953, 15.

177 **an all-time high of $15 million in 1953:** Ed Ward, Geoffrey Stokes, and Ken Tucker, *Rock of Ages*, 87.

177 **"The teen-age tide has swept":** Bob Rolontz and Joel Friedman, "Teen-Agers Demand Music with a Beat, Spur Rhythm-Blues," *Billboard*, April 24, 1954, 1.

177 **"The rhythm and blues market":** Steve Schickel, "A La Country & Western, R.&B. Music Invades Pop Market; Jukes, Disk Stores Feeling Trend," *Billboard*, August 14, 1954.

177 **"the r.&b. invasion":** Paul Ackerman, "Tin Pan Alley Days Fade on Pop Music Broader Horizons," *Billboard*, October 15, 1955, 1.

178 **"the popularity of the rock 'n' roll beat":** *Variety*, March 30, 1955, quoted in Albin Zak, *I Don't Sound Like Nobody*, 206.

178 **"From this point on":** "R&R Has 'Had It' Here, O'Seas Not Hot: ASCAP on Top," *Variety*, October 17, 1956, 54.

178 **In a 1956 interview . . . Johnny Green:** *Down Beat*, September 19, 1956, 44.

178 **"two words to a lyric":** Jim Walsh, "'Pops' on Pop Music Biz Today," *Variety*, June 5, 1957, 45.

178 **As *Billboard* had to acknowledge:** *Billboard*, September 9, 1957, 18.

178 **"The so-called 'tunes'":** Linda Martin and Kerry Segrave, *Anti-Rock*, 45.

179 **"The people of this country":** *The Instrumentalist*, September 1958, 92.

179 **"Rock 'n' roll smells phony and false":** Gertrude Samuels, "Why They Rock 'n' Roll—and Should They?" *New York Times Magazine*, January 12, 1958, 19. The Sinatra quotation was attributed to an unnamed "Paris magazine." It is an open question if he actually said it, and phrases like "imbecilic reiteration" and "martial

music" don't especially sound like Sinatra. But the quotation was in circulation for some four decades before his death, and he doesn't seem to have denied it.

179 **"Svengali grip on the teenagers"**: "Biz Big but So Are Kids' Riots," *Variety*, April 11, 1956, 1.

179 **"definitely influenced in their lawlessness"**: Ruth Stevens, "Editorially Speaking . . . ," *Music Journal* 16 (1958), 3.

180 **"leer-ics"**: The first installment appeared in *Variety* on February 22, 1955.

180 **Radio stations around the country**: Martin and Segrave, *Anti-Rock*, 21.

180 **"Wash-Out-the-Air" subcommittee**: Ibid., 23–24.

182 **"because she thought it was a children's song"**: http://www.rayevans.org/.

182 **"Paramount had told him"**: Typed manuscript, "Act Number Three," *Evans*.

182 **"Last Saturday when I heard"**: Harry Ruby to Ray Evans and Jay Livingston, September 10, 1956. *Evans*. "Cement Mixer" was a 1946 jazz novelty number by Slim Gaillard. "On the Street Where You Live" was from Lerner and Loewe's smash Broadway musical *My Fair Lady*; Vic Damone's rendition reached number four on the charts.

183 **selling more than 18 million records**: *Billboard*, December 21, 1968. The "Tammy" Oscar loss may have been the result of excessive zeal. Universal sent out more than two thousand copies of the record to Academy members, plus a letter purportedly handwritten by Tammy herself. "Stunt has the competition burning," wrote *The Hollywood Reporter*. "Feeling is this is electioneering and shouldn't be permitted." The song was satirized by Stan Freberg on his album *The Madison Ave. Werewolf*: "When I hold your sweet, hairy hands tight in mine . . . Clammy! Clammy!"

183 **"The kids are being short-changed"**: *Los Angeles Mirror-News*, March 14, 1958, quoted in *Evans*.

184 **"a call to veteran songwriters"**: "Vet Cleffers Must Get Hip to Market," *Billboard*, March 10, 1958.

184 **"probably the very first rock and roll record"**: Jonny Whiteside, *Cry*, 102.

184 **"paunchy prophet of doom"**: Mitch Miller, "June, Moon, Swoon and Ko Ko Mo," *New York Times Magazine*, April 24, 1955, 19. Intentionally or not, Miller had the paunchy prophet mangle the title of "Tweedlee Dee." LaVern Baker had recorded the song for Atlantic Records the year before; true to form, Georgia Gibbs's copycat cover version for Mercury was a bigger hit.

185 **"Emotion never makes you a hit"**: Will Friedwald, *Sinatra!*, 24–25.

185 **"To say you've grossly mishandled"**: "Deejay: Performer or Puppet?," *Variety*, March 12, 1958, 60.

186   **When a special master appointed by the court:** Russell Sanjek, *American Popular Music and Its Business*, 423.

186   **"adamant in their demands":** "Cleffers Nix Hanging on Webs' Bid to 'Divest' If Suit Is Withdrawn," *Variety*, October 3, 1956, 63.

187   **"an army of disc jockeys":** Marya Mannes, "Who Decides What Songs Are Hits?," *Reporter* 16 (1957), 36.

187   **"Have you, along with millions" . . . "under-the-counter bribes":** Booton Herndon, "The Battle over the Music You Hear," *Redbook*, December 1957, 88.

188   **"one of ASCAP's best friends":** Sanjek, *American Popular Music and Its Business*, 404.

188   **"an electronic curtain":** *Celler*, 4208.

188   **"rock and roll and the other musical monstrosities":** Ibid., 4425–26. Rose was referring to "Love Me, and the World Is Mine," a 1906 song by Ernest Ball that was popular among barbershop quartets; "He Beeped When He Shoulda Bopped," a 1940s number by Dizzy Gillespie; and "Be-Bop-A-Lula," a 1956 rock-and-roll song by Gene Vincent.

189   **"they managed to jam the airwaves":** Ibid., 4196.

189   **"A few years ago":** Ibid., 4219. "Smoke Gets in Your Eyes" and "Indian Love Call" were Harbach compositions.

190   **"That was a good song":** Ibid., 4912.

191   **"This is a BMI number":** Ibid., 4180.

191   **ASCAP's advantage was even greater:** Ibid., 4221.

192   **"From your reading the program logs":** Ibid., 4691.

192   **"Can you give us the call letters":** Ibid., 4962.

192   **"despite an apparent attitude of prejudgment":** Bob Chandler, "Celler Winds Probe with No Major Net Monopoly Findings, but Trouble Is Still Looming on D. of J. Front," *Variety*, October 3, 1956, 32.

193   **"What do you think is going to happen":** *Pastore*, 16.

193   **"the animal instinct in modern teenagers":** Ibid., 108–9.

194   **"Senators present listened in chill silence":** "'Payola' Hit at BMI Inquiry," *Billboard*, March 24, 1958.

194   **"I don't like rock and roll too much":** *Pastore*, 10–11.

195   **"a gratuitous insult to thousands":** Ibid., 141–42.

195 **"If you attack country music"**: Sanjek, *American Popular Music and Its Business*, 427.

195 **"Well, I tried to get into ASCAP"**: *Pastore*, 448.

195 **"I started writing my own material"**: Ibid., 497.

195 **"I . . . found that the welcome mat"**: Ibid., 524.

196 **"the extensive, if not prolific, affidavits and briefs"**: *Schwartz v. Broadcast Music, Inc.*, 180 F. Supp. 325 (S.D.N.Y. 1959).

196 **"No matter how phrased"**: Ibid., 332.

196 **However, the following March, Sylvester J. Ryan:** Ibid., 455.

197 **"We've entered the era"**: "Rackets Infest Music Industry, Says Nat Cole," *Variety*, March 25, 1959, 57.

197 **"The very general method"**: "Okeh Distribution Shifted to Indies in Two Markets," *Billboard*, October 4, 1952, 23.

197 **"relatively small fry"**: *New York Times*, November 20, 1959, quoted in Kerry Segrave, *Payola in the Music Industry*, 104.

198 **four deejays in Norfolk, Virginia:** Kingsport, Tennessee, *News*, November 26, 1959, via newspaperarchive.com.

198 **"What they call payola"**: Segrave, *Payola in the Music Industry*, 112.

199 **"going to school and giving the teacher a better gift"**: Ibid., 129.

199 **"junk music, rock and roll stuff"**: Ibid., 39.

200 **By 1955 . . . half of all record revenues:** Elijah Wald, *How the Beatles Destroyed Rock 'n' Roll*, 184.

201 **"the tunes got slower"**: Joseph Lanza, *Elevator Music*, 72.

201 **"reliance on strings without the jazz feel"**: Ibid., 74.

202 **"Slower, more hypnotic time signatures"**: Ibid., 69.

202 **"like the sound of pissing"**: William Henry, *The Great One*, 141.

205 **"Have found phenomenal 19 year old boy"**: www.johnnymathis.com.

206 **"the rock wave was cresting"**: Rosemary Clooney with Joan Barthel, *Girl Singer*, 171.

206 **"What we have been witnessing"**: Arnold Shaw, "Upheaval in Popular Music," *Harper's*, May 1959, 82.

207 **"the movie business, and by extension the movie-music business"**: Jon Burlingame, e-mail to author.

210 **By 1960, albums had surpassed singles:** Wald, *How the Beatles Destroyed Rock 'n' Roll*, 198.

211 **"Instead of fearing payola":** Abel Miller, "Jockeys Relearning 'Diskmanship' As Payola Probe Helps to Clear Air of Rock 'n' Roll 'Drivel': Mitch Miller," *Variety*, March 9, 1960, 59.

211 **"the wheel" was "starting to turn":** "Music Biz's Classy Comeback," *Variety*, March 16, 1960, 1.

211 **"knock rock 'n' roll out of the musical box":** Mike Gross, "FM Throws Block at Rock," *Variety*, August 16, 1961, 43. In 1961, "long-hair" was still a derisive epithet for classical music.

212 **"Her clear-lighted voice poured":** "Sibyl with Guitar," *Time*, November 23, 1962.

213 **"greatest ever preponderance":** Albin Zak, *I Don't Sound Like Nobody*, 230.

213 **"bands called the Byrds":** Tony Bennett with Will Friedwald, *The Good Life*, 179.

214 **selling a total of 13 million copies:** Andre Millard, *America on Record*, 234.

215 **Number of Broadway musicals:** IBDB.com.

215 **"In today's musical":** Quoted in William McBrien, *Cole Porter*, 363.

215 **"nothing has given me":** Ibid., 374.

216 **"the last musical he had really enjoyed":** Wilfrid Sheed, *The House That George Built*, 90–91.

216 **"At the moment, there's nothing":** Murray Schumach, "Composer Tells of Movie Abuses," *New York Times*, August 10, 1961, 17.

216 **"In the past four years":** John S. Wilson, "36 Years on the Hit Parade," *New York Times*, March 21, 1965, X13.

219 **"to hear this new music":** Clive Davis, *Clive*, 36–37.

VIII. Fly Me to the Moon, 1939–1965

222 **Gershwin, Arlen, Robin quotations:** Max Wilk, *They're Playing Our Song*, 93, 153, 110.

225 **"virtually the only artists to keep performing":** Will Friedwald, *Stardust Memories*, 355.

225 **In 1954 . . . Howard wrote a haunting song:** "Product of 20 Minutes: A Million-Dollar Song," *New York Times*, December 19, 1988.

226 **"never possessed a great voice":** Stephen Citron, *Jerry Herman*, 36.

226 **"Everything I learned":** James Haskins, *Mabel Mercer*, 114.

227 **"When Frank listened to the playback":** Peter J. Levinson, *September in the Rain*, 113.

230 **Granz hatched the idea—"for kicks":** Tad Hershorn, *Norman Granz*, 171.

231 **"I thought of jazz and popular song":** William Zinsser, *Easy to Remember*, 186.

231 **"performed a cultural transaction":** Frank Rich, "Journal: How High the Moon," *New York Times*, June 19, 1996.

232 **"had no hit records and was virtually forgotten":** Bill Simon and Paul Ackerman, "Too Much of a Good Thing Possible with Those Old Standards: Abundant Record Versions of Old Songs Raise Saturation Problems," *Billboard*, March 2, 1957, 1, 22.

234 **"I heard and saw jazz's":** http://www.jazzwax.com/2010/03/interview-george-avakian-part-3.html.

237 **"As you may know":** Sheldon Harnick to Carolyn Leigh, *Leigh*. Leigh responded in kind two days later, praising Harnick's skill with comic songs: "You are a source of inspiration and wonderment to *me*. Having noted your success with songs that tickle people's imaginations and make them laugh, I thought to try my hand at them too. The results have been edifying: what you arrive at through sheer talent, I shall only be able to skirt the eddies of through hard, hard work and successful mimicry. Yet I love the theatre, and what you do is so important to musical comedy that I shall go on using your work as an example to follow.

"So you see; you can't let us down. As for your ballads—it's utter nonsense that anyone with your talent can write a weak one. You simply underestimate your own capabilities—so let's hear no more foolishness on that subject."

238 **"I was tearing my hair out":** Thomas Vinciguerra, "The Elusive Girl from Ipanema," *Wall Street Journal*, July 2, 2012.

Epilogue: Do You Believe in Magic? 1957–1965

243 **In 2000 . . . Mojo asked . . . ten best songs:** Jonathan Gregg, "So, What Are Your Ten Best Songs of All Time?," *Time*, July 12, 2000.

243 **"R&B is an adult music":** Jerry Leiber and Mike Stoller, *Hound Dog*, 181.

244 **"moving closer to pop in style and content":** Bob Rolontz, "R & R Recedes Slowly; Still Packs Punch; Ballads Gain," *Billboard*, November 24, 1958, 3.

245 **"The office was a house in Goodlettsville":** Interview with Hank Cochran, Country Music Foundation Oral History Project, July 3, 1991.

246 **"The things they're writing":** Max Wilk, *They're Playing Our Song*, 110.

NOTES

247 **"The money one earned from writing":** Eljah Wald, *How the Beatles Destroyed Rock 'n' Roll*, 242.

248 **"he wanted to make R&B more appealing":** Leiber and Stoller, *Hound Dog*, 179.

249 **One morning Gordy found out:** Gerald Posner, *Motown*, 150–51.

250 **"That was the first time":** Burt Bacharach, *Anyone Who Had a Heart*, 53.

250 **"After I did that session":** Ibid., 75.

251 **"We take three days to two weeks":** Quoted in Kal Rudman, "David & Bachrach [*sic*] Profile: Part 1," *Billboard*, August 8, 1964, 14.

251 **"special kind of grace and elegance":** Bacharach, *Anyone Who Had a Heart*, 74.

251 **"Dionne could sing that high":** Ibid., 78.

253 **"Each was barely big enough":** Carole King, *A Natural Woman*, 90.

255 **"He wore his ambition like a topcoat":** Leiber and Stoller, *Hound Dog*, 170.

255 **"I yelled over the phone":** Marc Myers, "The Song That Conquered Radio," *Wall Street Journal*, July 12, 2012.

258 **"carrying my reel-to-reel tapes":** Jimmy Webb, *Tunesmith*, 345.

259 **"I had to pull over":** Marc Spitz, "Still Tingling Spines, 50 Years Later," *New York Times*, August 16, 2013.

263 ***Billboard* declared it a "modern standard":** Wald, *How the Beatles Destroyed Rock 'n' Roll*, 233.

BOOKS CITED

Adler, Richard, with Lee Davis. *You Gotta Have Heart: An Autobiography*. New York: D. I. Fine, 1989.

Bacharach, Burt. *Anyone Who Had a Heart: My Life and Music*. New York: HarperCollins, 2013.

Bennett, Tony, with Will Friedwald. *The Good Life*. New York: Pocket Books, 1998.

Bergreen, Laurence. *As Thousands Cheer: The Life of Irving Berlin*. New York: Viking, 1990.

Bryer, Jackson R., and Richard A. Davison. *The Art of the American Musical: Conversations with the Creators*. Piscataway, NJ: Rutgers University Press, 2005.

Cahn, Sammy. *I Should Care: The Sammy Cahn Story*. New York: Arbor House, 1974.

Citron, Stephen. *Jerry Herman: Poet of the Showtune*. New Haven, CT: Yale University Press, 2004.

Clarke, Donald. *The Rise and Fall of Popular Music*. New York: St. Martin's Press, 1995.

Clooney, Rosemary, with Joan Barthel. *Girl Singer: An Autobiography*. New York: Random House, 1999.

Davis, Clive. *Clive: Inside the Record Business*. New York: William Morrow, 1975.

Douglas, Ann. *Terrible Honesty: Mongrel Manhattan in the 1920s*. New York: Farrar, Straus & Giroux, 1995.

Dylan, Bob. *Chronicles: Volume One*. New York: Simon & Schuster, 2004.

Emerson, Ken. *Always Magic in the Air: The Bomp and Brilliance of the Brill Building Era*. New York: Viking, 2005.

Ennis, Philip H. *The Seventh Stream: The Emergence of Rocknroll in American Popular Music*. Hanover, NH: University Press of New England, 1992.

Epstein, Daniel Mark. *Nat King Cole*. New York: Farrar, Straus & Giroux, 1999.

Erenberg, Lewis A. *Swingin' the Dream: Big Band Jazz and the Rebirth of American Culture*. Chicago: University of Chicago Press, 1998.

Ewen, David. *The Life and Death of Tin Pan Alley: The Golden Age of American Popular Music*. New York: Funk & Wagnalls, 1964.

Forte, Allen. *The American Popular Ballad of the Golden Era, 1924–1950*. Princeton, NJ: Princeton University Press, 1995.

Fox, Ted. *In the Groove: The People Behind the Music*. New York: St. Martin's Press, 1986.

Friedwald, Will. *Sinatra! The Song Is You: A Singer's Art*. New York: Scribner, 1995.

———. *Stardust Melodies: The Biography of Twelve of America's Most Popular Songs*. New York: Random House, 2002.

Furia, Philip. *Skylark: The Life and Times of Johnny Mercer*. New York: St. Martin's Press, 2003.

———, and Laurie Patterson. *The Songs of Hollywood*. New York: Oxford University Press, 2010.

Gavin, James. *Intimate Nights: The Golden Age of New York Cabaret*. New York: Grove Weidenfeld, 1991.

Gershwin, Ira. *Lyrics on Several Occasions*. New York: Alfred A. Knopf, 1959.

Giddins, Gary. *Bing Crosby: A Pocketful of Dreams, The Early Years 1903–1940*. New York: Little, Brown, 2001.

Ginell, Cary. *Mr. B: The Music & Life of Billy Eckstine*. Milwaukee: Hal Leonard Books, 2013.

Goldberg, Isaac. *Tin Pan Alley: A Chronicle of the American Popular Music Racket*. New York: John Day, 1930.

Granata, Charles. *Sessions with Sinatra: Frank Sinatra and the Art of Recording*. Chicago: A Cappella, 1999.

Grant, Mark N. *The Rise and Fall of the Broadway Musical*. Boston: Northeastern University Press, 2005.

Greenspan, Charlotte. *Pick Yourself Up: Dorothy Fields and the American Musical*. New York: Oxford University Press, 2010.

Hamm, Charles. *Yesterdays: Popular Song in America*. New York: W. W. Norton, 1979.

Hammond, John, and Irving Townsend. *John Hammond on Record: An Autobiography*. New York: Summit Books, 1977.

Hanson, Bruce K. *Peter Pan on Stage and Screen, 1904–2010*. 2nd edition. Jefferson, NC: McFarland, 2011.

Harris, Charles K. *After the Ball: Forty Years of Melody*. New York: Frank-Maurice, 1926.

Hartman, Kent. *The Wrecking Crew: The Inside Story of Rock and Roll's Best-Kept Secret*. New York: St. Martin's Griffin, 2013.

Haskins, James. *Mabel Mercer: A Life*. New York: Atheneum, 1987.

Havers, Richard. *Verve: The Sound of America*. London: Thames & Hudson, 2013.

Henry, William. *The Great One: The Life and Legend of Jackie Gleason*. New York: Doubleday, 1992.

Hentoff, Nat, and Nat Shapiro. *Hear Me Talkin' to Ya: The Story of Jazz as Told by the Men Who Made It*. New York: Rinehart 1955.

Herman, Jerry. *Showtune: A Memoir*. New York: Donald I. Fine Books, 1996.

Hershorn, Tad. *Norman Granz: The Man Who Used Jazz for Justice*. Berkeley: University of California Press, 2011.

Hischak, Thomas. *The Oxford Companion to the American Musical: Theatre, Film, and Television*. New York: Oxford University Press, 2008.

Jablonski, Edward. *Harold Arlen: Rhythm, Rainbows, and Blues*. Boston: Northeastern University Press, 1996.

Jeness, David, and Don Velsey. *Classic American Popular Song: The Second Half-Century, 1950–2000*. New York: Routledge, 2006.

Jenkins, Bruce. *Goodbye: In Search of Gordon Jenkins*. Berkeley, CA: Frog Books, 2005.

Jowitt, Deborah. *Jerome Robbins: His Life, His Theater, His Dance*. New York: Simon & Schuster, 2004.

Kaplan, James. *Frank: The Voice*. New York: Doubleday, 2010.

Kimball, Robert, and Steve Nelson. *The Complete Lyrics of Frank Loesser*. New York: Alfred A. Knopf, 2003.

King, Carole. *A Natural Woman: A Memoir*. New York: Grand Central Publishing, 2012.

Kingsbury, Paul, Michael McCall, and John W. Rumble, eds. *The Encyclopedia of Country Music*. 2nd edition. New York: Oxford University Press, 2012.

Kirchner, Bill, ed. *The Oxford Companion to Jazz*. New York: Oxford University Press, 2000.

Kohn, Roy. *Songplugger, or How Much Is That Doggie in the Window?* Fort Worth: Bear-Manor Media, 2011.

Lanza, Joseph. *Elevator Music: A Surreal History of Muzak, Easy-Listening and Other Moodsong*. New York: St. Martin's Press, 1994.

Lawrence, Jack. *They All Sang My Songs*. Fort Lee, NJ: Barricade Books, 2004.

Lazarsfeld, Paul F., and Frank N. Stanton, eds. *Radio Research 1941*. New York: Duell, Sloan and Pearce, 1942.

Lees, Gene. *Portrait of Johnny: The Life of John Herndon Mercer*. New York: Pantheon, 2004.

———. *The World of Lerner and Loewe*. Lincoln: University of Nebraska Press, 1990.

Leiber, Jerry, and Mike Stoller, with David Ritz. *Hound Dog: The Leiber and Stoller Autobiography*. New York: Simon & Schuster, 2009.

Levinson, Peter J. *September in the Rain: The Life of Nelson Riddle*. New York: Billboard Books, 2001.

Liebling, A. J. *The Jollity Building*. New York: Ballantine Books, 1962.

Litoff, Judy, and David Smith. *Since You Went Away: World War II Letters from American Women on the Home Front*. New York: Oxford University Press, 1991.

Loesser, Susan. *A Most Remarkable Fellow: Frank Loesser and the Guys and Dolls in His Life*. 2nd edition. Milwaukee: Hal Leonard, 2000.

Mancini, Henry, with Gene Lees. *Did They Mention the Music?* Chicago: Contemporary Books, 1989.

Martin, Linda, and Kerry Segrave. *Anti-Rock: The Opposition to Rock 'n' Roll*. Hamden, CT: Archon Books, 1988.

Martin, Mary. *My Heart Belongs*. New York: William Morrow, 1976.

McBrien, William. *Cole Porter: A Biography*. New York: Alfred A. Knopf, 1998.

McClellan, Lawrence, Jr. *The Later Swing Era, 1942 to 1955*. Westport, CT: Greenwood Press, 2004.

Meyer, Hazel. *The Gold in Tin Pan Alley*. Philadelphia: J. B. Lippincott, 1958.

Millard, Andre. *America on Record: A History of Recorded Sound*. 2nd edition. New York: Cambridge University Press, 2005.

Nicholson, Stuart. *Ella Fitzgerald: A Biography of the First Lady of Jazz*. New York: Charles Scribner's Sons, 1994.

Palmer, Richard. *Such Deliberate Disguises: The Art of Philip Larkin*. London: Continuum, 2008.

Passman, Arnold. *The Deejays*. New York: Macmillan, 1971.

Posner, Gerald. *Motown: Music, Money, Sex, and Power*. New York: Random House, 2002.

Riccardi, Ricky. *What a Wonderful World: The Magic of Louis Armstrong's Later Years*. New York: Pantheon, 2011.

Richmond, Peter. *Fever: The Life and Music of Miss Peggy Lee*. New York: Henry Holt, 2006.

Riis, Thomas Laurence. *Frank Loesser*. New Haven, CT: Yale University Press, 2008.

Rodgers, Richard. *Musical Stages: An Autobiography*. New York: Random House, 1975.

Rosen, Gary A. *Unfair to Genius: The Strange and Litigious Career of Ira B. Arnstein*. New York: Oxford University Press, 2012.

Rotella, Mark. *Amore: The Story of Italian American Song*. New York: Farrar, Straus & Giroux, 2010.

Ruhlmann, William. *Breaking Records: 100 Years of Hits*. New York: Routledge, 2004.

Sanjek, Russell. *American Popular Music and Its Business: The First Four Hundred Years*. Vol. 3, *From 1900 to 1984*. New York: Oxford University Press, 1988.

———. *From Print to Plastic: Publishing and Promoting America's Popular Music, 1900–1980*. Brooklyn: Institute for Studies in American Music, Conservatory of Music, Brooklyn College of the City University of New York, 1983.

Schwartz, Jonathan. *All in Good Time: A Memoir*. New York: Random House, 2004.

Secrest, Meryle. *Somewhere for Me: A Biography of Richard Rodgers*. New York: Alfred A. Knopf, 2001.

Segrave, Kerry. *Payola in the Music Industry: A History, 1880–1991*. Jefferson, NC: McFarland, 1994.

Seldes, Gilbert. *The 7 Lively Arts*. New York: Harper & Brothers, 1924.

Shaw, Arnold. *Lingo of Tin-Pan Alley*. New York: Broadcast Music, 1950.

———. *The Rockin' 50s*. New York: Hawthorn Books, 1974.

Sheed, Wilfrid. *The House That George Built: With a Little Help from Irving, Cole, and a Crew of About Fifty*. New York: Random House, 2007.

Shipton, Alyn. *I Feel a Song Coming On: The Life of Jimmy McHugh*. Urbana: University of Illinois Press, 2009.

Simon, George T. *The Big Bands*. New York: Macmillan, 1967.

Sondheim, Stephen. *Finishing the Hat: Collected Lyrics (1954–1981), with Attendant Comments, Principles, Heresies, Grudges, Whines, and Anecdotes*. New York: Alfred A. Knopf, 2010.

Spitz, Bob. *The Beatles: The Biography*. New York: Little, Brown, 2005.

Suisman, David. *Selling Sounds: The Commercial Revolution in American Music*. Cambridge, MA: Harvard University Press, 2009.

Teachout, Terry. *Duke: A Life of Duke Ellington*. New York: Gotham Books, 2013.

Tormé, Mel. *My Singing Teachers*. New York: Oxford University Press, 1994.

Townsend, Peter. *Pearl Harbor Jazz: Change in Popular Music in the Early 1940s*. Jackson: University Press of Mississippi, 2007.

U.S. Congress. House Antitrust Subcommittee of the Committee on the Judiciary, House of Representatives. *Monopoly Problems in Regulated Industries*. Part 2, vol. 3, 84th Cong., 2nd sess., 1956.

U.S. Congress. Senate Subcommittee on Communications of the Committee on Interstate and Foreign Commerce. Amendment to the Communications Act of 1934 (Prohibiting Radio and Television Stations from Engaging in Music Publishing or Recording Business). 85th Cong., 2nd sess., 1958.

Wald, Elijah. *How the Beatles Destroyed Rock 'n' Roll: An Alternative History of American Popular Music*. New York: Oxford University Press, 2009.

Ward, Ed, Geoffrey Stokes, and Ken Tucker. *Rock of Ages: The Rolling Stone History of Rock & Roll*. New York: Rolling Stone Press/Summit Books, 1986.

Webb, Jimmy. *Tunesmith: Inside the Art of Songwriting*. New York: Hyperion, 1998.

Weller, Sheila. *Girls Like Us: Carole King, Joni Mitchell, Carly Simon—and the Journey of a Generation*. New York: Atria, 2008.

Weston, Paul, and Jo Stafford. *Song of the Open Road: An Autobiography and Other Writings*. Edited by Keith Pawlak. Albany, GA: BearManor Media, 2012.

Whitburn, Joel. *Pop Hits, 1940–1954*. Menomonee Falls, WI: Record Research, 1994.

Whiteman, Paul, and Mary Margaret McBride. *Jazz*. New York: J. H. Sears, 1926.

Whiteside, Jonny. *Cry: The Johnnie Ray Story*. New York: Barricade Books, 1994.

Wilder, Alec. *American Popular Song: The Great Innovators: 1900–1950*. New York: Oxford University Press, 1972.

Wilentz, Sean. *360 Sound: The Columbia Records Story*. San Francisco: Chronicle Books, 2011.

Wilk, Max. *They're Playing Our Song*. Revised edition. New York: New York Zoetrope, 1986.

Wilson, Edmund. *The Twenties: From Notebooks and Diaries of the Period*. New York: Farrar, Straus & Giroux, 1975.

Yardley, Jonathan. *Ring: A Biography of Ring Lardner*. New York: Random House, 1977.

Zak, Albin. *I Don't Sound Like Nobody: Remaking Music in 1950s America*. Ann Arbor: University of Michigan Press, 2010.

Zinsser, William. *Easy to Remember: The Great American Songwriters and Their Songs*. Jaffrey, NH: David R. Godine, 2001.

Zollo, Paul. *Songwriters on Songwriting*. Cincinnati: Writer's Digest Books, 1991.

INDEX

PHOTO CREDITS